MADAME GUYON

AN
AUTOBIOGRAPHY

moody press
chicago

ISBN: 0-8024-5135-7

Printed in the United States of America

INTRODUCTION

IN THE HISTORY of the world few persons have attained that high degree of spirituality reached by Madame Guyon.

Born in a corrupt age, in a nation marked for its degeneracy; nursed and reared in a church, as prof ligate as the world in which it was embedded; persecuted at every step of her career; groping as she did in spiritual desolation and ignorance, nevertheless, she arose to the highest pinnacle of pre-eminence in spirituality and Christian devotion.

She lived and died in the Catholic Church; yet was tormented and afflicted; was maltreated and abused; and was imprisoned for years by the highest authorities of that church.

Her sole crime was that of loving God. The ground of her offense was found in her supreme devotion, and unmeasured attachment to Christ. When they demanded her money and estate, she gladly surrendered them, even to her impoverishment, but it availed nothing. The crime of loving Him in whom

5

her whole being was absorbed, never could be mitigated, or forgiven.

She loved only to do good to her fellow-creatures, and to such an extent was she filled with the Holy Ghost, and with the power of God, that she wrought wonders in her day, and has not ceased to influence the ages that have followed.

Viewed from a human standpoint, it is a sublime spectacle, to see a solitary woman subvert all the machinations of kings and courtiers; laugh to scorn all the malignant enginery of the papal inquisition, and silence, and confound the pretentions of the most learned divines. She not only saw more clearly the sublimest truths of our most holy Christianity, but she basked in the clearest and most beautiful sunlight while they groped in darkness. She grasped with ease the deepest and sublimest truths of holy Writ, while they were lost in the mazes of their own profound ignorance.

One distinguished divine was delighted to sit at her feet. At first he heard her with distrust; then with admiration. Finally he opened his heart to the truth, and stretched forth his hand to be led by this saint of God into the Holy of Holies where she dwelt. We allude to the distinguished Archbishop Fenelon, whose sweet spirit and charming writings have been a blessing to every generation following him.

We offer no word of apology for publishing in the Autobiography of Madame Guyon, those expressions of devotion to her church, that found vent in her writings. She was a true Catholic when protestantism was in its infancy.

6

There can be no doubt that God, by a special interposition of His Providence, caused her to commit her life so minutely to writing. The duty was enjoined upon her by her spiritual director, whom the rules of her church made it obligatory upon her to obey. It was written while she was incarcerated in the cell of a lonely prison. The same all-wise Providence preserved it from destruction. We have not a shadow of doubt that it is destined to accomplish tenfold more in the future than it has accomplished in the past. Indeed, the Christian world is only beginning to understand and appreciate it, and the hope and prayer of the publisher is, that thousands may, through its instrumentality, be brought into the same intimate communion and fellowship with God, that was so richly enjoyed by Madame Guyon.

E.J.

MADAME GUYON

PART ONE

CHAPTER 1

THERE WERE OMISSIONS of impor-
tance in the former narration of my life. I willingly
comply with your desire, in giving you a more cir-
cumstantial relation; though the labor seems rather
painful, as I cannot use much study or reflection.
My earnest wish is to paint in true colors the goodness of God to me, and the depth of my own ingratitude — but it is impossible, as numberless little
circumstances have escaped my memory. You are
also unwilling I should give you a minute account of
my sins. I shall, however, try to leave out as few
faults as possible. I depend on you to destroy it,
when your soul hath drawn those spiritual advantages which God intended, and for which purpose
I am willing to sacrifice all things. I am fully persuaded of His designs toward you, as well for the
sanctification of others, as for your own sanctification.

Let me assure you, this is not attained, save
through pain, weariness and labor; and it will be
reached by a path that will wonderfully disappoint

your expectations. Nevertheless, if you are fully convinced that it is on the nothing in man that God establishes his greatest works, — you will be in part guarded against disappointment or surprise. He destroys that he might build; for when He is about to rear His sacred temple in us, He first totally razes that vain and pompous edifice, which human art and power had erected, and from its horrible ruins a new structure is formed, by His power only.

Oh, that you could comprehend the depth of this mystery, and learn the secrets of the conduct of God, revealed to babes, but hid from the wise and great of this world, who think themselves the Lord's counselor's, and capable of investigating His procedures, and suppose they have attained that divine wisdom hidden from the eyes of all who live in self, and are enveloped in their own works. Who by a lively genius and elevated faculties mount up to Heaven, and think to comprehend the height and depth and length and breadth of God.

This divine wisdom is unknown, even to those who pass in the world for persons of extraordinary illumination and knowledge. To whom then is she known, and who can tell us any tidings concerning her? Destruction and death assure us, that they have heard with their ears of her fame and renown. It is, then, in dying to all things, and in being truly lost to them, passing forward into God, and existing only in Him, that we attain to some knowledge of the true wisdom. Oh, how little are her ways known, and her dealings with her most chosen servants. Scarce do we discover anything thereof, but surprised at the dissimilitude betwixt the truth we thus discover and our former ideas of it, we cry out with St. Paul, "Oh, the depth of the knowledge and wisdom of God! how unsearchable are his judgments, and his ways past finding out." The Lord judgeth not of things as men do, who call good evil and evil good, and account that as righteousness which is abominable in His sight, and which according to the prophet He regards as filthy rags. He will enter into strict judgment with these self-righteous, and they shall, like the Pharisees, be rather subjects of His wrath, than objects of His love, or inheritors of His rewards. Doth not Christ Himself assure us, that "except our righteousness exceed that of the scribes and pharisees we shall in no case enter into the kingdom of heaven." And which of us even approaches them in righteousness; or, if we live in the practice of virtues, though much inferior to theirs, are we not tenfold more ostentatious? Who is not pleased to behold himself righteous in his own eyes, and in the eyes of others? or, who is it doubts that such righteousness is sufficient to please God? Yet, we see the indignation of our Lord manifested against such. He who was the perfect pattern of tenderness and meekness, such as flowed from the depth of the heart, and not that affected meekness, which under the form of a dove, hides the hawk's heart. He appears severe only to these self-righteous people, and He publicly dishonored them. In what strange colors does He represent them, while He beholds the poor sinner with mercy, compassion and love, and declares that for them only He was come, that it was the sick who

15

needed the physician; and that He came only to save the lost sheep of the house of Israel.

O thou Source of Love! Thou dost indeed seem so jealous of the salvation Thou hast purchased, that Thou dost prefer the sinner to the righteous! The poor sinner beholds himself vile and wretched, is in a manner constrained to detest himself; and finding his state so horrible, casts himself in his desperation into the arms of his Saviour, and plunges into the healing fountain, and comes forth "white as wool." Then confounded at the review of his disordered state, and overflowing with love for Him, who having alone the power, had also the compassion to save him—the excess of his love is proportioned to the enormity of his crimes, and the fullness of his gratitude to the extent of the debt remitted. The self-righteous, relying on the many good works he imagines he has performed, seems to hold salvation in his own hand, and considers Heaven as a just reward of his merits. In the bitterness of his zeal he exclaims against all sinners, and represents the gates of mercy as barred against them, and Heaven as a place to which they have no claim. What need have such self-righteous persons of a Saviour? they are already burdened with the load of their own merits. Oh, how long they bear the flattering load, while sinners divested of everything, fly rapidly on the wings of faith and love into their Saviour's arms, who freely bestows on them that which he has so freely promised!

How full of self-love are the self-righteous, and how void of the love of God! They esteem and admire themselves in their works of righteousness,

16

which they suppose to be a fountain of happiness. These works are no sooner exposed to the Sun of Righteousness, than they discover all to be so full of impurity and baseness, that it frets them to the heart. Meanwhile the poor sinner, Magdalene, is pardoned because she loves much, and her faith and love are accepted as righteousness. The inspired Paul, who so well understood these great truths and so fully investigated them, assures us that "the faith of Abraham was imputed to him for righteousness." This is truly beautiful for it is certain that all of that holy patriarch's actions were strictly righteous; yet, n)t seeing them as such, and being devoid of the love of them, and divested of selfishness, his faith was founded on the coming Christ. He hoped in Him even against hope itself, and this was imputed to him for righteousness, (Rom. 41: 18, 22,) a pure, simple and genuine righteousness, wrought by Christ, and not a righteousness wrought by himself, and regarded as of himself.

You may imagine this a digression wide of the subject, but it leads insensibly to it. It shows that God accomplishes His work either in converted sinners, whose past iniquities serve as a counterpoise to their elevation, or in persons whose self-righteousness He destroys, by totally overthrowing the proud building they had reared on a sandy foundation, instead of the Rock—CHRIST.

The establishment of all these ends, which He proposed in coming into the world, is effected by the apparent overthrow of that very structure which in reality He would erect. By means which seem to des-

17

troy His Church, He establishes it. How strangely does He found the new dispensation and give it His sanction! The legislator Himself is condemned by the learned and great, as a malefactor, and dies an ignominious death. Oh, that we fully understood how very opposite our self-righteousness is to the designs of God—it would be a subject for endless humiliation, and we should have an utter distrust in that which at present constitutes the whole of our dependence.

From a just love of His supreme power, and a righteous jealousy of mankind, who attribute to each other the gifts He Himself bestows upon them, it pleased Him to take one of the most unworthy of the creation. to make known the fact that His graces are the effects of His will, not the fruits of our merits. It is the property of His wisdom to destroy what is proudly built, and to build what is destroyed; to make use of weak things to confound the mighty and to employ in His service such as appear vile and contemptible.

This He does in a manner so astonishing, as to render them the objects of the scorn and contempt of the world. It is not to draw public approbation upon them, that He makes them instrumental in the salvation of others; but to render them the objects of their dislike and the subjects of their insults; as you will see in this life you have enjoined upon me to write.

CHAPTER 2

I WAS BORN on April 18, 1648. My parents, particularly my father, was extremely pious; but to him it was a manner hereditary. Many of his forefathers were saints.

My mother, in the eighth month, was accidentally frightened, which caused an abortion. It is generally imagined that a child born in that month cannot survive. Indeed, I was so excessively ill, immediately after my birth, that all about me despaired of my life, and were apprehensive I should die without baptism. Perceiving some signs of vitality, they ran to acquaint my father, who immediately brought a priest; but on entering the chamber they were told those symptoms which had raised their hopes were only expiring struggles, and all was over.

I had no sooner shown signs of life again, than I again relapsed, and remained so long in an uncertain state, that it was some time before they could find a proper opportunity to baptize me. I continued very unhealthy until I was two and a half years old, when they sent me to the convent of the Ursulines, where I remained a few months.

On my return, my mother neglected to pay due

attention to my education. She was not fond of daughters and abandoned me wholly to the care of servants. Indeed, I should have suffered severely from their inattention to me had not an all-watchful Providence been my protector: for through my liveliness, I met with various accidents. I frequently fell into a deep vault that held our firewood; however, I always escaped unhurt.

The Dutchess of Montbason came to the convent of the Benedictines, when I was about four years old. She had a great friendship for my father, and obtained his permission that I should go to the same convent. She took peculiar delight in my sportiveness and certain sweetness in my external deportment. I became her constant companion.

I was guilty of frequent and dangerous irregularities in this house, and committed serious faults. I had good examples before me, and being naturally well inclined, I followed them, when there were none to turn me aside. I loved to hear God spoken of, to be at church, and to be dressed in a religious garb. I was told of terrors of Hell which I imagined was intended to intimidate me as I was exceedingly lively, and full of a little petulant vivacity which they called wit. The succeeding night I dreamed of Hell, and though I was so young, time has never been able to efface the frightful ideas impressed upon my imagination. All appeared horrible darkness, where souls were punished, and my place among them was pointed out. At this I wept bitterly, and cried, "Oh, my God, if Thou wilt have mercy upon me, and spare me yet a little longer, I will never more offend Thee."

And thou didst, O Lord, in mercy hearken unto my cry, and pour upon me strength and courage to serve thee, in an uncommon manner for one of my age. I wanted to go privately to confession, but being little, the mistress of the boarders carried me to the priest, and stayed with me while I was heard. She was much astonished when I mentioned that I had suggestions against the faith, and the confessor began to laugh, and inquire what they were. I told him that till then I had doubted there was such a place as Hell, and supposed my mistress had spoken of it merely to make me good, but now my doubts were all removed. After confession my heart glowed with a kind of fervor, and at one time I felt a desire to suffer martyrdom. The good girls of the house, to amuse themselves, and to see how far this growing fervor would carry me, desired me to prepare for martyrdom. I found great fervency and delight in prayer, and was persuaded that this ardor, which was as new as it was pleasing, was a proof of God's love. This inspired me with such courage and resolution, that I earnestly besought them to proceed, that I might thereby enter into His sacred presence, But was there not latent hypocrisy here? Did I not imagine that it was possible they would not kill me, and that I would have the merit of martyrdom without suffering it? Indeed, it appeared there was something of this nature in it. Being placed kneeling on a cloth spread for the purpose, and seeing behind me a large sword lifted up which they had prepared to try how far my ardor would carry me I cried, "Hold! it is not right I should die without first obtaining my father's permission." I was quickly upbraided with having said this that I might escape, and that I was no longer a martyr. I continued long disconsolate, and would receive no comfort; something inwardly reproved me, for not having embraced that opportunity of going to Heaven, when it rested altogether on my own choice.

At my solicitation, and on account of my falling so frequently sick, I was at length taken home. On my return, my mother having a maid in whom she placed confidence, left me again to the care of servants. It is a great fault, of which mothers are guilty, when under pretext of external devotions, or other engagements, they suffer their daughters to be absent from them. I forbear not condemning that unjust partiality with which parents treat some of their children. It is frequently productive of divisions in families, and even the ruin of some. Impartiality, by uniting children's hearts together, lays the foundation of lasting harmony and unanimity.

I would I were able to convince parents, and all who have the care of youth, of the great attention they require, and how dangerous it is to let them be for any length of time from under their eye, or to suffer them to be without some kind of employment. This negligence is the ruin of multitudes of girls.

How greatly it is to be lamented, that mothers who are inclined to piety, should pervert even the means of salvation to their destruction—commit the greatest irregularities while apparently pursuing that which should produce the most regular and circumspect conduct.

Thus, because they experience certain gains in

prayer, they would be all day long at church; meanwhile their children are running to destruction. We glorify God most when we prevent what may offend Him. What must be the nature of that sacrifice which is the occasion of sin! God should be served in His own way. Let the devotion of mothers be regulated so as to prevent their daughters from straying. Treat them as sisters, not as slaves. Appear pleased with their little amusements. The children will delight then in the presence of their mothers, instead of avoiding it. If they find so much happiness with them, they will not dream of seeking it elsewhere. Mothers frequently deny their children any liberties. Like birds constantly confined to a cage, they no sooner find means of escape than off they go, never to return. In order to render them tame and docile when young, they should be permitted sometimes to take wing, but as their flight is weak, and closely watched, it is easy to retake them when they escape. Little flight gives them the habit of naturally returning to their cage which becomes an agreeable confinement. I believe young girls should be treated in a manner something similar to this. Mothers should indulge them in an innocent liberty, but should never lose sight of them.

To guard the tender minds of children from what is wrong, much care should be taken to employ them in agreeable and useful matters. They should not be loaded with food they cannot relish. Milk suited to babies should be administered to them not strong meat which may so disgust them, that when they arrive at an age when it would be proper nourishment, they will not so much as taste it. Every day they should be obliged to read a little in some good book, spend some time in prayer, which must be suited rather to stir the affections, than for meditation. Oh, were this method of education pursued, how speedily would many irregularities cease! These daughters becoming mothers, would educate their children as they themselves had been educated.

Parents should also avoid showing the smallest partiality in the treatment of their children. It begets a secret jealousy and hatred among them, which frequently augments with time, and even continues until death. How often do we see some children the idols of the house, behaving like absolute tyrants, treating their brothers and sisters as so many slaves according to the example of father and mother. And it happens many times, that the favorite proves a scourge to the parents while the poor despised and hated one becomes their consolation and support.

My mother was very defective in the education of her children. She suffered me whole days from her presence in company with the servants, whose conversation and example were particularly hurtful to one of my disposition. My mother's heart seemed wholly centered in my brother. I was scarcely ever favored with the smallest instance of her tenderness or affection. I therefore voluntarily absented myself from her. It is true, my brother was more amiable than I but the excess of her fondness for him, made her blind even to my outward good qualities. It served only to discover my faults, which would have been trifling had proper care been taken of me.

CHAPTER 3

My father who loved me tenderly and seeing how little my education was attended to sent me to a convent of the Ursulines. I was near seven years old. In this house were two half sisters of mine, the one by my father, the other by my mother. My father placed me under his daughter's care, a person of the great capacity and most exalted piety, excellently qualified for the instruction of youth. This was a singular dispensation of God's providence and love toward me, and proved the first means of my salvation. She loved me tenderly, and her affection made her discover in me many amiable qualities, which the Lord had implanted in me. She endeavored to improve these good qualities, and I believe that had I continued in such careful hands, I should have acquired as many virtuous habits as I afterward contracted evil ones.

This good sister employed her time in instructing me in piety and in such branches of learning as were suitable to my age and capacity. She had good talents and improved them well. She was frequent in prayer and her faith was as great as that of most persons. She denied herself every other pleasure to be with me and to instruct me. Such was her affection for me that it made her find more pleasure with me than anywhere else.

If I made her agreeable answers, though more from chance than from judgment, she thought herself well paid for all her labor. Under her care I soon became mistress of most studies suitable for me. Many grown persons of rank could not have answered the questions.

As my father often sent for me, desiring to see me at home, I found at one time the Queen of England there. I was near eight years of age. My father told the Queen's confessor that if he wanted a little amusement he might entertain himself with me. He tried me with several very difficult questions, to which I returned such pertinent answers that he carried me to the Queen, and said, "Your majesty must have some diversion with this child." She also tried me and was so well pleased with my lively answers, and my manners, that she demanded me of my father with no small importunity. She assured him that she would take particular care of me, designing me for maid of honor to the princess. My father resisted. Doubtless it was God who caused this refusal, and thereby turned off the stroke which might have probably intercepted my salvation. Being so weak, how could I have withstood the temptations and distractions of a court?

I went back to the Ursulines where my good sister continued her affection. But as she was not the mistress of the boarders, and I was obliged sometimes to go along with them, I contracted bad habits. I became addicted to lying, peevishness and indevotion, passing whole days without thinking on God; though He watched continually over me, as the sequel will manifest. I did not remain long under the power of such habits because my sister's care recovered me. I loved much to hear of God, was not weary of church, loved to pray, had tenderness for the poor, and a natural dislike for persons whose doctrine was judged unsound. God has always continued to me this grace, in my greatest infidelities.

There was at the end of the garden connected with this convent, a little chapel dedicated to the child Jesus. To this I betook myself for devotion and, for some time, carrying my breakfast thither every morning, I hid it all behind this image. I was so much a child, that I thought I made a considerable sacrifice in depriving myself of it. Delicate in my choice of food, I wished to mortify myself, but found self-love still too prevalent, to submit to such mortification. When they were cleaning out this chapel, they found behind the image what I had left there and presently guessed that it was I. They had seen me every day going thither. I believe that God, who lets nothing pass without a recompense, soon rewarded me with interest for this little infantine devotion.

I continued some time with my sister, where I retained the love and fear of God. My life was easy; I was educated agreeably with her. I improved much while I had my health, but very often I was sick, and seized with maladies as sudden as they were uncommon. In the evening well; in the morning swelled and full of bluish marks, symptoms of a fever which soon followed. At nine years, I was taken with so violent a hemorrhage that they thought I was going to die. I was rendered exceedingly weak.

A little before this severe attack, my other sister became jealous, wanting to have me in turn. Though she led a good life, yet she had not a talent for the education of children. At first she caressed me, but all her caresses made no impression upon my heart. My other sister did more with a look, than she with either caresses or threatenings. As she saw that I loved her not so well, she changed to rigorous treatment. She would not allow me to speak to my other sister. When she knew I had spoken to her, she had me whipped, or beat me herself. I could no longer hold out against severe usage, and therefore requited with apparent ingratitude all the favors of my paternal sister, going no more to see her. But this did not hinder her from giving me marks of her usual goodness, in the severe malady just mentioned. She kindly construed my ingratitude to be rather owing to my fear of chastisement, than to a bad heart. Indeed, I believe this was the only instance in which fear of chastisement operated so powerfully upon me. From that time I suffered more in occasioning pain to One I loved, than in suffering myself at their hand.

Thou knowest, O my Beloved, that it was not the dread of Thy chastisements that sunk so deep, either into my understanding or my heart; it was the sorrow for offending Thee which ever constituted the whole of my distress; which was so great. I imagine if there were neither Heaven nor Hell, I should always have retained the same fear of displeasing Thee Thou knowest that after my faults, when, in forgiving mercy, Thou wert pleased to visit my soul, Thy caresses were a thousand-fold more insupportable than Thy rod.

My father being informed of all that passed, took me home again. I was nearly ten years of age.

I stayed only a little while at home. A nun of the order of St. Dominie, of a great family, one of my father's intimate friends, solicited him to place me in her convent. She was the prioress and promised she would take care of me and make me lodge in her room. This lady had conceived a great affection for me. She was so taken up with her community, in its many troublesome events that she was not at liberty to take much care of me. I had the chickenpox, which made me keep to my bed three weeks, in which I had very bad care, though my father and mother thought I was under excellent care. The ladies of the house had such a dread of the smallpox, as they imagined mine to be, that they would not come near me. I passed almost all the time without seeing anybody. A lay-sister who only brought me my allowance of diet at the set hours immediately went off again. I providentially found a Bible and having both a fondness for reading and a happy memory. I spent whole days in reading it from morning to night. I learned entirely the historical part. Yet I was really very unhappy in this house. The other boarders, being large girls, distressed me with grievous persecutions. I was so much neglected, as to food, that I became quite emaciated.

CHAPTER 4

After about eight months, my father took me home. My mother kept me more with her, beginning to have a higher regard for me than before. She still preferred my brother; every one spoke of it. Even when I was sick and there was anything I liked, he damanded it. It was taken from me, and given to him, and he was in perfectly good health. One day he made me mount the top of the coach; then threw me down. By the fall I was very much bruised. At other times he beat me. But whatever he did, however wrong, it was winked at, or the most favorable construction was put upon it. This soured my temper. I had little disposition to do good, saying, "I was never the better for it."

It was not then for Thee alone, O God, that I did good; since I ceased to do it, when it met not with such a reception from others as I wanted. Had I known how to make a right use of this thy crucifying conduct, I should have made a good progress. Far from turning me out of the way, it would have made me turn more wholly to Thee.

I looked with jealous eyes on my brother, seeing

the difference between him and me. Whatever he did was considered well; but if there were blame, it fell on me. My stepsisters by the mother, gained her goodwill by caressing him and persecuting me. True, I was bad. I relapsed into my former faults of lying and peevishness. With all these faults I was very tender and charitable to the poor. I prayed to God assiduously, loved to hear any one speak of Him and to read good books.

I doubt not that you will be amazed at such a series of inconsistencies; but what succeeds will surprise you yet more, when you see this manner of acting gain ground with my years. As my reason ripened, it was so far from correcting this irrational conduct. Sin grew more powerful in me.

O my God, thy grace seemed to be redoubled in proportion to the increase of my ingratitude! It was with me as with a city besieged, Thou didst surround my heart, and I only studied how to defend myself against thy attacks. I raised fortifications about the wretched place, adding every day to the number of my iniquities to prevent Thee taking it. When there was an appearance of Thy becoming victorious over this ungrateful heart, I raised a counter-battery, and threw up ramparts to keep off thy goodness, and to hinder the course of thy grace. None other could have conquered than Thyself.

I cannot bear to hear it said, "We are not free to resist grace." I have had too long and fatal an experience of my liberty. I closed up the avenues of my heart, that I might not so much as hear that secret voice of God, which was calling me to Himself. I have indeed, from tenderest youth, passed through a series of grievances, either by maladies or by persecutions. The girl to whose care my mother left me, in arranging my hair used to beat me, and did not make me turn it except with rage and blows.

Everything seemed to punish me, but this instead of making me turn unto Thee, O my God, only served to afflict and embitter my mind.

My father knew nothing of all this; his love to me was such that he would not have suffered it. I loved him very much, but at the same time I feared him, so that I told him nothing of it. My mother was often teasing him with complaints of me, to which he made no other reply than, "There are twelve hours in the day; she'll grow wiser." This rigorous proceeding was not the worst for my soul, though it soured my temper, which was otherwise mild and easy. But what caused my greatest hurt was, that I chose to be among those who caressed me, in order to corrupt and spoil me.

My father, seeing I was now grown tall, placed me in Lent among the Ursulines, to receive my first communion at Easter, at which time I was to complete my eleventh year. And here my most dear sister, under whose inspection my father placed me, redoubled her cares, to cause me to make the best preparation possible for this act of devotion. I thought now of giving myself to God in good earnest. I often felt a combat between my good inclinations and my bad habits. I even did some penances. As I was almost always with my sister, and as the boarders in her class, which was the first, were very reasonable and civil, I became such also, while among them. It had been cruel to educate me badly; for my very nature was strongly disposed to goodness. Easily won with mildness, I did with pleasure whatever my good sister desired. At length Easter arrived; I received the communion with much joy and devotion. In this house I staid until Whitsuntide. But as my other sister was mistress of the second class, she demanded that in her week I should be with her in that class. Her manners, so opposite to the other's, made me relax my former piety. I felt no more that new and delightful ardor which had seized my heart at my first communion. Alas! it held but a short time. My faults and failings were soon reiterated and drew me from the care and duties of religion.

As I now grew very tall for my age, and more to my mother's liking than before, she took care to deck and dress me, to make me see company, and to take me abroad. She took an inordinate pride in that beauty with which God had formed me, to bless and praise Him. However it was perverted by me into a source of pride and vanity. Several suitors came to me; but as I was not yet twelve years my father would not listen to any proposals. I loved reading and shut myself up alone every day to read without interruption.

What proved effectual to gain me entirely to God, at least for a time, was that a nephew of my father's passed by our home on a mission to Cochin China. I happened at that time to be taking a walk with my companions, which I seldom did. At my return he was gone. They gave me an account of his sanctity, and the things he had said. I was so touched that I was overcome with sorrow. I cried all the rest of the day and night. Early in the morning I went in great distress to seek my confessor. I said to him, "What! my father, am I the only person in our family to be lost? Alas; help me in my salvation." He was greatly surprised to see me so much afflicted, and comforted me in the best manner he could, not thinking me so bad as I was. In my backslidings I was docile, punctual in obedience, careful to confess often. Since I went to him my life was more regular.

Oh, thou God of love, how often hast Thou knocked at the door of my heart! How often terrified me with appearances of sudden death! All these only made a transient impression. I presently returned again to my infidelities. This time thou didst take and quite carried off my heart. Alas, what grief I now sustained for having displeased Thee! what regrets, what exclamations, what sobbings! Who would have thought, to see me, but that my conversion would have lasted as long as my life? Why didst thou not, O my God, utterly take this heart to thyself, when I gave it to Thee so fully. Or, if Thou didst take it then, oh, why didst Thou let it revolt again? Thou wast surely strong enough to hold it, but Thou wouldst perhaps, in leaving me to myself, display thy mercy that the depth of my iniquity might serve as a trophy to thy goodness.

I immediately applied myself to every part of my duty. I made a general confession with great compunction of heart. I frankly confessed all that I knew with many tears. I became so changed that I was scarcely known. I would not for ever so much have made the least voluntary slip. They found not any matter for absolution when I confessed. I discovered the very smallest faults and God did me the favor to enable me to conquer myself in many things. There were left only some remains of passion, which gave me some trouble to conquer. But as soon as I had by means thereof, given any displeasure, even to the domestics, I begged their pardon, in order to subdue my wrath and pride; for wrath is the daughter of pride. A person truly humbled permits not anything to put him in a rage. As it is pride which dies the last in the soul, so it is passion which is last destroyed in the outward conduct. A soul thoroughly dead to itself, finds nothing of rage left.

There are persons who, being very much filled with grace and with peace, at their entrance of the resigned path of light and love, think they are come thus far. But they are greatly mistaken, in this view of their state. This they will readily discover, if they are heartily willing to examine two things. First, if their nature is lively, warm and violent, (I speak not of stupid tempers) they will find, from time to time, that they make slips, in which trouble and emotion have some share. Even then they are useful to humble and annihilate them. (But when annihilation is perfected all passion is gone—it is incompatible with this state.) They will find that there often arises in them certain motions of anger, but the sweetness of grace holds them back. They would easily transgress, if in any wise they gave way to these motions. There are persons who think themselves very mild because nothing thwarts them. It is not of such that I am speaking. Mildness which has never been put to the proof, is often only counterfeit. Those persons who, when unmolested, appear to be saints are no sooner exercised by vexing occurences than there starts up in them a strange number of faults. They had thought them dead which only lay dormant because nothing awakened them.

—I followed my religious exercises. I shut myself up all day to read and pray. I gave all I had to the poor taking even linen to their houses. I taught them the catechism and when my parents dined out I made them eat with me and served them with great respect. I read the works of St. Francis de Sales and the life of Madam de Chantal. There I first learned what mental prayer was, and I besought my confessor to teach me that kind of prayer. As he did not, I used my own endeavors to practice it, though without success, as I then thought, because I could not exercise the imagination, I persuaded myself, that that prayer could not be made without forming to one's self certain ideas and reasoning much. This difficulty gave me no small trouble, for a long time. I was very assiduous and prayed earnestly to God to give me the gift of prayer. All that I saw in the life of M. de Chantal charmed me. I was so much a child, that I thought I ought to do everything I saw in it. All the vows she had made I made also. One day as I was reading that she had put the name of Jesus on her heart, to follow the counsel, "Set me as a seal upon thy heart." For this purpose she had taken a hot iron, whereupon the holy name was engraven. I was very much afflicted that I could not do the same. I decided to write that sacred and adorable name, in large characters, on paper, then with ribbons and a needle I fastened it to my skin in four places. In that position it continued a long time.

After this, I turned all my thoughts to become a nun. Because the love which I had for St. Francis de Sales did not permit me to think of any other community than the one of which he was the founder, I frequently went to beg the nuns there to receive me into their convent. Often I stole out of my father's house to go and repeatedly solicit my admission there. Though it was what they eagerly desired, even as a temporal advantage, yet they never dared let me enter, as they very much feared my father, to whose fondness for me they were no strangers.

There was at that house a niece of my father's, to whom I am under great obligations. Fortune had not been very favorable to her father. It had reduced her in some measure to depend on mine, to whom she made known my desire. Although he would not for anything in the world have hindered a right vocation, yet he could not hear of my design without shedding tears. As he happened at this time to be abroad, my cousin went to my confessor, to desire him to forbid my going to the visitation. He dared not, however, do it plainly, for fear of drawing on himself the resentment of that community. I still wanted to be a nun, and importuned my mother excessively to take me to that house. She would not do it, for fear of grieving my father, who was absent.

CHAPTER 5

No sooner was my father returned home, than he became violently ill. My mother was at the same time indisposed in another part of the house. I was all alone with him, ready to render him every kind of service I was capable of, and to give him all the dutiful marks of a most sincere affection. I do not doubt but my assiduity was very agreeable to him. I performed the most menial offices unperceived by him taking the time for it when the servants were not at hand; as well to mortify myself as to pay due honor to what (Jesus Christ said, that He came not to be ministered to, but to minister) When father made me read to him, I read with such heartfelt devotion that he was surprised. I remembered the instruction my sister had given me, and the ejaculatory prayers and praises I had learned.

— She had taught me to praise Thee, O my God, in all Thy works. All that I saw called upon me to render Thee homage. If it rained, I wished every drop to be changed into love and praises. My heart was nourished insensibly with Thy love; and my spirit was incessantly engrossed with the remembrance of

Thee. I seemed to join and partake in all the good that was done in the world, and could have wished to have the united hearts of all men to love Thee. This habit rooted itself so strongly in me, that I retained it throughout my greatest wanderings.

My cousin helped not a little, to support me in these good sentiments; I was often with her, and loved her, as she took great care of me, and treated me with much gentleness. Her fortune being equal neither to her birth nor her virtue, she did with charity and affection what her condition obliged her to do. My mother grew jealous, fearing I should love my cousin too well and herself too little. She who had left me in my young years to the care of her maids, and since that to my own, only requiring if I was in the house. Troubling herself no further, now required me always to stay with her, and never suffered me to be with my cousin but with great reluctance. My cousin fell ill. My mother took that occasion to send her home, which was a very severe stroke to my heart, as well as to that grace which began to dawn in me.

My mother was a very virtuous woman. She was one of the most charitable women of her age. She not only gave the surplus, but even the necessities of the house. Never were the needy neglected. Never any wretched one came to her without succor. She furnished poor mechanics wherewith to carry on their work, and needy tradesmen wherewith to supply their shops. From her, I think, I inherited my charity and love for the poor. God favored me with the blessing of being her successor in that holy exercise. There was not one in the town, or its environs, who did not praise her for this virtue. She sometimes gave to the last penny in the house, though she had a large family to maintain, and yet she did not fail in her faith.

My mother's only care about me had been all along to have me in the house, which indeed is one material point for a girl. This habit of being so constantly kept within, proved of great service after my marriage. It would have been better had she kept me more in her own apartment, with an agreeable freedom and inquired oftener what part of the house I was in.

After my cousin left me, God granted me the grace to forgive injuries with such readiness, that my confessor was surprised. He knew that some young ladies had, out of envy, traduced me and that I spoke well of them as occasion offered. I was seized with an ague, which lasted four months, in which I suffered much. During that time, I was enabled to suffer with much resignation and patience. In this frame of mind and manner of life I persevered, so long as I continued the practice of mental prayer.

Later we went to pass some days in the country. My father took along with us one of his relations, a very accomplished young gentleman. He had a great desire to marry me; but my father, resolved not to give me to any near kinsman on account of the difficulty obtaining dispensations, put him off, without alleging any false or frivolous reasons for it. As this young gentleman was very devout, and every day said the office of the Virgin, I said it with him. To have time for it, I left off prayer which was to me the first inlet of evils. Yet, I kept up for a long time some share of the spirit of piety; for I went to seek out the little shepherdesses, to instruct them in their religious duties. This spirit gradually decayed, not being nourished by prayer. I became cold toward God. All my old faults revived to which I added an excessive vanity. The love I began to have for myself extinguished what remained in me of the love of God.

I did not wholly leave off mental prayer, without asking my confessor's leave. I told him I thought it better to say the office of the Virgin every day than to practice prayer; I had not time for both. I saw not that this was a stratagem of the enemy to draw me from God, to entangle me in the snares he had laid for me. I had time sufficient for both, as I had no other occupation than what I prescribed to myself. My confessor was easy in the matter. Not being a man of prayer he gave his consent to my great hurt.

Oh, my God, if the value of prayer were but known, the great advantage which accrues to the soul from conversing with Thee, and what consequence it is of to salvation, everyone would be assiduous in it. It is a stronghold into which the enemy cannot enter. He may attack it, besiege it, make a noise about its walls; but while we are faithful and hold our station, he cannot hurt us. It is alike requisite to dictate to children the necessity of prayer as of their salvation. Alas! unhappily, it is thought sufficient to tell them that there is a Heaven and a

Hell; that they must endeavor to avoid the latter and attain the former; yet they are not taught the shortest and easiest way of arriving at it. The only way to Heaven is prayer; a prayer of the heart, which every one is capable of, and not of reasonings which are the fruits of study, or exercise of the imagination, which, in filling the mind with wandering objects, rarely settle it; instead of warming the heart with love to God, they leave it cold and languishing. Let the poor come, let the ignorant and carnal come; let the children without reason or knowledge come, let the dull or hard hearts which can retain nothing come to the practice of prayer and they shall become wise.

O ye great, wise and rich, Have ye not a heart capable of loving what is proper for you and of hating what is destructive? Love the sovereign good, hate all evil, and ye will be truly wise. When ye love anyone, is it because ye know the reasons of love and its definitions? No, certainly. Ye love because your heart is formed to love what it finds amiable. Surely you cannot but know that there is nought lovely in the universe but God. Know ye not that He has created you, that He has died for you? But if these reasons are not sufficient, which of you has not some necessity, some trouble, or some misfortune? Which of you does not know how to tell his malady, and beg relief? Come, then, to this Fountain of all good, without complaining to weak and impotent creatures, who cannot help you; come to prayer; lay before God your troubles, beg His grace—and above all, that you may love Him. None can exempt himself from loving; for none can live without a heart, nor the heart without love.

Why should any amuse themselves, in seeking reasons for loving Love itself? Let us love without reasoning about it, and we shall find ourselves filled with love, before the others have learned the reasons which induced to it. Make trial of this love, and you will be wiser in it than the most skillful philosophers. In love, as in everything else, experience instructs better than reasoning. Come then, drink at this fountain of living waters, instead of the broken cisterns of the creature, which far from allaying your thirst, only tend continually to augment it. Did ye once drink at this fountain, ye would not seek elsewhere for anything to quench your thirst; for while ye still continue to draw from this source, ye would thirst no longer after the world. But if ye quit it, alas! the enemy has the ascendant. He will give you of his poisoned draughts, which may have an apparent sweetness, but will assuredly rob you of life.

I forsook the the fountain of living water when I left off prayer. I became as a vineyard exposed to pillage, hedges torn down with liberty to all the passengers to ravage it. I began to seek in the creature what I had found in God. He left me to myself, because I first left him. It was His will by permitting me to sink into the horrible pit, to make me feel the necessity I was in of approaching Him in prayer.

Thou hast said, that Thou wilt destroy those adulterous souls who depart from Thee. Alas! it is their departure alone which causes their destruction, since, in departing from Thee, O Sun of Righteousness, they enter into the regions of darkness and the coldness of death, from which they would never rise, if Thou didst not revisit them. If Thou didst not by thy divine light, illuminate their darkness, and by thy enlivening warmth, melt their icy hearts, and restore them to life, they would never rise.

I fell then into the greatest of all misfortunes. I wandered yet farther and farther from Thee, O my God, and thou didst gradually retire from a heart which had quitted Thee. Yet such is thy goodness, that it seemed as if Thou hadst left me with regret; and when this heart was desirous to return again unto Thee, with what speed didst Thou come to meet it. This proof of Thy love and mercy, shall be to me an everlasting testimony of thy goodness and of my own ingratitude.

I became still more passionate than I had ever been, as age gave more force to nature. I was frequently guilty of lying. I felt my heart corrupt and vain. The spark of divine grace was almost extinguished in me, and I fell into a state of indifference and indevotion, though I still carefully kept up outside appearances. The habit I had acquired of behaving at church made me appear better than I was. Vanity, which had been excluded to my heart now resumed its seat. I began to pass a great part of my time before a looking glass. I found so much pleasure in viewing myself, that I thought others were in the right who practiced the same. Instead of making use of this exterior, which God had given me, that I might love Him the more, it became to me only the means of a vain complacency. All seemed to me to look beautiful in my person, but I saw not that it covered a polluted soul. This rendered me so inwardly vain, that I doubt whether any ever exceeded me therein. There was an affected modesty in my outward deportment that would have deceived the world.

The high esteem I had for myself made me find faults in everyone else of my own sex. I had no eyes but to see my own good qualities, and to discover the defects of others. I hid my own faults from myself, or if I remarked any, yet to me they appeared little in comparison of others. I excused, and even figured them to myself as perfections. Every idea I had of others and of myself was false. I loved reading to such excess, particularly romances, that I spent whole days and nights at them. Sometimes the day broke while I continued to read, insomuch, that for a length of time I almost lost the habit of sleeping. I was ever eager to get to the end of the book, in hopes of finding something to satisfy a certain craving which I found within me. My thirst for reading was only increased the more I read. Books are strange inventions to destroy youth. If they caused no other hurt than the loss of precious time, is not that too much? I was not restrained, but rather encouraged to read them under this fallacious pretext, that they taught one to speak well.

Meanwhile, through thy abundant mercy, O my God, Thou camest to seek me from time to time, Thou didst indeed knock at the door of my heart. I was often penetrated with the most lively sorrow and shed abundance of tears. I was afflicted to find my state so different from what it was when I enjoyed Thy sacred presence; but my tears were fruitless and my grief in vain. I could not of myself get out of this wretched state. I wished some hand as charitable as powerful would extricate me; as for myself I had no power. If I had had any friend, who would have examined the cause of this evil, and made me have recourse again to prayer, which was the only means of relief, all would have been well. I was (like the prophet) in a deep abyss of mire, which I could not get out off. I met with reprimands for being in it, but none were kind enough to reach out to free me. And when I tried vain efforts to get out, I only sunk the deeper, and each fruitless attempt only made me see my own impotence, and rendered me more afflicted.

Oh, how much compassion has this sad experience given me for sinners. It has taught me why so few of them emerge from the miserable state into which they have fallen. Such as see it only cry out against their disorders, and frighten them with threats of future punishment! These cries and threats at first make some impression, and they use some weak efforts after liberty, but, after having experienced their insufficiency, they gradually abate in their design, and lose their courage for trying any more. All that man can say to them afterward is but lost labor, though one preach to them incessantly. When any for relief run to confess, the only true remedy for them is prayer; to present themselves before God as criminals, beg strength of Him to rise out of this state. Then would they soon be changed, and brought out of the mire and clay. But the devil has falsely persuaded the doctors and the wise men of the age, that, in order to pray, it is necessary first to be perfectly converted. Hence people are dissuaded from it, and hence there is rarely any conversion that is durable. The devil is outrageous only against prayer, and those that exercise it; because he knows it is the true means of taking his prey from him. He lets us undergo all the austerities we will. He neither persecutes those that enjoy them nor those that practice them. But no sooner does one enter into a spiritual life, a life of prayer, but they must prepare for strange crosses. All manner of persecutions and contempts in this world are reserved for that life.

Miserable as the condition was to which I was reduced by my infidelities, and the little help I had from my confessor, I did not fail to say my vocal prayers every day, to confess pretty often, and to partake of the communion almost every fortnight. Sometimes I went to church to weep, and to pray to the Blessed Virgin to obtain my conversion. I loved to hear anyone speak of God, and would never tire of the conversation. When my father spoke of Him, I was transported with joy; and when he and my mother went on any pilgrimage, and were to set off early in the morning, I either did not go to bed the night before, or hired the girls to awake me early. My father's conversation at such times was always of divine matters, which afforded me the highest delight, and I preferred that subject to any other. I also loved the poor, and was charitable, even while I was so very faulty. How strange may this seem to some, and how hard to reconcile things so very opposite.

CHAPTER 6

A<small>FTERWARD</small> we came to Paris where
my vanity increased. No course was spared to make
me appear to advantage. I was forward enough to
show myself and expose my pride, in making a pa-
rade of this vain beauty. I wanted to be loved of
everyone and to love none. Several apparently advantageous offers of marriage were made for me; but
God unwilling to have me lost did not permit matters to succeed. My father still found difficulties,
which my all-wise Creator raised for my salvation.
Had I married any of these persons, I should have
been much exposed, and my vanity would have
had means to extend itself.

There was one person who had asked for me in
marriage for several years. My father, for family reasons, had always refused him. His manners were opposite to my vanity. A fear lest I should leave my
country, together with the affluent circumstances of
this gentleman, induced my father, in spite of both
his own and my mother's reluctance, to promise me
to him. This was done without consulting me. They
made me sign the marriage articles without letting

me know what they were. I was well pleased with the thoughts of marriage, flattering myself with a hope of being thereby set at full liberty, and delivered from the ill-treatment of my mother which I drew upon myself. God ordered it far otherwise. The condition which I found myself in afterward, frustrated my hopes.

Pleasing as marriage was to my thoughts, I was all the time, after my being promised, and even long after my marriage, in extreme confusion, which arose from two causes. First, my natural modesty, which I did not lose. I had much reserve toward men. The other, my vanity. Though the husband provided was a more advantageous match than I merited, yet I did not think him such. The figure which the others made, who had offered to me before, was vastly more engaging. Their rank would have placed me in view. Whatever did not flatter my vanity, was to me insupportable. Yet this very vanity was, I think, of some advantage; it hindered me from falling into such things as cause the ruin of families. I would not do anything which in the eye of the world, might render me culpable. As I was modest at church and had not been used to go abroad without my mother, as the reputation of our house was great, I passed for virtuous.

I did not see my spouse elect (at Paris) till two or three days before our marriage. I caused masses to be said all the time after my being contracted, to know the will of God. I wished to do it in this affair at least.

Oh, my God, how great was thy goodness, to bear

50

with me at this time, and to allow me to pray to Thee with as much boldness, as if I had been one of thy friends, I who had rebelled against Thee as thy greatest enemy.

The joy of our nuptials was universal through our village. Amid this general rejoicing, there appeared none sad but myself. I could neither laugh as others did, nor even eat; so much was I depressed. I knew not the cause. It was a foretaste which God gave me of what was to befall me. The remembrance of the desire I had of being a nun, came pouring in. All who came to compliment me, the day after, could not forbear rallying me. I wept bitterly. I answered, "Alas! I had desired so much to be a nun; why then am I now married? By what fatality has such a revolution befallen me? No sooner was I at the house of my new spouse, than I perceived that it would be for me a house of mourning.

I was obliged to change my conduct. Their manner of living was very different from that in my father's house. My mother-in-law, who had long been a widow, regarded nothing else but economy. At my father's house they lived in a noble manner and great elegance. What my husband and mother-in-law called pride, and I called politeness, was observed there. I was very much surprised at this change, and so much the more, as my vanity wished to increase, rather than to be diminished.

At the time of my marriage I was a little past fifteen years of age. My surprise increased greatly, when I saw I must lose what I had acquired with so much application. At my father's house we were

51

obliged to behave in a genteel way, and to speak with propriety. All that I said was applauded. Here they never hearkened to me, but to contradict and find fault. If I spoke well, they said it was to give them a lesson. If any questions were started at my father's, he encouraged me to speak freely. Here, if I spoke my sentiments, they said it was to enter into a dispute. They put me to silence in an abrupt and shameful manner, and scolded me from morning till night.

I should have some difficulty to give you an account, which cannot be done without wounding charity, if you had not forbidden me to omit any one. I request you not to look at things on the side of the creature, which would make these persons appear worse than they were. My mother-in-law had virtue, my husband had religion, and not any vice. It is requisite to look at everything on the side of God. He permitted these things only for my salvation, and because He would not have me lost. I had beside so much pride, that had I received any other treatment, I should have continued therein, and should not, perhaps, have turned to God as I was induced to do, by the oppression of a multitude of crosses.

My mother-in-law conceived such a desire to oppose me in everything, that, in order to vex me, she made me perform the most humiliating offices. Her disposition was so extraordinary, having never surmounted it in her youth, that she could hardly live with anybody. Saying none than vocal prayers, she did not see this fault; or seeing it, and not drawing from the forces of prayer, she could not get the better of it. It was a pity, for she had both sense and merit. I was made the victim of her humors. All her occupation was to thwart me and she inspired the like sentiments in her son. They would make persons my inferiors take place above me. My mother, who had a high sense of honor, could not endure that. When she heard it from others (for I told her nothing) she chided me thinking I did it because I did not know how to keep my rank and had no spirit. I dared not tell her how it was; but I was almost ready to die with the agonies of grief and continual vexation. What aggravated all was the remembrance of the persons who had proposed for me, the difference of their dispositions and manners, the love they had for me, with their agreeableness and politeness. All this made my burden intolerable. My mother-in-law upbraided me in regard to my family, and spoke to me incessantly to the disadvantage of my father and mother. I never went to see them, but I had some bitter speeches to bear on my return.

My mother complained that I did not come often enough to see her. She said I did not love her, that I was alienated from my family by being too much attached to my husband.

What augmented my crosses was that my mother related to my mother-in-law the pains I had cost her from infancy. They then reproached me, saying, I was a changeling, and an evil spirit. My husband obliged me to stay all day long in my mother-in-law's room, without any liberty of retiring into my own apartment. She spoke disadvantageously of me, to lessen the affection and esteem which some had entertained for me. She galled me with the grossest affronts before the finest company. This did not have the effect she wanted; the more patiently they saw me bear it, the higher esteem they had for me.

She found the secret of extinguishing my vivacity, and rendering me stupid. Some of my former acquaintances hardly knew me. Those who had not seen me before said, "Is this the person famed for such abundance of wit? She can't say two words. She is a fine picture." I was not yet sixteen years old. I was so much intimidated, that I dared not go out without my mother-in-law, and in her presence I could not speak. I knew not what I said; so much fear had I.

To complete my affliction, they presented me with a waiting-maid who was everything with them. She kept me in sight like a governess. For the most part I bore with patience these evils which I had no way to avoid. But sometimes I let some hasty answer escape me, a source of grievous crosses to me. When I went out, the footmen had orders to give an account of everything I did. It was then I began to eat the bread of sorrows, and to mingle tears with my drink. At the table they always did something which covered me with confusion. I could not forbear tears. I had no one to confide in who might share my affliction, and assist me to bear it. When I would impart some hint of it to my mother, I drew upon myself new crosses. I resolved to have no confidant. It was not from any natural cruelty that my husband treated me thus; he loved me passionately, but he was warm and hasty, and my mother-in-law continually irritated him about me.

54

It was in a condition so deplorable, O my God, that I began to perceive the need I had of Thy assistance. For this situation was perilous for me. I met with none but admirers abroad, those that flattered me to my hurt. It were to be feared lest at such a tender age, amid all the strange domestic crosses I had to bear, I might be drawn away. But Thou, by Thy goodness and love, gave it quite another turn. By these redoubled strokes Thou didst draw me to Thyself, and by Thy crosses effected what Thy caresses could not effect. Nay, Thou madest use of my natural pride, to keep me within the limits of my duty. I knew that a woman of honor ought never to give suspicion to her husband. I was so very circumspect that I often carried it to excess, so far as to refuse my hand to such as in politeness offered me theirs. There happened to me an adventure which, by carrying my prudence too far, might have ruined me, for things were taken contrary to their intent. My husband was sensible both of my innocence and of the falsehood of the insinuations of my mother-in-law.

Such weighty crosses made me return to God. I began to deplore the sins of my youth. Since my marriage I had not committed any voluntarily. Yet I still had some sentiments of vanity remaining, which I did not wish. However, my troubles now counter-balanced them. Moreover, many of them appeared my just dessert according to the little light I then had. I was not illuminated to penetrate the essence of my vanity; I fixed my thoughts only on its appearance. I tried to amend my life by penance, and by a general confession, the most exact that I ever yet had made. I laid aside the reading of romances, for which I lately had such a fondness. Though some time before my marriage that had been dampened by reading the Gospel, I was so much affected therewith, and discovered truth therein, that put me out of patience with all the other books. Novels appeared then to me only full of lies and deceit. I now put away even indifferent books, to have none but such as were profitable. I resumed the practice of prayer, and endeavored to offend God no more. I felt His love gradually recovering the ascendant in my heart, and banishing every other. Yet I had still an intolerable vanity and self-complacency, which has been my most grievous and obstinate sin.

My crosses redoubled. What rendered them more painful was that my mother-in-law, not content with the bitterest speeches which she uttered against me, both in public and private, would break out in anger about the smallest trifles, and scarcely be pacified for a fortnight. I used a part of my time in bewailing myself when I could be alone; and my grief became every day more bitter. Sometimes I could not contain myself, when the girls, my domestics, who owed me submission, treated me ill. I did what I could to subdue my temper which has cost me not a little.

Such stunning blows so impaired the vivacity of my nature, that I became like a lamb that is shorn. I prayed to our Lord to assist me, and He was my refuge. As my age differed from theirs (for my huband was twenty-two years older than I) I saw well that

there was no probability of changing their dispositions, which were fortified with years. I found that
whatever I said was offensive, not excepting those
things which others would have been pleased with.

One day, weighed down with grief and in despair,
about six months after I was married, being alone,
I was tempted even to cut out my tongue so I might
no longer irritate those who seized every word I uttered with rage and resentment.

But Thou, O God, didst stop me short and showed
me my folly. I prayed continually, and wished even
to become dumb, so simple and ignorant was I.
Though I have had my share of crosses, I never found
any so difficult to support as that of perpetual contrariety without relaxation of doing all one can to
please, without succeeding, but still offending by
the very means designed to oblige. Being kept with
such persons, in a most severe confinement, from
morning till night, without ever daring to quit them
is most difficult. I have found that great crosses over-
whelm, and stifle all anger. Such a continual contrariety irritates and stirs up sourness in the heart.
It has such strange effect, that it requires the utmost
efforts of self-restraint, not to break out into vexation and rage.

My condition in marriage was rather that of a
slave than of a free person. I perceived, four months
after my marriage, that my husband was gouty. This
malady caused many crosses within and without.
He had the gout twice the first year, six weeks each
time. He was so much plagued with it, that he came
no more out of his room, nor out of his bed. He was

in bed usually for several months. I carefully attended him although so very young. I did not fail to exert myself to the utmost in the performance of my duty. Alas! all this did not gain me friendship. I had not the consolation to know whether what I did was agreeable. I denied myself all the most innocent diversions to continue with my husband. I did whatever I thought would please him. Sometimes he quietly suffered me, and then I esteemed myself very happy. At other times I seemed insupportable to him. My particular friends said, "I was of a fine age indeed to be a nurse to an invalid, and that it was a shameful thing that I did not set more value on my talents." I answered, "Since I have a husband, I ought to share his painful as well as his pleasing circumstances." Besides this, my mother, instead of pitying me, reprimanded me sharply for my assiduity to my husband.

But, O my God, how different were Thy thoughts from theirs,—how different that which was without, from what passed within! My husband had that foible, that when anyone said anything to him against me, he flew into a rage at once. It was the conduct of providence over me; for he was a man of reason and loved me much. When I was sick, he was inconsolable. I believe, had it not been for my mother-in-law, and the girl I have spoken of, I should have been very happy with him. Most men have their moods and emotions, and it is the duty of a reasonable woman to bear them peaceably, without irritating them more by cross replies.

These things Thou hast ordered, O my God, in such a manner, by Thy goodness, that I have since seen it was necessary, to make me die to my vain and haughty nature. I should not have had power to destroy it myself, if thou hadst not accomplished it by an all-wise economy of thy providence. I prayed for patience with great earnestness; nevertheless, some sallies of my natural liveliness escaped me, and vanquished the resolutions I had taken of being silent. This was doubtless permitted, that my self-love might not be nourished by my patience. Even a moment's slip caused me months of humiliation, reproach and sorrow, and proved the occasion of new crosses.

CHAPTER 7

DURING THE FIRST YEAR I was still vain. I sometimes lied to excuse myself to my husband and mother-in-law. I stood strangely in awe of them. Sometimes I fell into a temper, their conduct appeared so very unreasonable, and especially their countenancing the most provoking treatment of the girl who served me. As to my mother-in-law, her age and rank rendered her conduct more tolerable.

But Thou, O my God, opened my eyes to see things in a very different light. I found in Thee reasons for suffering, which I had never found in the creature. I afterward saw clearly and reflected with joy, that this conduct, as unreasonable as it seemed, and as mortifying as it was, was quite necessary for me. Had I been applauded here as I was at my father's, I should have grown intolerably proud. I had a fault common to most of our sex—I could not hear a beautiful woman praised, without finding fault, to lessen the good which was said of her. This fault continued long, and was the fruit of gross and malignant pride. Extravagantly extolling anyone proceeds from a like source.

Just before the birth of my first child, they were induced to take great care of me. My crosses were somewhat mitigated. Indeed, I was so ill that it was enough to excite the compassion of the most indifferent. They had so great a desire of having children to inherit their fortunes, that they were continually afraid lest I should any way hurt myself. Yet, when the time of my delivery drew near, this care and tenderness of me abated. Once, as my mother-in-law had treated me in a very grating manner, I had the malice to feign a cholic, to give them some alarm; but as I saw this little artifice gave them too much pain, I told them I was better. No creature could be more heavily laden with sickness than I was. Beside continual heavings, I had so strange a distaste, except for some fruit, that I could not bear the sight of food. I had continual swoonings and violent pains. After my delivery I continued weak a long time. There was indeed sufficient to exercise patience, and I was enabled to offer up my sufferings to our Lord. I took a fever, which rendered me so weak, that after several weeks I could scarcely bear to be moved or to have my bed made. When I began to recover, an abscess fell upon my breast, which was forced to be laid open in two places, which gave me great pain. Yet all the maladies seemed to me only a shadow of troubles, in comparison with those I suffered in the family which daily increased. Indeed, life was so wearisome to me, that those maladies which were thought mortal did not frighten me.

The event improved my appearance, and consequently served to increase my vanity. I was glad to call forth expressions of regard. I went to the public promenades (though but seldom) and when in the streets, I pulled off my mask out of vanity. I drew off my gloves to show my hands. Could there be greater folly? After falling into these weaknesses, I used to weep bitterly at home. Yet, when occasion offered, I fell into them again.

My husband lost considerably. This cost me strange crosses, not that I cared for the losses, but I seemed to be the butt of all the ill-humors of the family. With what pleasure did I sacrifice temporal blessings. How often I felt willing to have begged my bread, if God had so ordered it. But my mother-in-law was inconsolable. She bid me pray to God for these things. To me that was wholly impossible.

O my dearest Lord, never could I pray to Thee about the world, or the things thereof; nor sully my sacred addresses to Thy majesty with the dirt of the earth. No; I rather wish to renounce it all, and everything beside whatsoever, for the sake of Thy love, and the enjoyment of Thy presence in that kingdom which is not of this world. I wholly sacrificed myself to Thee, even earnestly begging Thee rather to reduce our family to beggary, than suffer it to offend thee.

In my own mind I excused my mother-in-law, saying to myself, "If I had taken the pains to scrape and save, I would not be so indifferent at seeing so much lost. I enjoy what cost me nothing, and reap what I have not sowed" Yet all these thoughts could not make me sensible to our losses. I even formed agreeable ideas of our going to the hospital. No state appeared to me so poor and miserable, which I should not have thought easy, in comparison with the continual domestic persecutions I underwent. My father, who loved me tenderly, and whom I honored beyond expression, knew nothing of it. God so permitted it, that I should have him also displeased with me for some time. My mother was continually telling him that I was an ungrateful creature, showing no regard for them, but all for my husband's family. Appearances were against me. I did not go to see them as often as I should. They knew not the captivity I was in; what I was obliged to bear in defending them. These complaints of my mother, and a trivial affair that fell out, lessened a little my father's fond regard for me; but it did not last long. My mother-in-law reproached me, saying, "No afflictions befell them till I came into the house. All misfortunes came with me." On the other hand my mother wanted me to exclaim against my husband which I could never submit to do.

We continued to meet with loss after loss, the king retrenching a considerable share of our revenues, besides great sums of money, which we lost by L'Hotel de Ville. I could have no rest or peace, in such great afflictions. I had no mortal to console me, or to advise me. My sister, who had educated me, had departed this life. She died two months before my marriage. I had no other for a confidant.

I declare, that I find much repugnance in saying so many things of my mother-in-law. I have no doubt that my own indiscretion, my caprice, and the occasional sallies of a warm temper, drew many of the crosses upon me. Although I had what the world calls patience, yet I had neither a relish nor love for the cross. Their conduct toward me, which appeared so unreasonable, should not be looked upon with worldly eyes. We should look higher and then we shall see that it was directed by Providence for my eternal advantage.

I now dressed my hair in the most modest manner, never painted, and to subdue the vanity which still had possession of me, I rarely looked in the glass. My reading was confined to books of devotion, such as Thomas a'Kempis, and the works of St. Francis de Sales. I read these aloud for the improvement of the servants, while the maid was dressing my hair. I suffered myself to be dressed just as she pleased, which freed me from a great deal of trouble. It took away the occasions wherein my vanity used to be exercised. I knew not how things were; but they always liked me, and thought all well in point of dress. If on some particular days I wanted to appear better, it proved worse. The more indifferent I was about dress the better I appeared. How often have I gone to church, not so much to worship God as to be seen. Other women, jealous of me, affirmed that I painted; they told my confessor, who chided me for it, though I assured him I was innocent. I often spoke in my own praise, and sought to raise myself by depreciating others. Yet these faults gradually deceased; for I was very sorry afterward for having committed them. I often examined myself very strictly, writing down my faults from week to week, and from month to month, to see how much I was improved or reformed. Alas! this labor, though fatiguing, was of but little service, because I trusted in my own efforts. I wished indeed to be reformed, but my good desires were weak and languid.

At one time my husband's absence was so long, and in the meantime my crosses and vexations at home so great, that I determined to go to him. My mother-in-law strongly opposed it. This once my father interfering, and insisting on it, she let me go. On my arrival I found he had almost died. Through vexation and fretting he was very much changed. He could not finish his affairs, having no liberty in attending to them, keeping himself concealed at the Hotel de Longueville, where Madame de Longueville was extremely kind to me. I came publicly, and he was in great fear lest I should make him known. In a rage he bid me return home. Love and my long absence from him surmounting every other reason, he soon relented and suffered me to stay with him. He kept me eight days without letting me stir out of his sight. Fearing the effects of such a close confinement on my constitution, he desired me to go and take a walk in the garden There I met Madame de Longueville, who testified great joy on seeing me.

I cannot express all the kindness I met with in this house All the domestics served me with emulation, and applauded me on account of my appearance, and exterior deportment. Yet I was much on my guard against too much attention. I never entered into discourse with any man when alone. I admitted none into my coach, not even my relations, unless my husband were in it. There was not any rule of discretion which I did not duly observe, to avoid giving suspicion to my husband, or subject of calumny to others. Everyone studied there how to contribute to divert or oblige me. Outwardly everything appeared agreeable. Chagrin had so overcome and ruffled my husband that I had continually something to bear. Sometimes he threatened to throw the supper out of the windows. I said, he would then do me an injury, as I had a keen appetite." I made him laugh and I laughed with him. Before that, melancholy prevailed over all my endeavors, and over the love he had for me. God both armed me with patience and gave me the grace to return him no answer. The devil, who attempted to draw me into some offence, was forced to retire in confusion, through the signal assistance of that grace.

I loved my God and was unwilling to displease Him, and I was inwardly grieved on account of that vanity, which still I found myself unable to eradicate. Inward distresses, together with oppressive crosses, which I had daily to encounter, at length threw me into sickness. As I was unwilling to incommode the Hotel de Longueville I had myself moved to another house. The disease proved violent and tedious, insomuch that the physicians despaired of my life. The priest, a pious man, seemed fully satisfied with the state of my mind. He said, "I should die like a saint." But my sins were too present and too painful to my heart to have such presumption. At midnight they administered the sacrament to me as they hourly expected my departure. It was a scene of general distress in the family and among all who knew me. There were none indifferent to my death but myself. I beheld it without fear, and was insensible to its approach. It was far otherwise with my husband. He was inconsolable when he saw there was no hope. I no sooner began to recover, than notwithstanding all his love, his usual fretfulness returned. I recovered almost miraculously and to me this disorder proved a great blessing. Beside a very great patience under violent pains, it served to instruct me much in my view of the emptiness of all worldly things. It detached me from myself and gave me new courage to suffer better than I had done. The love of God gathered strength in my heart, with a desire to please and be faithful to Him in my condition. I reaped several other advantages from it which I need not relate, I had yet six months to drag along with a slow fever. It was thought that it would terminate in death.

Thy time, O my God, had not yet arrived for taking me to Thyself. Thy designs over me were widely different from the expectations of those about me; it being Thy determination to make me both the object of Thy mercy and the victim of Thy justice.

CHAPTER 8

Aᴄ FTER LONG LANQUISHING, at length I regained my former health. About this time my dear mother departed this life in great tranquility of mind. Beside her other good qualities, she had been particularly charitable to the poor. This virtue, so acceptable to God, He was graciously pleased to commence rewarding even in this life. Though she was but twenty-four hours sick, she was made perfectly easy about everything that was near and dear to her in this world.

I now applied myself to my duties, never failing to practice that of prayer twice a day. I watched over myself, to subdue my spirit continually. I went to visit the poor in their houses, assisting them in their distresses. I did (according to my understanding) all the good I knew.

Thou, O my God, increased both my love and my patience, in proportion to my sufferings. I regretted not the temporal advantages with which my mother distinguished my brother above me. Yet they fell on on me about that, as about everything else. I also had for some time a severe ague. I did not indeed serve Thee yet with that fervor which Thou didst give me soon after. For I would still have been glad to reconcile Thy love with the love of myself and of the creature. Unhappily I always found some who loved me, and whom I could not forbear wishing to please. It was not that I loved them, but it was for the love that I bore to myself.

A lady, an exile, came to my father's house. He offered her an apartment which she accepted, and she stayed a long time. She was one of true piety and inward devotion. She had a great esteem for me, because I desired to love God. She remarked that I had the virtues of an active and bustling life; but I had not yet attained the simplicity of prayer which she experienced. Sometimes she dropped a word to me on that subject. As my time had not yet come, I did not understand her. Her example instructed me more than her words. I observed on her countenance something which marked a great enjoyment of the presence of God. By the exertion of studied reflection and thoughts I tried to attain it but to little purpose. I wanted to have, by my own efforts, what I could not acquire except by ceasing from all efforts.

My father's nephew, of whom I have made mention before, was returned from Cochin China, to take over some priests from Europe. I was exceedingly glad to see him, and remembered what good he had done me. The lady mentioned was no less rejoiced than I. They understood each other immediately and conversed in a spiritual language. The virtue of this excellent relation charmed me. I admired his continual prayer without being able to comprehend it. I endeavored to meditate, and to think on God without intermission, to utter prayers and ejaculations. I could not acquire, by all my toil, what God at length gave me Himself, and which is experienced only in simplicity. My cousin did all he could to attach me more strongly to God. He conceived great affection for me. The purity he observed in me from the corruptions of the age, the abhorrence of sin at a time of life when others are beginning to relish the pleasures of it, (I was not yet eighteen), gave him a great tenderness for me. I complained to him of my faults ingenuously. These I saw clearly. He cheered and exhorted me to support myself, and to persevere in my good endeavors. He would fain have introduced me into a more simple manner of prayer, but I was not yet ready for it. I believe his prayers were more effectual than his words.

No sooner was he gone out of my father's house, than thou, O Divine Love, manifested thy favor. The desire I had to please Thee, the tears I shed, the manifold pains I underwent, the labors I sustained, and the little fruit I reaped from them, moved Thee with compassion. This was the state of my soul when Thy goodness, surpassing all my vileness and infidelities, and abounding in proportion to my wretchedness, granted me in a moment, what all my own efforts could never procure. Beholding me rowing with laborious toil, the breath of Thy divine operations turned in my favor, and carried me full sail over this sea of affliction.

I had often spoken to my confessor about the great

anxiety it gave me to find I could not meditate, nor exert my imagination in order to pray. Subjects of prayer which were too extensive were useless to me. Those which were short and pithy suited me better.

At length, God permitted a very religious person, of the order of St. Francis, to pass by my father's dwelling. He had intended going another way that was shorter, but a secret power changed his design. He saw there was something for him to do, and imagined that God had called him for the conversion of a man of some distinction in that country. His labors there proved fruitless. It was the conquest of my soul which was designed. As soon as he arrived he came to see my father who rejoiced at his coming. At this time I was about to be delivered of my second son, and my father was dangerously ill, expected to die. For some time they concealed his sickness from me. An indiscreet person abruptly told me. Instantly I arose, weak as I was, and went to see him. A dangerous illness came upon me. My father was recovered, but not entirely, enough to give me new marks of his affection. I told him of the strong desire I had to love God, and my great sorrow at not being able to do it fully. He thought he could not give me a more solid indication of his love than in procuring me an acquaintance with this worthy man. He told me what he knew of him, and urged me to go and see him.

At first I made a difficulty of doing it, being intent on observing the rules of the strictest prudence. However, my father's repeated requests had with me the weight of a positive command. I thought I could not

do that amiss, which I only did in obedience to him.
I took a kinswoman with me. At first he seemed a
little confused; for he was reserved toward women.
Being newly come out of a five years' solitude, he was
surprised that I was the first to address him. He
spoke not a word for some time. I knew not to what
attribute his silence. I did not hesitate to speak to
him, and to tell him a few words, my difficulties
about prayer. Presently he replied, "It is, madame,
because you seek without what you have within.
Accustom yourself to seek God in your heart, and
you will there find Him."

Having said these words, he left me. They were to
me like the stroke of a dart, which penetrated
through my heart. I felt a very deep wound, a wound
so delightful that I desired not to be cured. These
words brought into my heart what I had been seeking so many years. Rather they discovered to me
what was there, and which I had not enjoyed for
want of knowing it.

O my Lord, Thou wast in my heart, and demanded
only a simple turning of my mind inward, to make me
perceive Thy presence. Oh, Infinite Goodness! how
was I running hither and thither to seek Thee, my
life was a burden to me, although my happiness was
within myself. I was poor in riches, and ready to perish with hunger, near a table plentifully spread, and
a continual feast. O Beauty, ancient and new; why
have I known Thee so late? Alas! I sought Thee
where Thou wert not, and did not seek Thee where
thou wert. It was for want of understanding these
words of Thy Gospel, "The kingdom of God cometh

72

not with observation . . . The kingdom of God is within you." This I now experienced. Thou becamest my King, and my heart Thy kingdom, wherein Thou didst reign supreme, and performed all Thy sacred will.

I told this man, that I did not know what he had done to me, that my heart was quite changed, that God was there. He had given me an experience of His presence in my soul; not by thought or any application of mind, but as a thing really possessed after the sweetest manner. I experienced these words in the Canticles (Song of Solomon): "Thy name is as precious ointment poured forth; therefore do the virgins love thee." I felt in my soul an unction which, as a salutary balsam, healed in a moment all my wounds.

I slept not that whole night, because Thy love, O my God, flowed in me like a delicious oil, and burned as a fire which was going to devour all that was left of self. I was suddenly so altered that I was hardly to be known either by myself or others. I found no longer those troublesome faults or reluctances They disappeared, being consumed like chaff in a great fire.

I now became desirous that the instrument hereof might become my director, preferable to any other. This good father could not readily resolve to charge himself with my conduct although he saw so surprising a change effected by the hand of God. Several reasons induced him to excuse himself. First, my person, then my youth, for I was only nineteen years. Lastly, a promise he had made to God, from a distrust of himself, never to take upon himself the direction of any of our sex, unless God, by some particular providence, should charge him therewith. However, upon my earnest and repeated request to him to become my director, he said he would pray to God and desired that I should do so. As he was at prayer, it was said to him, "Fear not that charge; she is my spouse." When I heard this, it affected me greatly. "What (said I to myself) a frightful monster of iniquity, who has done so much to offend my God, in abusing His favors, and requiting them with ingratitude, now to be declared his spouse!" After this he consented to my request.

Nothing was more easy to me than prayer. Hours passed away like moments, while I could hardly do anything else but pray. The fervency of my love allowed me no intermission. It was a prayer of rejoicing and possessing, devoid of all busy imaginations and forced reflections; it was a prayer of the will, and not of the head. The taste of God was so great, so pure, unblended and uninterrupted, that it drew and absorbed the power of my soul into a profound recollection without act or discourse. I had now no sight but of Jesus Christ alone. All else was excluded, in order to love with the greater extent, without any selfish motives or reasons for loving.

The will, absorbed the two others, the memory and understanding into itself, and concentrated them in LOVE;—not but that they still subsisted, but their operations were in a manner imperceptible and passive. They were no longer stopped or retarded by the multiplicity, but collected and united in one. So the rising of the sun does not extinguish the stars, but overpowers and absorbs them in the luster of his incomparable glory.

CHAPTER 9

Sᴜᴄʜ ᴡᴀs ᴛʜᴇ ᴘʀᴀʏᴇʀ that was given me at once, far above ecstacies, transports or visions. All these gifts are less pure, and more subject to illusion or deceits from the enemy.

Visions are in the inferior powers of the soul, and cannot produce true union. The soul must not dwell or rely upon them, or be retarded by them; they are but favors and gifts. The Giver alone must be our object and aim.

It is of such that Paul speaks, "Satan transforms himself into an angel of light," II Cor. 11:18; which is generally the case with such as are fond of visions, and lay a stress on them; because they are apt to convey a vanity to the soul, or at least hinder it from humbly attending to God only.

Ecstacies arise from a sensible relish. They may be termed a kind of spiritual sensuality, wherein the soul letting itself go too far, by reason of the sweetness it finds in them, falls imperceptibly into decay. The crafty enemy presents such sort of interior elevations and raptures for baits to entrap the soul, to

76

fill it with vanity and self-love, to fix its esteem and attention on the gifts of God, and to hinder it from following Jesus Christ in the way of renunciation and of death to all things.

And as to distinct interior words, they too are subject to illusion; the enemy can form and counterfeit them. Or if they come from a good angel (for God Himself never speaks thus) we may mistake and misapprehend them. They are spoken in a divine manner, but we construe them in a human and carnal manner.

But the immediate word of God has neither tone nor articulation. It is mute, silent, and unutterable. It is Jesus Christ Himself, the real and essential Word who in the center of the soul that is disposed for receiving Him, never one moment ceases from His living, fruitful, and divine operation.

Oh, thou Word made flesh, whose silence is inexpressible eloquence, Thou canst never be misapprehended or mistaken. Thou becomest the life of our life, and the soul of our soul. How infinitely is thy language elevated above all the utterances of human and finite articulation. Thy adorable power, all efficacious in the soul that has received it, communicates itself through them to others. As a divine seed it becomes fruitful to eternal life.

The revelations of things to come are also very dangerous. The Devil can counterfeit them, as he did formerly in the heathen temples, where he uttered oracles. Frequently they raise false ideas, vain hopes, and frivolous expectations. They take up the mind with future events, hinder it from dying to self, and

77

prevent it following Jesus Christ in His poverty, abnegation, and death.

Widely different is the revelation of Jesus Christ, made to the soul when the eternal Word is communicated. (Gal 1:16.) It makes us new creatures, created anew in Him. This revelation is what the Devil cannot counterfeit. From hence proceeds the only safe transport of ecstasy, which is operated by naked faith alone, and dying even to the gifts of God. As long as the soul continues resting in gifts, it does not fully renounce itself. Never passing into God the soul loses the real enjoyment of the Giver, by attachments to the gifts. This is truly an unutterable loss.

Lest I should let my mind go after these gifts, and steal myself from thy love, O my God, Thou wast pleased to fix me in a continual adherence to Thyself alone. Souls thus directed get the shortest way. They are to expect great sufferings, especially if they are mighty in faith, in mortification and deadness to all but God. A pure and disinterested love, and intenseness of mind for the advancement of thy interest alone. These are the dispositions Thou didst implant in me, and even a fervent desire of suffering for Thee. The cross, which I had hitherto borne only with resignation, was become my delight, and the special object of my rejoicing.

CHAPTER 10

I WROTE AN ACCOUNT of my wonderful change, in point of happiness, to that good father who had been made the instrument of it. It filled him both with joy and astonishment.

O my God, what penances did the love of suffering induce me to undergo! I was impelled to deprive myself of the most innocent indulgences. All that could gratify my taste was denied and I took everything that could mortify and disgust it. My appetite, which had been extremely delicate, was so far conquered that I could scarcely prefer one thing to another.

I dressed loathsome sores and wounds, and gave remedies to the sick. When I first engaged in this sort of employment, it was with the greatest difficulty I was able to bear it. As soon as my aversion ceased, and I could stand the most offensive things, other channels of employment were opened to me. (For I did nothing of myself, but left myself to be wholly governed by my Sovereign.)

When that good father asked me how I loved God, I answered, "Far more than the most passionate lover his beloved; and that even this comparison was inadequate, since the love of the creature never can attain to this, either in strength or in depth." This love of God occupied my heart so constantly and so strongly, that I could think of nothing else. Indeed, I judged nothing else worthy of my thoughts.

The good father mentioned was an excellent preacher. He was desired to preach in the parish to which I belonged. When I came, I was so strongly absorbed in God, that I could neither open my eyes, nor hear anything he said.

—I found that Thy Word, O my God, made its own impression on my heart, and there had its effect, without the mediation of words or any attention to them. And I have found it so ever since, but after a different manner, according to the different degrees and states I have passed through. So deeply was I settled in the inward spirit of prayer, that I could scarce any more pronounce the vocal prayers.

This immersion in God absorbed all things therein. Although I tenderly loved certain saints, as St. Peter, St. Paul, St. Mary Magdalene, St. Teresa, yet I could not form to myself images of them, nor invoke any of them out of God.

A few weeks after I had received that interior wound of the heart, which had begun my change, the feast of the Blessed Virgin was held, in the convent in which was that good father my director. I went in the morning to get the indulgences and was much surprised when I came there and found that I could not attempt it; though I stayed above five hours in the church. I was penetrated with so lively a dart of pure love, that I could not resolve to abridge by in-

dulgences, the pain due to my sins. "O my Love,"
I cried, "I am willing to suffer for Thee. I find no
other pleasure but in suffering for Thee. Indulgences
may be good for those who know not the value of
sufferings, who choose not that thy divine justice
should be satisfied; who, having mercenary souls, are
not so much afraid of displeasing Thee, as of the
pains annexed to sin." Yet, fearing I might be mistaken, and commit a fault in not getting the indulgences, for I had never heard of anyone being in
such a way before, I returned again to try to get
them, but in vain. Not knowing what to do, I resigned
myself to our Lord. When I returned home, I
wrote to the good father that he had made what I
had written a part of his sermon, reciting it verbatum
as I had written it.

I now quitted all company, bade farewell forever to
all plays and diversions, dancing, unprofitable walks
and parties of pleasure. For two years I had left off
dressing my hair. It became me, and my husband approved it.

My only pleasure now was to steal some moments
to be alone with Thee, O thou who art my only Love!
All other pleasure was a pain to me. I lost not Thy
presence, which was given me by a continual infu-
sion, not as I had imagined, by the efforts of the
head, or by force of thought in meditating on God,
but in the will, where I tasted with unutterable
sweetness the enjoyment of the beloved object. In a
happy experience I knew that that the soul was
created to enjoy its God.

The union of the will subjects the soul to God, con-

81

forms it to all His pleasure, causes self-will gradually to die. Lastly in drawing with it the other powers, by means of the charity with which it is filled. It causes them gradually to be reunited in the Center, and lost there as to their own nature and operations.

This loss is called the annihilation of the powers. Although in themselves they still subsist, yet they seem annihilated to us, in proportion as charity fills and inflames; it becomes so strong, as by degrees to surmount all the activities of the will of man, subjecting it to that of God. When the soul is docile, and leaves itself to be purified, and emptied of all that which it has of its own, opposite to the will of God, it finds itself by little and little, detached from every emotion of its own, and placed in a holy indifference, wishing nothing but what God does and wills. This never can be effected by the activity of our own will, even though it were employed in continual acts or resignation. These though very virtuous, are so far one's own actions, and cause the will to subsist in a multiplicity, in a kind of separate distinction or dissimilitude from God.

When the will of the creature entirely submits to that of the Creator, suffering freely and voluntarily and yielding only a concurrence to the divine will (which is its absolute submission) suffering itself to be totally surmounted and destroyed, by the operations of love; this absorbs the will into self, consummates it in that of God, and purifies it from all narrowness, dissimilitude, and selfishness.

The case is the same with the other two powers. By means of charity, the two other theological virtues, faith and hope, are introduced. Faith so strongly siezes on the understanding, as to make it decline all reasonings, all particular illuminations and illustrattions, however sublime. This sufficiently demonstrates how far visions, revelations and ecstasies, differ from this, and hinder the soul from being lost in God. Although by them it appears lost in Him for some transient moments, yet it is not a true loss, since the soul which is entirely lost in God no more finds itself again. Faith then makes the soul lose every distinct light, in order to place it in its own pure light.

The memory, too, finds all its little activities surmounted by degrees, and absorbed in hope. Finally the powers are all concentrated and lost in pure love. It engulfs them into itself by means of their sovereign, the WILL. The will is the sovereign of the powers and charity is the queen of the virtues, and unites them all in herself.

This reunion thus made, is called the central union or unity. By means of the will and love, all are reunited in the center of the soul in God who is our ultimate end. According to St. John, "He who dwelleth in love, dwelleth in God, for God is love."

This union of my will to Thine, O my God, and this ineffable presence was so sweet and powerful, that I was compelled to yield to its delightful power, power which was strict and severe to my minutest faults.

CHAPTER 11

My senses (as I have described) were continually mortified, and under perpetual restraint. To conquer them totally, it is necessary to deny them the smallest relaxation, until the victory is completed. We see those who content themselves practicing great outward austerities, yet by indulging their senses in what is called innocent and necessary, they remain forever unsubdued. Austerities, however severe, will not conquer the senses. To destroy their power, the most effectual means is, in general, to deny them firmly what will please, and to persevere in this, until they are reduced to be without desire or repugnance. If we attempt, during the warfare, to grant them any relaxation, we act like those, who, under pretext of strengthening a man, who was condemned to be starved to death, should give him from time to time a little nourishment. It indeed would prolong his torments, and postpone his death.

It is just the same with the death of the senses, the powers, the understanding, and self-will. If we do not eradicate every remains of self subsisting in these, we support them in a dying life to the end. This state and its termination are clearly set forth by Paul. He speaks of bearing about in the body the dying of the Lord Jesus. (II Cor. 4:10.). But, lest we should rest here, he fully distinguishes this from the state of being dead and having our life hid with Christ in God. It is only by a total death to self we can be lost in God.

He who is thus dead has no further need of mortification. The very end of mortification is accomplished in him, and all is become new. It is an unhappy error in those good souls, who have arrived at a conquest of the bodily senses, through this unremitted and continual mortification, that they should still continue attached to the exercise of it. They should rather drop their attention thereto, and remain in indifference, accepting with equality the good as the bad, the sweet as the bitter, and bend their whole attention to a labor of greater importance; namely, the mortification of the mind and self-will. They should begin by dropping all the activity of self, which can never be done without the most profound prayer; no more than the death of the senses can be perfected without profound recollection joined to mortification. Indeed, recollection is the chief means whereby we attain to a conquest of the senses. It detaches and separates us from them, and sweetly saps the very cause from whence they derive their influence over us.

The more Thou didst augment my love, and my patience, O my Lord, the less respite had I from the most oppressive crosses; but love rendered them easy to bear.

O ye poor souls, who exhaust yourselves with needless vexation, if you would but seek God in your hearts, there would be a speedy end to all your troubles. The increase of crosses would proportionately increase your delight.

Love, at the beginning, athirst for mortification impelled me to seek and invent various kinds. It is surprising, that as soon as the bitterness of any new mode of mortification was exhausted, another kind was pointed to me, and I was inwardly led to pursue it. Divine love so enlightened my heart, and so scrutinized into its secret springs, that the smallest defects became exposed. If I was about to speak, something wrong was instantly pointed to me, and I was compelled to silence. If I kept silence, faults were presently discovered—in every action there was something defective—in my mortifications, my penances, my alms-giving, my retirement, I was faulty. When I walked, I observed there was something wrong; if I spoke any way in my own favor, I saw pride. If I said within myself, alas, I will speak no more, here was self. If I was cheerful and open, I was condemned. Pure love always found matter for reproof in me, and was jealous that nothing should escape unnoticed. It was not that I was particularly attentive over myself, for it was even with constraint that I could look at all at myself. My attention toward God, by an attachment of my will to His, was without intermission. I waited continually upon Him, and He watched incessantly over me, and He so led me by His providence, that I forgot all things. I knew not how to communicate what I felt to anyone. I was so lost to myself, that I could scarcely go about self-examination. When I attempted it all ideas of myself immediately disappeared. I found myself occupied with my ONE OBJECT, without distinction of ideas. I was absorbed in peace inexpressible; I saw by the eye of faith that it was God that thus wholly possessed me; but I did not reason at all about it. It must not, however, be supposed that divine love suffered my faults to go unpunished.

O Lord! with what rigor, dost Thou punish the most faithful, the most loving and beloved of Thy children. I mean not externally, for this would be inadequate to the smallest fault, in a soul that God is about to purify radically. The punishments it can inflict on itself, are rather gratifications and refreshments than otherwise. Indeed, the manner in which He corrects His chosen, must be felt, or it is impossible to conceive how dreadful it is. In my attempt to explain it, I shall be unintelligible, except to experienced souls. It is an internal burning, a secret fire sent from God to purge away the fault, giving extreme pain, until this purification is complete. It is like a dislocated joint, which is in incessant torment, until the bone is replaced. This pain is so severe, that the soul would do anything to satisfy God for the fault, and would rather be torn in pieces than endure the torment. Sometimes the soul flies to others, and opens her state that she may find consolation. Thereby she frustrates God's designs toward her. It is of the utmost consequence to know what use to make of the distress. The whole of one's spiritual advancement depends on it. We should at these seasons of internal anguish, obscurity and mourning, co-operate with God, endure this consuming torture in its utmost extent (while it continues) without attempting to lessen or increase it. Bear it passively, nor seek to satisfy God by anything we can do of ourselves. To continue passive at such a time is extremely difficult, and requires great firmness and courage. I knew some who never advanced farther in the spiritual process because they grew impatient, and sought means of consolation.

CHAPTER 12

THE TREATMENT OF MY HUSBAND and mother-in-law, however rigorous and insulting, I now bore silently. I made no replies and this was not so difficult for me, because the greatness of my interior occupation, and what passed within, rendered me insensible to all the rest. There were times when I was left to myself. Then I could not refrain from tears. I did the lowest offices for them to humble myself. All this did not win their favor. When they were in a rage, although I could not find that I had given them any occasion, yet I did not fail to beg their pardon, even from the girl of whom I have spoken. I had a good deal of pain to surmount myself, as to the last. She became the more insolent for it; reproaching me with things which ought to have made her blush and have covered her with shame. As she saw that I contradicted and resisted her no more in anything, she proceeded to treat me worse. And when I asked her pardon she triumphed, saying, "I knew very well I was in the right." Her arrogance rose to the height that I would not have treated the meanest slave.

89

One day, as she was dressing me, she pulled me roughly, and spoke to me insolently. I said, "It is not my account that I am willing to answer you, for you give me no pain, but lest you should act thus before persons to whom it would give offence. Moreover, as I am your mistress, God is assuredly offended with you." She left me that moment, and ran like a mad woman to meet my husband telling him she would stay no longer, I treated her so ill, that I hated her for the care she took of him in his continual indispositions, wanting her not to do any service for him. My husband was very hasty, so he took fire at these words. I finished dresing alone. Since she had left me I dared not call another girl; she would not suffer another girl to come near me. I saw my husband coming like a lion, he was never in such a rage as this. I thought he was going to strike me; I awaited the blow with tranquillity; he threatened with his uplifted crutch; I thought he was going to knock me down. Holding myself closely united to God, I beheld it without pain. He did not strike me for he had presence of mind enough to see what indignity it would be. In his rage he threw it at me. It fell near me, but it did not touch me. He then discharged himself in language as if I had been a street beggar, or the most infamous of creatures. I kept profound silence, being recollected in the Lord.

The girl in the meantime came in. At the sight of her his rage redoubled. I kept near to God, as a victim disposed to suffer whatever He would permit. My husband ordered me to beg her pardon, which I readily did, and thereby appeased him. I went into my closet, where I no sooner was, than my divine Director impelled me to make this girl a present, to recompense her for the cross which she had caused me. She was a little astonished, but her heart was too hard to be gained.

I often acted thus because she frequently gave me opportunities. She had a singular dexterity in attending the sick. My husband, ailing almost continually, would suffer no other person to administer to him. He had a very great regard for her. She was artful; in his presence she affected an extraordinary respect for me. When he was not present, if I said a word to her, though with the greatest mildness and if she heard him coming, she cried out with all her might that she was unhappy She acted like one distressed so that, without informing himself of the truth, he was irritated against me, as was also my mother-in-law.

The violence I did to my proud and hasty nature was so great, that I could hold out no longer. I was quite spent with it. It seemed sometimes as if I was inwardly rent, and I have often fallen sick with the struggle. She did not forbear exclaiming against me, even before persons of distinction, who came to see me. If I was silent, she took offence at that yet more, and said that I despised her. She cried me down, and made complaints to everybody. All this redounded to my honor and her own disgrace. My reputation was so well established, on account of my exterior modesty, my devotion, and the great acts of charity which I did, that nothing could shake it.

Sometimes she ran out into the street, crying out

against me. At one time she exclamied, "Am not I very unhappy to have such a mistress?" People gathered about her to know what I had done to her; and not knowing what to say, she answered that I had not spoken to her all the day. They returned, laughing, and said, "She has done you no great harm then."

I am surprised at the blindness of confessors, and at their permitting their penitents to conceal so much of the truth from them. The confessor of this girl made her pass for a saint. This he said in my hearing. I answered nothing; for love would not permit me to speak of my troubles. I should consecrate them all to God by a profound silence.

My husband was out of humor with my devotion. "What," said he, "you love God so much, that you love me no longer." So little did he comprehend that the true conjugal love is that which the Lord Himself forms in the heart that loves Him.

Oh, Thou who art pure and holy, Thou didst imprint in me from the first such a love of chastity, that there was nothing in the world which I would not have undergone to possess and preserve it.

I endeavored to be agreeable to my husband in anything, and to please him in everything he could require of me. God gave me such a purity of soul at that time, that I had not so much as a bad thought. Sometimes my husband said to me, "One sees plainly that you never lose the presence of God."

The world, seeing I quit it, persecuted and turned me into ridicule. I was its entertainment, and the subject of its fables. It could not bear that a woman, scarce twenty years of age, should thus make war against it, and overcome. My mother-in-law took part with the world, and blamed me for not doing many things that in her heart she would have been highly offended had I done them. I was as one lost, and alone; so little communion had I with the creature, farther than necessity required. I seemed to experience literally those words of Paul, "I live yet, no more I, but Christ liveth in me." His operations were so powerful, so sweet, and so secret, all together, that I could not express them. We went into the country on some business. Oh! what unutterable communications did I there experience in retirement!

I was insatiable for prayer. I arose at four o'clock in the morning to pray. I went very far to the church, which was so situated, that the coach could not come to it. There was a steep hill to go down and another to ascend. All that cost me nothing; I had such a longing desire to meet with my God, as my only good, who on His part was graciously forward to give Himself to His poor creature, and for it to do even visible miracles. Such as saw me lead a life so very different from the women of the world said I was a fool. They attributed it to stupidity. Sometimes they said, "What can all this mean? Some people think this lady has parts, but nothing of them appears." If I went into company, often I could not speak; so much was I engaged within, so inward with the Lord, as not to attend to anything else. If any near me spoke, I heard nothing. I generally took one with me, that this might not appear. I took some work, to hide under that appearance the real employ of my heart. When I was alone, the work dropped out of my hand. I wanted to persuade a relation of my husband's to practice prayer. She thought me a fool, for depriving myself of all the amusements of the age. But the Lord opened her eyes, to make her despise them. I could have wished to teach all the world to love God; and thought it depended only on them to feel what I felt. The Lord made use of my thinking to gain many souls to Himself.

The good father I have spoken of, who was the instrument of my conversion, made me acquainted with Genevieve Granger, prioress of the Benedictines, one of the greatest servants of God of her time. She proved of very great service to me. My confessor, who had told everyone that I was a saint before, when so full of miseries, and so far from the condition to which the Lord in His mercy had now brought me, seeing I placed a confidence in the father of whom I have spoken, and that I steered in a road which was unknown to him, declared openly against me. The monks of his order persecuted me much. They even preached publicly against me, as a person under a delusion.

My husband and mother-in-law, who till now had been indifferent about this confessor, then joined him and ordered me to leave off prayer, and the exercise of piety; that I could not do. There was carried on a conversation within me, very different from that which passed without. I did what I could to hinder it from appearing, but could not. The presence of so great a Master manifested itself, even on my countenance. That pained my husband, he sometimes told me. I did what I could to hinder it from being noticed, but was not able completely to hide it. I was so much inwardly occupied that I knew not what I ate. I made as if I ate some kinds of meat, though I did not take any. This deep inward attention suffered me scarcely to hear or see anything. I still continued to use many severe mortifications and austerities. They did not in the least diminish the freshness of my countenance.

I had often grievous fits of sickness and no consolation in life, except in the practice of prayer, and in seeing Mother Granger. How dear did these cost me, especially the former! Is this esteeming the cross as I ought?—should I not rather say that prayer to me was recompensed with the cross, and the cross with prayer. Inseparable gifts united in my heart and life! When your eternal light arose in my soul, how perfectly it reconciled me and made you the object of my love! From the moment I received Thee I have never been free from the cross, nor it seems without prayer—though for a long time I thought myself deprived thereof, which exceedingly augmented my afflictions.

My confessor at first exerted his efforts to hinder me from practicing prayer, and from seeing Mother Granger. He violently stirred up my husband and mother-in-law to hinder me from praying. The method they took was to watch me from morning until night. I dared not go out from my mother-in-law's room, or from my husband's bedside. Sometimes I carried my work to the window, under a pretense of seeing better, in order to relieve myself with some moment's repose. They came to watch me very closely, to see if I did not pray instead of working. When my husband and mother-in-law played cards, if I did turn toward the fire, they watched to see if I continued my work or shut my eyes. If they observed I closed them, they would be in a fury against me for several hours. What is most strange, when my husband went out, having some days of health, he would not allow me to pray in his absence. He marked my work, and sometimes, after he was just gone out, returning immediately, if he found me in prayer he would be in a rage. In vain I said, "Surely, sir, what matters it what I do when you are absent, if I be assiduous in attending you when you are present?" That would not satisfy him; he insisted that I should no more pray in his absence than in his presence.

I believe there is hardly a torment equal to that of being ardently drawn to retirement, and not having it in one's power to be retired.

O my God, the war they raised to hinder me from loving Thee did but augment my love. While they were striving to prevent my addresses to Thee, thou drewest me into an inexpressible silence. The more they labored to separate me from Thee, the more closely didst Thou unite me to Thyself. The flame of Thy love was kindled, and kept up by everything that was done to extinguish it.

Often through compliance I played at piquet with my husband. At such times I was even more interiorly attracted than if I had been at church. I was scarce able to contain the fire which burned in my soul, which had all the fervor of what men call love, but

96

nothing of its impetuosity. The more ardent, the more peaceable it was. This fire gained strength from everything that was done to suppress it. And the spirit of prayer was nourished and increased from their contrivances and endeavors to disallow me any time for practicing it. I loved without considering a motive or reason for loving. Nothing passed in my head, but much in the innermost recesses of my soul. I thought not about any recompense, gift, or favor, which He could bestow or I receive. The Well-beloved was Himself the only object which attracted my heart. I could not contemplate His attributes. I knew nothing else, but to love and to suffer. Ignorance more truly learned than any science of the doctors, since it taught me so well Jesus Christ crucified and brought me to be in love with His holy cross. I could then have wished to die, in order to be inseparably united to Him who so powerfully attracted my heart. As all this passed in the will, the imagination and the understanding being absorbed in it, I knew not what to say, having never read or heard of such a state as I experienced. I dreaded delusion and feared that all was not right, for before this I had known nothing of the operations of God in souls. I had only read St. Francis de Sales, Thomas a'Kempis, *The Spiritual Combat,* and the Holy Scriptures. I was quite a stranger to those spiritual books wherein such states are described.

Then all those amusements and pleasures that are prized and esteemed appeared to me dull and insipid. I wondered how it could be that I had ever enjoyed them. And indeed since that time, I could never find any satisfaction or enjoyment out of God. I have sometimes been unfaithful enough to find it. I was not astonished that martyrs gave their lives for Jesus Christ. I thought them happy, and sighed after their privilege of suffering for Him, I so esteemed the cross that my greatest trouble was the want of suffering as much as my heart thirsted for.

This respect and esteem for the cross continually increased. Afterward I lost the sensible relish and enjoyment, yet the love and esteem no more left me than the cross itself. Indeed, it has ever been my faithful companion, changing and augmenting, in proportion to the changes and dispositions of my inward state. O blessed cross, thou hast never quitted me, since I surrendered myself to my divine, crucified Master. I still hope that thou wilt never abandon me. So eager was I for the cross, that I endeavored to make myself feel the utmost rigor of every mortification. This only served to awaken my desire for suffering, and to show me that it is God alone that can prepare and send crosses suitable to a soul that thirsts for a following of His sufferings, and a conformity to His death. The more my state of prayer augmented, my desire of suffering grew stronger, as the full weight of heavy crosses from every side came thundering upon me.

The peculiar property of this prayer of the heart is to give a strong faith. Mine was without limits, as was also my resignation to God, and my confidence in Him—my love of His will, and of the order of His providence over me. I was very timorous before, but now feared nothing. It is in such a case that one feels the efficacy of these words, "My yoke is easy, and my burden is light" (Matt. 11:30).

CHAPTER 13

I HAD A SECRET DESIRE given me from that time to be wholly devoted to the disposal of my God, let that be what it would. I said, "What couldst Thou demand of me, that I would not willingly offer Thee? Oh, spare me not." The cross and humiliations were represented to my mind in the most frightful colors, but this deterred me not. I yielded myself up as willing and indeed our Lord seemed to accept of my sacrifice, for His divine providence furnished me incessantly with occasions and opportunities for putting it to the test.

I had difficulty to say vocal prayers I had been used to repeat. As soon as I opened my lips to pronounce them, the love of God seized me strongly. I was swallowed up in a profound silence and an inexpressible peace. I made fresh attempts but still in vain. I began again and again, but could not go on. I had never before heard of such a state, I knew not what to do. My inability increased because my love to the Lord was growing more strong, more violent and more overpowering. There was made in me, without the sound of words, a continual prayer. It

100

seemed to me to be the prayer of our Lord Jesus Christ Himself; a prayer of the Word, which is made by the Spirit. According to St. Paul it "asketh for us that which is good, perfect, and conformable to the will of God" (Rom. 8:26-27).

My domestic crosses continued. I was prevented from seeing or even writing to Mrs. Granger. My very going to divine service or the sacrament, were a source of woeful offences. The only amusement I had left me, was the visiting and attending the sick poor, and performing the lowest offices for them.

My prayer-time began to be exceedingly distressing. I compelled myself to continue at it, though deprived of all comfort and consolation. When I was not employed therein, I felt an ardent desire and longing for it. I suffered inexpressible anguish in my mind, and endeavored with the severest inflictions of corporeal austerities to mitigate and divert it—but in vain. I found no more that enlivening vigor which had hitherto carried me on with great swiftness. I seemed to myself to be like those young brides, who find a great deal of difficulty to lay aside their self-love, and to follow their husbands to the war. I relapsed into a vain complacency and fondness for myself. My propensity to pride and vanity, which seemed quite dead, while I was so filled with love of God, now showed itself again, and gave me severe exercise. This made me lament the exterior beauty of my person, and pray to God incessantly, that he would remove from me that obstacle, and make me ugly. I could even have wished to be deaf, blind and dumb, that nothing might divert me from my love of God.

I set out on a journey, which we had then to make, and I appeared more than ever like those lamps which emit a glimmering flash, when they are just on the point of extinguishing. Alas! how many snares were laid in my way! I met them at every step. I even committed infidelities through unwatchfulness.

O my Lord, with what rigor didst Thou punish them! A useless glance was checked as a sin. How many tears did those inadvertent faults cost me, through a weak compliance, and even against my will! Thou knowest that Thy rigor, exercised after my slips, was not the motive of those tears which I shed. With what pleasure would I have suffered the most rigorous severity to have been cured of my infidelity. To what severe chastisement did I not condemn myself! Sometimes Thou didst treat me like a father who pities the child, and caresses it after its involuntary faults. How often didst Thou make me sensible of Thy love toward me, notwithstanding my blemishes! It was the sweetness of this love after my falls which caused my greatest pain; for the more the amiableness of Thy love was extended to me, the more inconsolable I was for having departed ever so little from Thee. When I had let some inadvertence escape me, I found Thee ready to receive me. I have often cried out, "O my Lord! is it possible thou canst be so gracious to such an offender, and so indulgent to my faults; so propitious to one who has wandered astray from Thee, by vain complaisances, and an unworthy fondess for frivolous objects? Yet no sooner do I return, than I find Thee waiting, with open arms ready to receive me.

O sinner, sinner! hast thou any reason to complain of God? If there yet remains in thee any justice, confess the truth, and admit that it is owing to thyself if thou goest wrong; that in departing from Him thou disobeyest His call. When thou returnest, He is ready to receive thee; and if thou returnest not, He makes use of the most engaging motives to win thee. Yet thou turnest a deaf ear to His voice; thou wilt not hear Him. Thou sayest He speaks not to thee, though He calls loudly. It is therefore only because thou daily rebellest, and art growing daily more and more deaf to the voice.

When I was in Paris, and the clergy saw me so young, they appeared astonished. Those to whom I opened my state told me, that I could never enough thank God for the graces conferred on me; that if I knew them I should be amazed at them; and that if I were not faithful, I should be the most ungrateful of all creatures. Some declared that they never knew any woman whom God held so closely, and in so great a purity of conscience.

I believe what rendered it so was the continual care Thou hadst over me, O my God, making me feel Thy presence, even as Thou hast promised it to us in Thy Gospel,—"if a man love me, my Father will love him, and we will come unto him, and make our abode with him (John 14:23). The continual experience of Thy presence in me was what preserved me. I became deeply assured of what the prophet had said, "Except the Lord keep the city, the watchman waketh but in vain (Ps. 127:1). Thou, O my Love, wert my faithful keeper, who didst defend my heart against all sorts of enemies, preventing the least faults, or correcting them when vivacity had occasioned their being committed. But alas! when Thou didst cease to watch for me, or left me to myself, how weak was I, and how easily did my enemies prevail over me! Let others ascribe their victory to their own fidelity. As for me, I shall never attribute them to anything else than thy paternal care. I have too often experienced, to my cost, what I should be without Thee, to presume in the least on any cares of my own. It is to Thee, and to Thee only, that I owe everything, O my Deliverer; and my being indebted to Thee for it gives me infinite joy.

While in Paris, I relaxed and did many things which I should not. I knew the extreme fondness which some had for me, and suffered them to express it without checking it as I ought. I fell into other faults too, as having my neck a little too bare, though not near so much as others had. I plainly saw I was too remiss; and that was my torment. I sought all about for Him who had secretly inflamed my heart. But, alas! hardly anybody knew Him. I cried, "Oh, Thou best beloved of my soul, hadst Thou been near me these disasters had not befallen me." When I say that I spoke thus to Him, it is but to explain myself. In reality, it all passed almost in silence, for I could not speak. My heart had a language which was carried on without the sound of words, understood of Him, as He understands the language of the Word, which speaks incessantly in the innermost recesses of the soul. Oh, sacred language! Experience only gives the comprehension of it! Let not any think it a barren language, and effect of the mere imagination. Far different—it is the silent expression of the Word in the soul. As He never ceases to speak, so He never ceases to operate. If people once came to know the operations of the Lord, in souls wholly resigned to His guiding, it would fill them with reverential admiration and awe.

I saw that the purity of my state was like to be sullied by too great a commerce with the creatures, so I made haste to finish what detained me in Paris, in order to return to the country. "Tis true, O my Lord, I felt that Thou hadst given me strength enough to avoid the occasions of evil—but when I had so far yielded as to get into them, I found I could not resist the vain complaisances, and a number of other foibles which they ensnared me into." The pain which I felt after my faults was inexpressible. It was not an anguish that arose from any distinct idea or conception, from any particular motive or affection—but a kind of devouring fire which ceased not, till the fault was consumed and the soul purified. It was a banishment of my soul from the presence of its Beloved. I could have no access to Him, neither could I have any rest out of Him. I knew not what to do. I was like the dove out of the ark, which finding no rest for the soul of her foot, was constrained to return to the ark; but, finding the window shut, could only fly about. In the meantime, through an infidelity which will ever render me culpable, I strove to find some satisfaction without, but could not. This served to convince me of my folly and of the vanity of those pleasures which are called innocent. When I was prevailed on to taste them, I felt a strong repulse which, joined with my remorse for the transgression, changed the diversion into torment. "Oh, my Father," said I, "this is not Thee; and nothing else, beside Thee, can give solid pleasure."

One day, as much through unfaithfulness as complaisance, I went to take a walk at some of the public parks, rather from excess of vanity to show myself than to take the pleasure of the place. Oh, my Lord! how didst Thou make me sensible of this fault? But far from punishing me in letting me partake of the amusement, Thou didst it in holding me so close to Thyself, that I could give no attention to anything but my fault and Thy displeasure. After this I was invited with some other ladies to an entertainment at St. Cloud. Through vanity and weak compliance, I yielded and went. The affair was magnificent; they, though wise in the eye of the world, could relish it. I was filled with bitterness. I could eat nothing, I could enjoy nothing. Oh, what tears! For beyond three months my Beloved withdrew His favoring presence, and I could see nothing but an angry God.

I was on this occasion, and in another journey which I took with my husband into Touraine, like those animals destined for slaughter. On certain days people adorn them with greens and flowers, and bring in pomp into the city before they kill them. This weak beauty, on the eve of decline, shone forth with new brightness, in order to become the sooner extinct. I was shortly after afflicted with the smallpox.

One day as I walked to church, followed by a footman I was met by a poor man. I went to give him alms; he thanked me but refused them and then spoke to me in a wonderful manner of God and of divine things. He displayed to me my whole heart, my love to God, my charity, my too great fondness for my beauty and all my faults; he told me it was not enough to avoid Hell, but that the Lord required of me the utmost purity and height of perfection. My heart assented to his reproofs. I heard him with silence and respect, his words penetrated my very soul. When I arrived at the church I fainted away. I have never seen the man since.

CHAPTER 14

My HUSBAND ENJOYING some intermission of his almost continual ailments, had a mind to go to Orleans, and then into Touraine. In this journey my vanity made its last blaze. I received abundance of visits and applauses. But how clearly did I see the folly of men who are so taken with vain beauty! I disliked the disposition, yet not that which caused it, though I sometimes ardently desired to be delivered from it. The continual combat of nature and grace cost me no small affliction. Nature was pleased with public applause; grace made me dread it. What augmented the temptation was that they esteemed in me virtue, joined with youth and beauty. They did not know that all the virtue is only in God, and His protection, and all the weakness in myself.

I went in search of confessors, to accuse myself of my failing, and to bewail my backslidings. They were utterly insensible of my pain. They esteemed what God condemned. They treated as a virtue what to me appeared detestable in His sight. Far from measuring my faults by His graces, they only considered what I was, in comparison of what I might have been. Hence, instead of blaming me, they only flattered my pride. They justified me in what incurred His rebuke, or only treated as a slight fault what in me was highly displeasing to Him, from whom I had received such signal mercies.

The heinousness of sins is not to be measured singly by their nature, but also by the state of the person who commits them. The least unfaithfulness in a spouse is more injurious to her husband, than far greater ones in his domestics. I told them all the trouble I had been under for not having entirely covered my neck. It was covered much more than was covered by other women of my age. They assured me that I was very modestly dressed. As my husband liked my dress there could be nothing amiss in it. My inward Director taught me quite the contrary. I had not courage enough to follow Him, and to dress myself differently from others, at my age. My vanity furnished me with pretences seemingly just for following fashions. If pastors knew what hurt they do in humoring female vanity, they would be more severe against it! Had I found but one person honest enough to deal plainly with me, I should not have gone on. But my vanity, siding with the declared opinion of all others, induced me to think them right, and my own scruples mere fancy.

We met with accidents in this journey, sufficient to have terrified anyone. Though corrupt nature prevailed so far as I have just mentioned, yet my resignation to God was so strong, that I passed fearless, even where there was apparently no possibility of escape. At one time we got into a narrow pass, and did not perceive, until we were too far advanced to draw back, that the road was undermined by the river Loire, which ran beneath, and the banks had fallen in; so that in some places the footmen were obliged to support one side of the carriage. All those around me were terrified to the highest degree, yet God kept me perfectly tranquil. I secretly rejoiced at the prospect of losing my life by a singular stroke of His providence.

On my return, I went to see Mrs. Granger, to whom I related how it had been with me while abroad. She strengthened and encouraged me to pursue my first design. She advised me to cover my neck, which I have done ever since notwithstanding the singularity of it.

The Lord, who had so long deferred the chastisement merited by such a series of infidelities, now began to punish me for the abuse of his grace. Sometimes I wished to retire to a convent, and thought it lawful. I found wherein I was weak, and that my faults were always of the same nature. I wished to hide myself in some cave, or to be confined in a dreary prison, rather than enjoy a liberty by which I suffered so much. Divine love gently drew me inward, and vanity dragged me outward. My heart was rent asunder by the contest, as I neither gave myself wholly up to the one nor the other.

I besought my God to deprive me of power to displease Him, and cried, "Art thou not strong enough wholly to eradicate this unjust duplicity out of my heart?" For my vanity broke forth when occasions offered; yet I quickly returned to God. He, instead of repulsing or upbraiding me, often received me with open arms, and gave me fresh testimonials of His love. They filled me with the most painful reflections on my offense. Though this wretched vanity was still so prevalent, yet my love to God was such, that after my wanderings, I would rather have chosen His rod than His caresses. His interests were more dear to me than my own, and I wished He would have done Himself justice upon me. My heart was full of grief and of love. I was stung to the quick for offending Him, who showered His grace so profusely upon me. That those who know not God should offend Him by sin is not to be wondered at, but that a heart which loved Him more than itself, and so fully experienced His love, should be seduced by propensities which it detests, is a cruel martyrdom.

When I felt most strongly Thy presence, and Thy love, O Lord, said I, how wonderfully Thou bestowest Thy favors on such a wretched creature, who requites Thee only with ingratitude. For if anyone reads this life with attention, he will see on God's part, nothing but goodness, mercy, and love; on my part, nothing but weakness, sin and infidelity. I have nothing to glory in but my infirmities and my unworthiness, since, in that everlasting marriage-union thou hast made with me, I brought with me nothing but weakness, sin and misery. How I rejoice to owe all to Thee, and that Thou favorest my heart with a sight of the treasures and boundless riches of Thy grace and love! Thou hast dealt by me, as if a magnificent king should marry a poor slave, forget her slavery, give her all the ornaments which may render her pleasing in his eyes, and freely pardon her all the faults and ill qualities which her ignorance and bad education had given her. This Thou hast made my case. My poverty is become my riches, and in the extremity of my weakness I have found my strength. Oh, if any knew, with what confusion the indulgent favors of God cover the soul after its faults! Such a soul would wish with all its power to satisfy the divine justice. I made verses and little songs to bewail myself. I exercised austerities, but they did not satisfy my heart. They were like those drops of water which only serve to make the fire hotter. When I take a view of God, and myself, I am obliged to cry out, "Oh, admirable conduct of Love toward an ungrateful wretch! Oh, horrible ingratitude toward such unparalleled goodness." A great part of my life is only a mixture of such things as might be enough to sink me to the grave between grief and love.

CHAPTER 15

On my arrival at home, I found my husband taken with the gout, and his other complaints. My little daughter ill, and like to die of the smallpox; my eldest son, too, took it; and it was of so malignant a type, that it rendered him as disfigured, as before he was beautiful. As soon as I perceived the smallpox was in the house, I had no doubt but I should take it. Mrs. Granger advised me to leave if I could. My father offered to take me home, with my second son, whom I tenderly loved. My mother-in-law would not suffer it. She persuaded my husband it was useless, and sent for a physician, who seconded her in it, saying, "I should as readily take it at a distance as here, if I were disposed to take it." I may say, she proved at that time a second Jephtha, and that she sacrificed us both, though innocently. Had she known what followed, I doubt not but she would have acted otherwise. All the town stirred in this affair. Everyone begged her to send me out of the house, and cried out that it was cruel to expose me thus. They set upon me, too, imagining I was unwilling to go. I had not told that she was so averse to it. I had at that time no other disposition than to sacrifice myself to divine Providence. Though I might have removed, notwithstanding my mother-in-law's resistance, yet I would not without her consent; because it looked to me as if her resistance was an order of Heaven.

I continued in this spirit of sacrifice to God, waiting from moment to moment in an entire resignation, for whatever He should be pleased to ordain. I cannot express what nature suffered. I was like one who sees both certain death and an easy remedy, without being able to avoid the former, or try the latter. I had no less apprehension for my younger son than for myself. My mother-in-law so excessively doted on the eldest, that the rest of us were indifferent to her. Yet I am assured, if she had known the younger would have died of the smallpox, she would not have acted as she did. God makes use of creatures, and their natural inclinations to accomplish His designs. When I see in the creatures a conduct which appears unreasonable and mortifying, I mount higher, and look upon them as instruments both of the mercy and justice of God. His justice is full of mercy.

I told my husband that my stomach was sick, and that I was taking the smallpox. He said it was only imagination. I let Mrs. Granger know the situation I was in. As she had a tender heart, she was affected by the treatment I met with, and encouraged me to offer myself up to the Lord. At length, nature finding there was no resource, consented to the sacrifice which my spirit had already made. The disorder gained ground apace. I was seized with a great shivering, and pain both in my head and stomach. They would not yet believe that I was sick. In a few hours it went so far, that they thought my life in danger. I was also taken with an inflammation on my lungs, and the remedies for the one disorder were contrary to the other. My mother-in-law's favorite physician was not in town, nor the resident surgeon. Another surgeon said that I must be bled; but my mother-in-law would not suffer it at that time. I was on the point of death for the want of proper assistance. My husband, not being able to see me, left me entirely to his mother. She would not allow any physician but her own to prescribe for me, and yet did not send for him, though he was within a day's journey. In this extremity I opened not my mouth. I looked for life or death from the hand of God, without testifying the least uneasiness. The peace I enjoyed within, on account of that perfect resignation, in which God kept me by His grace, was so great, that it made me forget myself, in the midst of oppressive disorders.

The Lord's protection was indeed wonderful. How oft have I been reduced to extremity, yet He never failed to succor, when things appeared most desperate. It pleased Him so to order it, that the skillful surgeon, who had attended me before, passing by our house, inquired after me. They told him I was extremely ill. He alighted immediately, and came in to see me. Never was a man more surprised, when he saw the condition I was in. The smallpox, which could not come out, had fallen on my nose with such force, that it was quite black. He thought there had been gangrene and that it was going to fall off. My eyes were like two coals; but I was not alarmed. At that time I could have made a sacrifice of all things, and was pleased that God should avenge Himself on that face, which had betrayed me into so many infidelities. He also was so affrighted that he went into my mother-in-law's room and told her, that it was most shameful to let me die in that manner, for want of bleeding. She still opposed it violently so that in short she told him flatly that she would not suffer it, until the physician returned. He flew into such a rage at seeing me thus left without sending for the physician that he reproved my mother-in-law in the severest manner. But it was all in vain. He came up again presently and said, "If you choose, I will bleed you, and save your life." I held out my arm to him; and though it was extremely swelled, he bled me in an instant. My mother-in-law was in a violent passion. The smallpox came out immediately. He ordered that they should have me bled again in the evening, but she would not suffer it. Fear of displeasing my mother-in-law, and a total resignation of myself into the hands of God, I did not retain him.

I am more particular to show how advantageous it is to resign one's self to God without reserve. Though in appearance He leaves us for a time to prove and exercise our faith, yet He never fails us, when our need of Him is the more pressing. One may say with the Scripture, "It is God who bringeth down to the gates of death, and raiseth up again." The blackness and swelling of my nose went away and I believe, had they continued to bleed me, I had been pretty easy. For want of that I grew worse again. The malady fell into my eyes, and inflamed them with such severe pain, that I thought I should lose them both.

I had violent pains for three weeks during which time I got little sleep. I could not shut my eyes, they were so full of the smallpox, nor open them by reason of the pain. My throat, palate, and gums were likewise so filled with the pock, that I could not swallow broth, or take nourishment without suffering extremely. My whole body looked leprous. All that saw me said that they had never seen such a shocking spectacle. But as to my soul, it was kept in a contentment not to be expressed. The hopes of its liberty, by the loss of that beauty, which had so frequently brought me under bondage, rendered me so satisfied, and so united to God, that I would not have changed my condition for that of the most happy prince in the world.

Everyone thought I would be inconsolable. Several expressed their sympathy in my sad condition, as they judged it. I lay still in the secret fruition of a joy unspeakable, in this total deprivation of what had been a snare to my pride, and to the passions of men. I praised God in profound silence. None ever heard any complaints from me, either of my pains or the loss I sustained. The only thing that I said was, that I rejoiced at, and was exceedingly thankful for the interior liberty I gained thereby; and they construed this as a great crime. My confessor, who had been dissatisfied with me before, came to see me. He asked me if I was not sorry for having the smallpox; and he now taxed me with pride for my answer.

117

My youngest little boy took the distemper the same day with myself, and died for want of care. This blow indeed struck me to the heart, but yet, drawing strength from my weakness, I offered him up, and said to God as Job did, "Thou gavest him to me, and thou takest him from me; blessed be thy holy name." The spirit of sacrifice possessed me so strongly, that, though I loved this child tenderly, I never shed a tear at hearing of his death. The day he was buried, the doctor sent to tell me he had not placed a tombstone upon his grave, because my little girl could not survive him two days. My eldest son was not yet out of danger, so that I saw myself stripped of all my children at once, my husband indisposed, and myself extremely so. The Lord did not take my little girl then. He prolonged her life some years.

At last my mother-in-law's physician arrived, at a time wherein he could be of but little service to me. When he saw the strange inflammation in my eyes, he bled me several times; but it was too late. And those bleedings which would have been so proper at first, did nothing but weaken me now. They could not even bleed me in the condition I was in but with the greatest difficulty. My arms were so swelled that the surgeon was obliged to push in the lance to a great depth. Moreover, the bleeding being out of season had liked to have caused my death. This, I confess, would have been very agreeable to me. I looked upon death as the greatest blessing for me. Yet I saw well I had nothing to hope in that side; and that, instead of meeting with so desirable an event, I must prepare myself to support the trials of life.

After my eldest son was better, he got up and came into my room. I was surprised at the extraordinary change I saw in him. His face, lately so fair and beautiful, was become like a coarse spot of earth, all full of furrows. That gave me the curiosity to view myself. I felt shocked, for I saw that God had ordered the sacrifice in all its reality.

Some things fell out by the contrariety of my mother-in-law that caused me severe crosses. They put the finishing stroke to my son's face. However, my heart was firm in God, and strengthened itself by the number and greatness of my sufferings. I was as a victim incessantly offered upon the altar, to HIM who first sacrificed Himself for love. "What shall I render to the Lord, for all his benefits toward me? I will take the cup of salvation, and call upon the name of the Lord." These words, I can truly say, O my God, have been the delight of my heart, and have had their effect on me, through my whole life; for I have been continually heaped with thy blessings and thy cross. My principal attraction, besides that of suffering for Thee, has been to yield myself up without resistance, interiorly and exteriorly, to all Thy divine disposals. These gifts which I was favored with from the beginning, have continued and increased until now Thou hast Thyself guided my continual crosses, and led me through paths impenetrable to all but thee.

They sent me pomatums to recover my complexion, and to fill up the hollows of the smallpox. I had seen wonderful effects from it upon others, and therefore at first had a mind to try them. But, jealous of God's work, I would not suffer it. There was a voice in my heart which said, "If I would have had thee fair, I would have left thee as thou wert." I was therefore obliged to lay aside every remedy, and to go into the air, which made the pitting worse; to expose myself in the street when the redness of the smallpox was at the worst, in order to make my humiliation triumph, where I had exalted my pride.

My husband kept to his bed almost all that time, and made good use of his indisposition. Only as he now lost that, which before gave him so much pleasure in viewing me, he grew much more susceptible to impressions which any gave him against me. In consequence of this, the persons who spoke to him to my disadvantage, finding themselves now better hearkened to, spoke more boldly and more frequently.

There was only Thou, O my God, who changed not for me. Thou didst redouble my interior graces, in proportion as Thou didst augment my exterior crosses.

CHAPTER 16

My maid became every day more haughty. Seeing that her scoldings and outcries did not now torment me, she thought, if she could hinder me from going to the communion, she would give me the greatest of all vexations.

She was not mistaken, O divine Spouse of pure souls, since the only satisfaction of my life was to receive and to honor Thee. I gave everything, of the finest I had, to furnish the churches with ornaments, and contributed to the utmost extent of my abilities, to make them have silver plates and chalices.

"Oh, my Love," I cried, "let me be thy victim! Spare nothing to annihilate me." I felt an inexpressible longing to be more reduced, and to become, as it were, nothing.

This girl then knew my affection for the holy sacrament, where, when I could have liberty for it, I passed several hours on my knees. She took it in her head to watch me daily. When she discovered me going, she ran to tell my mother-in-law and my husband. There needed no more to chagrin them. Their invectives lasted the whole day. If a word escaped me in my own justification, it was enough to make them say that I was guilty of sacrilege, and to raise an outcry against all devotion. If I made them no answer at all, they still heightened their indignation, and said the most grating things they could devise. If I fell sick, which often happened, they took occasion to come to quarrel with me at my bed, saying, my communion and prayers were what made me sick. They spoke as if there had been nothing else could make me ill, but my devotion to Thee, O my Beloved!

She told me one day that she was going to write to my director to get him to stop me from going to the communion. When I made no answer, she cried out as loud as she could, that I treated her ill and despised her. When I went to prayers, (though I had taken care to arrange everything about the house) she ran to tell my husband that I was going and had left nothing in order. When I returned home his rage fell on me in all its violence. They would hear none of my reasons, but said, "they were all a pack of lies." My mother-in-law persuaded my husband that I let everything go to wreck. If she did not take the care of things he would be ruined. He believed it, and I bore all with patience, endeavoring, as well as I could, to do my duty. What gave most trouble was the not knowing what course to take; for when I ordered anything without her, she complained that I showed her no respect, that I did things of my own head and that they were done always the worse for it. Then she would order them contrary. If I consulted her to know what, or how she would have anything to be done, she said that I compelled her to have the care and trouble of everything."

I had scarcely any rest but what I found in the love of Thy will, O my God, and submission to Thy orders, however rigorous they might be. They incessantly watched my words and actions, to find occasion against me. They chided me all the day long, continually repeating, and harping over and over the same things, even before the servants. How often have I made my meals on my tears, which were interpreted as the most criminal in the world! They said, I would be damned; as if the tears would open Hell for me, which surely they were more likely to extinguish. If I recited anything I had heard, they would render me accountable for the truth of it. If I kept silence, they taxed me with contempt and perverseness; if I knew anything without telling it, that was a crime; if I told it, then they said I had forged it. Sometimes they tormented me for several days successively, without giving me any relaxation. The girls said, "I ought to feign sickness, to get a little rest." I made no reply. The love of God so closely possessed me, that it would not allow me to seek relief by a single word, or even by a look. Sometimes I said in myself, "Oh, that I had but any one who could take notice of me, or to whom I might unburden myself,—what a relief it would be to me!" But it was not granted me.

Yet, if I happened to be for some days freed from the exterior cross, it was a most sensible distress to me, and indeed a punishment more difficult to bear than the severest trials. I then comprehended what St. Teresa says, "Let me suffer or die." For this absence of the cross was so grievous to me, that I languished with desire for its return. But no sooner was this earnest longing granted, and the blessed cross returned again, than strange as it may seem, it appeared so weighty and burdensome, as to be almost insupportable.

Though I loved my father extremely, and he loved me tenderly, yet I never spoke to him of my sufferings. One of my relations, who loved me very much, perceived the little moderation they used toward me. They spoke very roughly to me before him. He was highly displeased, and told my father of it, adding, that I would pass for a fool. Soon after I went to see my father, who, contrary to his custom, sharply reprimanded me, "for suffering them to treat me in such a manner, without saying anything in my own defence." I answered, "If they knew what my husband said to me, that was confusion enough for me, without my bringing any more of it on myself by replies; that if they did not notice it, I ought not to cause it to be observed, nor expose my husband's weakness; that remaining silent stopped all disputes, whereas I might cause them to be continued and increased by my replies." My father answered that I did well, and that I should continue to act as God should inspire me. And after that, he never spoke to me of it any more.

They were ever talking to me against my father, against my relations, and all such as I esteemed most. I felt this more keenly than all they could say against myself. I could not forbear defending them, and therein I did wrong; as whatever I said served only to provoke them. If any complained of my father or relations, they were always in the right. If any, whom they had disliked before, spoke against them, they were presently approved of. If any showed friendship to me, such were not welcome. A relation whom I greatly loved for her piety, coming to see me, they openly bid her begone. They treated her in such a manner as obliged her to go, which gave me no small uneasiness. When any person of distinction came, they would speak against me; even to those who knew me not, which surprised them. But when they saw me they pitied me.

It mattered not what they said against me, love would not allow me to justify myself. I spoke not to my husband of what either my mother-in-law or the girl did to me, except the first year, when I was not sufficiently touched with the power of God to suffer. My mother-in-law and my husband often quarrelled. Then I was in favor, and to me they made their mutual complaints. I never told the one what the other had said. And though it might have been of service to me, humanly speaking, to take advantage of such opportunities, I never made use of them to complain of either. Nay, on the contrary, I did not rest till I had reconciled them. I spoke many obliging things of the one to the other, which made them friends again. I knew by frequent experience that I should pay dear for their reunion. Scarcely were they reconciled when they joined together against me.

I was so deeply engaged within, as often to forget

things without, yet not anything which was of consequence. My husband was hasty, and inattention frequently irritated him. I walked into the garden, without observing anything. When my husband, who could not go thither, asked me about it, I knew not what to say, at which he was angry. I went thither on purpose to notice everything, in order to tell him and yet when there did not think of looking. I went ten times one day, to see and bring him an account and yet forgot it. But when I did remember to look, I was much pleased. Yet it happened I was then asked nothing about them.

All my crosses to me would have seemed little, if I might have had liberty to pray, and to be alone, to indulge the interior attraction which I felt. But I was obliged to continue in their presence, with such a subjection as is scarcely conceivable. My husband looked at his watch, if at any time I had liberty allowed me for prayer, to see if I stayed more than half an hour. If I exceeded, he grew very uneasy. Sometimes I said, "Grant me one hour to divert and employ myself as I have a mind." Though he would have granted it to me for other diversions, yet for prayer he would not. I confess that inexperience caused me much trouble. I have often thereby given occasion for what they made me suffer. For ought I not to have looked on my captivity as an effect of the will of my God, to content myself and to make it my only desire and prayer? But I often fell back again into the anxiety of wishing to get time for prayer, which was not agreeable to my husband. Those faults were more frequent in the beginning. Afterward I prayed to God in His own retreat, in the temple of my heart, and I went out no more.

CHAPTER 17

W<small>E WENT INTO THE COUNTRY</small>, where
I committed many faults. I thought I might do it
then because my husband diverted himself with
building. If I stayed from him he was dissatisfied.
That sometimes happened as he was continually talking with the workmen. I set myself in a corner, and
there had my work with me, but could scarcely do
anything by reason of the force of the attraction
which made the work fall out of my hands. I passed
whole hours this way, without being able either to
open my eyes or know what passed; but I had nothing to wish for, nor yet to be afraid of. Everywhere
I found my proper center, because everywhere I
found God.

My heart could then desire nothing but what it
had. This disposition extinguished all its desires; and
I sometimes said to myself, "What wantest thou?
What fearest thou?" I was surprised to find upon
trial that I had nothing to fear. Every place I was in
was my proper place.

As I had generally no time allowed me for prayer
but with difficulty, and would not be suffered to rise

till seven o'clock, I stole up at four, and kneeling in my bed, I wished not to offend my husband and strove to be punctual and assiduous in everything. But this soon affected my health and injured my eyes, which were still weak. It was but eight months since I had the smallpox. This loss of rest brought a heavy trial upon me. Even my sleeping hours were much broken, by the fear of not waking in time, I insensibly dropped asleep at my prayers. In the half hour that I got after dinner, though I felt quite wakeful, the drowsiness overpowered me. I endeavored to remedy this by the severest bodily inflictions, but in vain.

As we had not yet built the chapel, and were far from any church, I could not go to prayers or sacrament without the permission of my husband. He was very reluctant to permit me, except on Sundays and holidays. I could not go out in the coach, so that I was obliged to make use of some stratagems, and to get service performed very early in the morning, to which, feeble as I was, I made an effort to creep on foot. It was a quarter of a league distant. Really God wrought wonders for me. Generally, in the mornings when I went to prayers, my husband did not awake until after I was returned. Often, as I was going out, the weather was so cloudy, that the girl I took with me told me that I could not go; or if I did, I should be soaked with the rain. I answered her with my usual confidence, "God will assist us." I generally reached the chapel without being wet. While there the rain fell excessively. When I returned it ceased. When I got home it began again with fresh violence.

During several years that I have acted this way, I have never been deceived in my confidence. When I was in town, and could find nobody, I was surprized that there came to me priests to ask me if I was willing to receive the communion, and that if I was they would give it to me. I had no mind to refuse the opportunity which Thou thyself offered me; for I had no doubt of its being Thee who inspired them to propose it. Before I had contrived to get divine service at the chapel I have mentioned, I have often suddenly awoke with a strong impulse to go to prayers. My maid would say, "But, madam, you are going to tire yourself in vain. There will be no service." For that chapel was not yet regularly served. I went full of faith and at my arrival have found them just ready to begin. If I could particularly enumerate the remarkable providences which were hereupon given in my favor there would be enough to fill whole volumes.

When I wanted to hear from, or write to Mother Granger, I often felt a strong propensity to go to the door. There to find a messenger with a letter from her. This is only a small instance of these kind of continual providences. She was the only person I could be free to open my heart to, when I could get to see her, which was with the greatest difficulty. It was through providential assistance; because prohibited by my confessor and husband. I placed an extreme confidence in Mother Granger. I concealed nothing from her either of sins or pains. I did not now practice any austerities but those she was willing to allow me. My interior dispositions I was scarcely able to tell because I knew not how to explain myself, being very ignorant of those matters, having never read or heard of them.

One day when they thought I was going to see my father, I ran off to Mother Granger. It was discovered, and cost me crosses. Their rage against me was so excessive, that it would seem incredible. Even my writing to her was extremely difficult. I had the utmost abhorrence of a lie, so I forbade the footman to tell any. When they were met they were asked whither they were going, and if they had any letters. My mother-in-law set herself in a little passage, through which those who went out must necessarily pass. She asked them whither they were going and what they carried. Sometimes going on foot to the Benedictines, I caused shoes to be carried, that they might not perceive by the dirty ones that I had been far. I dared not go alone; those who attended me had orders to tell of every place I went. If they were discovered to fail, they were either corrected or discharged.

My husband and mother-in-law were always inveighing against that good woman, though in reality they esteemed her. I sometimes made my own complaint and she replied, "How should you content them, when I have been doing all in my power for twenty years to satisfy them without success?" For as my mother-in-law had two daughters under her care, she was always finding something to say against everything she did in regard to them.

But the most sensible cross to me now was the revolting of my own son against me. They inspired him with so great a contempt for me, that I could not bear to see him without extreme affliction. When I was in my room with some of my friends, they sent him to listen to what we said. As he saw this pleased them, he invented a hundred things to tell them. If I caught him in a lie, as I frequently did, he would upbraid me, saying, "My grandmother says you have been a greater liar than I." I answered, "Therefore I know the deformity of that vice, and how hard a thing it is to get the better of it; and for this reason, I would not have you suffer the like." He spoke to me things very offensive. Because he saw the awe I stood in of his grandmother and his father, if in their absence I found fault with him for anything, he insultingly upbraided me. He said that now I wanted to be set up over him because they were not there. All this they approved of. One day he went to see my father and rashly began talking against me to him, as he was used to doing to his grandmother. But there it did not meet with the same recompense. It affected my father to tears. Father came to our house to desire he might be corrected for it. They promised it should be done, and yet they never did it. I was grievously afraid of the consequences of so bad an education. I told Mother Granger of it, who said that since I could not remedy it, I must suffer and leave everything to God. This child would be my cross.

Another great cross was the difficulty I had in attending my husband. I knew he was displeased when I was not with him; yet when I was with him, he never expressed any pleasure. On the contrary, he only rejected with scorn whatever office I performed. He was so difficult with me about everything, that I sometimes trembled when I approached him. I could do nothing to his liking; and when I did not attend him he was angry. He had taken such a dislike to soups, that he could not bear the sight of them. Those that offered them had a rough reception. Neither his mother nor any of the domestics would carry them to him. There was none but I who did not refuse that office. I brought them and let his anger pass; then I tried in some agreeable manner to prevail on him to take them. I said to him, "I had rather be reprimanded several times a day, than let you suffer by not bringing you what is proper." Sometimes he took; at other times he pushed them back.

When he was in a good humor and I was carrying something agreeable to him, then my mother-in-law would snatch it out of my hands. She would carry it herself. As he thought I was not so careful and studious to please him he would fly in a rage against me and express great thankfulness to his mother. I used all my skill and endeavors to gain my mother-in-law's favor by my presents, my services; but could not succeed.

"How bitter and grievous, O my God, would such a life be were it not for Thee! Thou hast sweetened and reconciled it to me." I had a few short intervals from this severe and mortifying life. These served only to make the reverses more keen and bitter.

CHAPTER 18

About eight or nine months after my recovery from the smallpox, Father LaCombe, passing by our house, brought me a letter from Father de la Motte, recommending him to my esteem, and expressing the highest friendship for him. I hesitated because I was very loath to make new acquaintances. The fear of offending my brother prevailed. After a short conversation we both desired a farther opportunity. I thought that he either loved God, or was disposed to love Him, and I wished everybody to love Him. God had already made use of me for the conversion of three of his order. The strong desire he had of seeing me again induced him to come to our country house about half a league from the town. A little incident which happened opened a way for me to speak to him. As he was in discourse with my husband, who relished his company, he was taken ill and retired into the garden. My husband bade me go and see what was the matter. He told me he had noticed in my countenance a deep inwardness and presence of God, which had given him a strong desire of seeing me again. God then assisted me to open to him the interior path of the soul, and conveyed so much grace to him through this poor channel, that he went away changed into quite another man. I preserved an esteem for him; for it appeared to me that he would be devoted to God; but little did I then forsee, that I should ever be led to the place where he was to reside.

My disposition at this time was a continual prayer, without knowing it to be such. The presence of God was so plentifully given that it seemed to be more in me than my very self. The sensibility thereof was so powerful, so penetrating, it seemed to me irresistible. Love took from me all liberty of my own. At other times I was so dry, I felt nothing but the pain of absence, which was the keener to me, as the divine presence had before been so sensible. In these alternatives I forgot all my troubles and pains. It appeared to me as if I had never experienced any. In its absence, it seemed as if it would never return again. I still thought it was through some fault of mine it was withdrawn, and that rendered me inconsolable. Had I known it had been a state through which it was necessary to pass, I should not have been troubled. My strong love to the will of God would have rendered everything easy to me. The property of this prayer was to give a great love to the order of God, with so sublime and perfect a reliance on Him, as to fear nothing, whether danger, thunders, spirits, or death. It gives a great abstraction from one's self, our own interests and reputation, with an utter disregard to everything of the kind—all being swallowed up in the esteem of the will of God.

At home, I was accused of everything that was ill done, spoiled or broken. At first I told the truth, and said it was not I. They persisted, and accused me of lying. I then made no reply. Besides, they told all their tales to such as came to the house. But when I was afterward alone with the same persons, I never undeceived them. I often heard such things said of me, before my friends, as were enough to make them entertain a bad opinion. My heart kept its habitation in the tacit consciousness of my own innocence, not concerning myself whether they thought well or ill of me; excluding all the world, all opinions or censures, out of my view, I minded nothing else but the friendship of God.

If through infidelity I happened at any time to justify myself, I always failed, and drew upon myself new crosses, both within and without. But notwithstanding all this, I was so enamored with it, that the greatest cross of all would have been to be without any. When the cross was taken from me for any short space, it seemed to me that it was because of the bad use I made of it; that my unfaithfulness deprived me of so great an advantage. I never knew its value better than its loss.

I cried punish me any way, but take not the cross from me. This amiable cross returned to me with so much the more weight, as my desire was more vehement. I could not reconcile two things, they appeared to me so very opposite. 1) To desire the cross with so much ardor. 2) To support it with so much difficulty and pain.

God knows well, in the admirable economy he observes, how to render the crosses more weighty, conformable to the ability of the creature to bear them. Hereby my soul began to be more resigned, to comprehend that the state of absence, and of wanting what I longed for, was in its turn more profitable than that of always abounding. This latter nourished self-love. If God did not act thus, the soul would never die to itself. That principle of self-love is so crafty and dangerous, that it cleaves to everything.

What gave me most uneasiness, in this time of darkness and cruifixion, both within and without, was an inconceivable readiness to be quick and hasty. When any answer a little too lively escaped me, (which served not a little to humble me,) they said "I was fallen into a mortal sin." A conduct no less rigorous than this was quite necessary for me. I was so proud, passionate, and of a humor naturally thwarting, wanting always to carry matters my own way, thinking my own reasons better than those of others. Hadst thou, O my God, spared the strokes of thy hammer, I should never have been formed to Thy will, to be an instrument for Thy use; for I was ridiculously vain. Applause rendered me intolerable. I praised my friends to excess, and blamed others without reason. But, the more criminal I have been, the more I am indebted to Thee, and the less of any good can I attribute to myself. How blind are men who attribute to others the holiness that God gives them! I believe, my God, that thou hast had children, who under thy grace, owed much to their own fidelity. As for me, I owe all to Thee; I glory to confess it; I cannot acknowledge it too much.

In acts of charity I was very assiduous. So great was my tenderness for the poor, that I wished to have supplied all their wants. I could not see their necessity without reproaching myself for the plenty I enjoyed. I deprived myself of all I could to help them. The very best at my table was distributed. There were few of the poor where I lived, who did not partake of my liberality. It seemed as if Thou hadst made me thy only almoner there, for being refused by others, they came to me. I cried, "it is Thy substance; I am only the steward. I ought to distribute it according to Thy will." I found means to relieve them without letting myself be known, because I had one who dispensed my alms privately. When there were families who were ashamed to take it in this way, I sent it to them as if I owed them a debt. I clothed such as were naked, and caused young girls to be taught how to earn their livelihood, especially those who were handsome; to the end that being employed, and having whereon to live, they might not be under a temptation to throw themselves away. God made use of me to reclaim several from their disorderly lives. I went to visit the sick, to comfort them, to make their beds. I made ointments, dressed their wounds, buried their dead. I privately furnished tradesmen and mechanics wherewith to keep up their shops. My heart was much opened toward my fellow creatures in distress. Few indeed could carry charity much farther than our Lord enabled me to do, according to my state, both while married and since.

To purify me the more from the mixture I might

make of His gifts with my own self-love, He gave me interior probations, which were very heavy. I began to experience an insupportable weight, in that very piety which had formerly been so easy and delightful to me; not that I did not love it extremely, but I found myself defective in that noble practice of it. The more I loved it, the more I labored to acquire what I saw failed in. But, alas! I seemed continually to be overcome by that which was the contrary to it. My heart, indeed, was detached from all sensual pleasures. For these several years past, it has seemed to me that my mind is so detached and absent from the body, that I do things as if I did them not. If I eat, or refresh myself, it is done with such an absence, or separation, as I wonder at, with an entire mortification of the keenness of sensation in all the natural functions.

CHAPTER 19

To RESUME MY HISTORY, the smallpox had so much hurt one of my eyes, that it was feared I would lose it. The gland at the corner of my eye was injured. An imposthume arose from time to time between the nose and the eye, which gave me great pain till it was lanced. It swelled all my head to that degree that I could not bear even a pillow. The least noise was agony to me, though sometimes they made a great commotion in my chamber. Yet this was a precious time to me, for two reasons. First, because I was left in bed alone, where I had a sweet retreat without interruption; the other, because it answered the desire I had for suffering,—which desire was so great, that all the austerities of the body would have been but as a drop of water to quench so great a fire. Indeed the severities and rigors which I then exercised were extreme, but they did not appease this appetite for the cross. It is Thou alone, O Crucified Saviour, who canst make the cross truly effectual for the death of self. Let others bless themselves in their ease or gaiety, grandeur or pleasures, poor temporary heavens; for me, my desires were all turned another way, even to the silent path of suffering for Christ, and to be united to Him, through the mortification of all that was of nature in me, that my senses, appetites and will, being dead to these, might wholly live in Him.

I obtained leave to go to Paris for the cure of my eye; and yet it was much more through the desire I had to see Monsieur Bertot, a man of profound experience, whom Mother Granger had lately assigned to me for my director. I went to take leave of my father, who embraced me with peculiar tenderness, little thinking then that it would be our last adieu.

Paris was a place now no longer to be dreaded as in times past. The throngs only served to draw me into a deep recollection, and the noise of the streets agumented my inward prayer. I saw Monsieur Bertot, who did not prove of that service to me, which he would have been if I had then the power to explain myself. Though I wished earnestly to hide nothing from him, yet God held me so closely to Him, that I could scarcely tell anything at all. As soon as I spoke to him, everything vanished from my mind, so that I could remember nothing but some few faults. As I saw him very seldom, and nothing stayed in my recollection, and as I read of nothing any way resembling my case, I knew not how to explain myself. Besides, I desired to make nothing known, but the evil which was in me. Therefore Monsieur Bertot knew me not, even till his death. This was of great utility to me, by taking away every support, and making me truly die to myself.

I went to pass the ten days, from the Ascension to

141

Whitsuntide, at an abbey four leagues from Paris, the abbess of which had a particular friendship for me. Here my union with God seemed to be deeper and more continued, becoming always simple, at the same time more close and intimate.

One day I awoke suddenly at four o'clock in the morning, with a strong impression on my mind that my father was dead. At the same time my soul was in a very great contentment, yet my love for him affected it with sorrow, and my body with weakness. Under the strokes and daily troubles which befell me, my will was so subservient to Thine, O my God, that it appeared absolutely united to it. There seemed, indeed, to be no will left in me but Thine only. My own disappeared, and no desires, tendencies or inclinations were left, but to the one sole object of whatever was most pleasing to Thee, be it what it would. If I had a will, it was in union with thine, as two well tuned lutes in concert. That which is not touched renders the same sound as that which is touched; it is but one and the same sound, one pure harmony. It is this union of the will which establishes in perfect peace. Yet, though my own will was lost I have found since, in the strange states I have been obliged to pass through, how much it had yet to cost me to have it totally lost. How many souls are there which think their own wills quite lost, while they are yet very far from it! They would find they still subsist, if they met with severe trials. Who is there who does not wish something for himself, either of interest, wealth, honor, pleasure, conveniency and liberty. He who thinks his mind loose from all these objects, because he possesses them, would soon perceive his attachment to them, were he stripped of those he possessed. If there are found in a whole age three persons so dead to everything, as to be utterly resigned to providence without any exception, they may well pass for prodigies of grace.

In the afternoon as I was with the abbess, I told her I had strong presentiments of my father's death. Indeed I could hardly speak, I was so affected within. Presently one came to tell her that she was wanted in the parlor. It was a messenger come in haste, with an account from my husband that my father was ill. And as I afterward found, he suffered only twelve hours. He was therefore by this time dead. The abbess returning, said, "Here is a letter from your husband, who writes that your father is taken violently ill." I said to her, "He is dead, I cannot have a doubt about it."

I sent away to Paris immediately, to hire a coach, to go the sooner; mine waited for me at the midway. I went off at nine o'clock at night. They said. I "was going to destroy myself." I had no acquaintance with me as I had sent away my maid to Paris, to put everything in order there. Being in a religious house, I had no mind to keep a footman with me. The abbess told me, that "since I thought my father was dead, it would be rashness in me to expose myself, and run the risk of my life in that manner. Coaches could hardly pass the way I was going, it being no beaten road." I answered, "It was my indispensible duty to go to assist my father, and that I ought not, on a bare apprehension, to exempt myself from it." I then went alone, abandoned to Providence, with people unknown. My weakness was so great, that I could hardly keep my seat in the coach. I was often forced to alight, on account of dangerous places in the road.

In this way I was obliged, about midnight, to cross a forest, notorious for murders and robberies. The most intrepid dreaded it; but my resignation left me scarce any room to think at all about it. What fears and uneasiness does a resigned soul spare itself! All alone I arrived within five leagues of my own habitation, where I found my confessor who had opposed me, with one of my relations, waiting for me. The sweet consolation I had enjoyed, when alone, was now interrupted. My confessor, ignorant of my state, restrained me entirely. My grief was of such a nature that I could not shed a tear. And I was ashamed to hear a thing which I knew but too well, without giving any exterior mark of grief. The inward and profound peace I enjoyed dawned on my countenance. The state I was in did not permit me to speak, or to do such things as are usually expected from persons of piety. I could do nothing but love and be silent.

I found on my arrival at home, that my father was already buried because of the excessive heat. It was ten o'clock at night. All wore the habit of mourning. I had traveled thirty leagues in a day and a night. As I was very weak, not having taken any nourishment, I was instantly put to bed.

About two o'clock in the morning my husband got up, and having gone out of my chamber, he returned presently, crying out with all his might, "My daughter is dead!" She was my only daughter, as dearly beloved as truly lovely. She had so many graces both of body and mind conferred on her, that one must have been insensible not to have loved her. She had an extraordinary share of love to God. Often was she found in corners at prayer. As soon as she perceived me at prayer, she came and joined. If she discovered that I had been without her, she would weep bitterly and cry, "Ah, mamma, you pray but I don't." When we were alone and she saw my eyes closed she would whisper, "Are you asleep?" Then she would cry out, "Ah no, you are praying to our dear Jesus." Dropping on her knees before me she would begin to pray too. She was several times whipped by her grandmother, because she said, she would never have any other husband but our Lord. She could never make her say otherwise. She was innocent and modest as a little angel; very dutiful and endearing, and withal very beautiful. Her father doted on her, to me she was very dear, much more for the qualities of her mind than those of her beautiful person. I looked upon her as my only consolation on earth. She had as much affection for me, as her brother had aversion and contempt. She died of an unseasonable bleeding. But what shall I say? She died by the hands of Him who was pleased, for wise reasons of His own, to strip me of all.

There now remained to me only the son of my sorrow. He fell ill to the point of death, but was restored at the prayer of Mother Granger who was now my only consolation after God. I no more wept for my child than for my father. I could only say,

"Thou, O Lord, gave her to me; it pleases Thee to take her back again, for she was Thine." As for my father, his virtue was so generally known, that I must rather be silent, than enter upon the subject. His reliance on God, his faith and patience were wonderful. Both died in July, 1672. Henceforth crosses were not spared me, and though I had abundance of them hitherto, yet they were only the shadows of those which I have been since obliged to pass through. In this spiritual marriage I claimed for my dowry only crosses, scourges, persecutions, ignominies, lowliness, and nothingness of self, which in God's great goodness, and for wise ends, as I have seen, has been pleased to grant and confer upon me.

One day, being in great distress on account of the redoubling of outward and inward crosses, I went into my closet to give vent to my grief. M. Bertot was brought into my mind, with this wish, "Oh, that he was sensible of what I suffer!" Though he wrote but very seldom, and with great difficulty, yet he wrote me a letter dated the same day about the cross. It was the finest and most consolatory he ever wrote me on that subject. Sometimes my spirit was so oppressed with continual crosses, which scarcely gave me any relaxation, that when alone my eyes turned every way, to see if they could find anything to give relief. A word, a sigh, a trifle, or to know that anyone took part in my grief, would have been some comfort. That was not granted me, not even to look toward Heaven, or to make any complaint. Love held me then so closely, that it would have this miserable nature to perish, without giving it any support or nourishment.

Oh, my dearest Lord! Thou yet gavest my soul a victorious support, which made it triumph over all the weaknesses of nature, and seized Thy knife to sacrifice it without sparing. And yet this nature so perverse, and full of artifices to save its life, at last took the course of nourishing itself on its own despair, on its fidelity under such heavy and continual oppression. It sought to conceal the value it attributed thereto. But thy eyes were too penetrating not to detect the subtilty. Wherefore, thou, O my Shepherd, changed Thy conduct toward it. Thou sometimes comforted it with thy crook and Thy staff; that is to say, by Thy conduct as loving as crucifying; but it was only to reduce it to the last extremity, as I shall show hereafter.

CHAPTER 20

A LADY OF RANK, whom I sometimes visited, took a particular liking to me, because (as she was pleased to say) my person and manners were agreeable. She said that she observed in me something extraordinary and uncommon. I believe it was the inward attraction of my soul that appeared on my very countenance. One day a gentleman of fashion said to my husband's aunt, "I saw the lady your niece; and it is very evident that she lives in the presence of God." I was surprised at this, as I little thought such an one as he could know what it was to have God thus present. This lady of rank began to be touched with the sense of God. Wanting once to take me to the play, I refused to go; (I never went to plays) making use of the pretext of my husband's continual indispositions. She pressed me exceedingly, and said, "I should not be prevented by his sickness from taking some amusement and I was not of an age to be confined with the sick like a nurse." I told her my reasons. She then perceived that it was more from a principle of piety, than the indispositions of my husband. Insisting to know my

148

sentiment of plays, I told her, I entirely disapproved of them, and especially for a Christian woman. And as she was far more advanced in years than I was, what I then said made such an impression on her mind, she never went again.

Once with her and another lady, who was fond of talking and who had read "the fathers," they spoke much of God. This lady spoke learnedly of Him. I said scarcely anything, being inwardly drawn to silence, and troubled at this conversation about God. My acquaintance came next day to see me. The Lord had so touched her heart, she could hold out no longer. I attributed this to something the other lady had said, but she said to me, "Your silence had something in it which penetrated to the bottom of my soul. I could not relish what the other said." We spoke to one another with open hearts.

It was then that God left indelible impressions of His grace on her soul, and she continued so athirst for Him, that she could scarcely endure to converse on any other subject. That she might become wholly His, He deprived her of a most affectionate husband. He visited her with such severe crosses, and at the same time poured His grace so abundantly into her heart, that He soon became the sole master thereof. After the death of her husband, and the loss of most of her fortune, she went to reside four leagues from our house, on a small estate, which was left. She obtained my husband's consent to my going to spend a week with her, to console her. God gave her by my means all she wanted. She had a great share of understanding, but was surprised at my expressing things to her so far above my natural capacity. I should have been surprised at it myself. It was God who gave me the gift for her sake, diffusing a flood of grace into her soul, without regarding the unworthiness of the channel of which He was pleased to make use. Since that time her soul has been the temple of the Holy Ghost, and our hearts have been indissolubly united.

My husband and I took a little journey together, in which both my resignation and humility were exercised, yet without difficulty or constraint, so powerful was the influence of divine grace. We had all liked to have perished in a river. The rest of the company in desperate fright threw themselves out of the coach, which sunk in the moving sand. I continued so much inwardly occupied, that I did not once think of the danger. God delivered me from it without my thought of avoiding it. I was quite content to be drowned, had He permitted it. It may be said, "I was rash." I believe I was so; yet I rather chose to perish, trusting in God, than make my escape in a dependence on myself. What say I? We do not perish, but for want of trusting Him. My pleasure is to be indebted to Him for everything. This renders me content in my miseries, which I would rather endure all my life long, in a state of resignation to Him, than put an end to them, in a dependence on myself. However, I would not advise others to act thus, unless they were in the same disposition which I was in.

As my husband's maladies daily increased, he resolved to go to St. Reine. He appeared very desirous

150

of having none but me with him, and told me one day, "If they never spoke to me against you, I should be more easy, and you more happy." In this journey I committed many faults of self-love and self-seeking. I was become like a poor traveler that had lost his way in the night and could find no way, path, or track. My husband, in his return from St. Reine, passed by St. Edm. Having now no children but my firstborn son, who was often at the gates of death, he wished exceedingly for heirs, and prayed for them earnestly. God granted his desire, and gave me a second son. As I was several weeks without any one daring to speak to me, on account of my great weakness, it was a time of retreat and of silence. I tried to indemnify myself for the loss of time I had sustained in the others, to pray to Thee, O my God, and to continue alone with Thee. I may say that God took a new possession of me, and left me not. It was a time of continual joy without interruption. As I had experienced many inward difficulties and weaknesses it was a new life. It seemed as if I was already in the fruition of beatitude. How dear did this happy time cost me, since it was only a preparative to a total privation of comfort for several years, without any support, or hope of return! It began with the death of Mrs. Granger, who had been my only consolation under God. Before my return from St. Reine I heard she was dead.

When I received this news, I confess it was the most afflicting stroke I had ever felt. I thought that had I been with her at her death I might have spoken to her and recieved her last instructions. God has so

151

ordered it that I was deprived of her assistance in almost all my losses, in order to render the strokes more painful. Some months indeed before her death, it was shown to me, that though I could not see her but with difficulty, and suffering for it, yet she was still some support to me. The Lord let me know that it would be profitable for me to be deprived of her. But at the time she died I did not think so. It was in that trying season when my paths were all blocked up, she was taken from me. She who might have guided me in my lonesome and difficult road, bounded as it were with precipices, and entangled with briars and thorns.

Adorable conduct of my God! there must be no guide for the person whom Thou art leading into the regions of darkness and death, no conductor for the man whom thou art determined to destroy, (that is, to cause to die totally to himself). After having saved me with much mercy, after having led me by the hand in rugged paths, it seems Thou wast bent on my destruction. May it not be said that Thou dost not save but to destroy, nor go to seek the lost sheep, but to cause it to be yet more lost; that Thou art pleased in building what is demolished, and in demolishing what is built. Thou wouldst overturn the temple built by human endeavors, with so much care and industry, in order as it were miraculously to erect a divine structure, a house not built with hands, eternal in the Heavens. Secrets of the incomprehensible wisdom of God, unknown to any besides Himself! Man, sprung up only of a few days, wants to penetrate, and to set bounds to it. Who is it that hath known the mind of the Lord, or who hath been His counselor? Is it a wisdom only to be known through death to everything, and through the entire loss of all self?

My brother now openly showed his hatred for me. He married at Orleans and my husband had the complaisance to go to his marriage. He was in a poor state of health, the roads bad, and so covered over with snow, that we had like to have been overturned twelve or fifteen times. Yet far from appearing obliged by his politeness, my brother quarreled with him more than ever, and without reason. I was the butt of both their resentments. While I was at Orleans, meeting with one whom at that time I thought highly of, I was too forward and free in speaking to him of spiritual things, thinking I was doing well, but had a remorse for it afterwards. How often we mistake nature for grace! One must be dead to self, when such forwardness comes from God only.

My brother treated me with the utmost contempt. Yet, my mind was so fully drawn inward, that although we had much more danger on the road than when going, I had no thought about myself, but all about my husband. Seeing the coach overturning, I said, "Fear not, it is on my side that it falls; it will not hurt you." I believe, had all perished, I should not have been moved. My peace was so profound that nothing could shake it. If these times continued, we should be too strong. They now began to come but seldom and were followed with long and wearisome privations. Since that time my brother has changed for the better, and has turned on the side of God, but he has never turned to me. It has been by particular permission of God, and the conduct of His providence over my soul, that has caused him and other religious persons, who have persecuted me, to think they were rendering glory to God, and doing acts of justice therein. Indeed, it is just that all creatures should be treacherous to me, and declare against me, who have too many times been treacherous to God, and sided with His enemy.

After this there was a very perplexing affair. To me it caused great crosses, and seemed designed for nothing else. A certain person conceived so much malice against my husband, that he was determined to ruin him if possible. He found no other way to attempt it, but by entering into a private engagement with my brother. He obtained a power to demand, in the name of the king's brother, two hundred thousand livres, which he pretended that my brother and I owed him. My brother signed the processes, upon an assurance given him that he should not pay anything. I think his youth engaged him in what he did not understand. This affair so chagrined my husband, that I have reason to believe it shortened his days. He was so angry with me (although I was innocent), that he could not speak to me except in a fury. He would give me no light into the affair, and I did not know in what it consisted. In the height of his rage, he said he would not meddle with it, but give me my portion, and let me live as I could. On the other side, my brother would not move in it, nor suffer anything to be done. The day of the trial, after prayer, I felt myself strongly pressed to go to the judges. I was wonderfully assisted even so as to discover and unravel all the turns and artifices of this affair, without knowing how I could have been able to do it. The first judge was so surprised to see the affair so different from what he had thought it before, that he himself exhorted me to go to the other judges, and especially to the intendant, who was just then going to court. He was quite misinformed about the matter. God enabled me to manifest the truth in so clear a light, and gave such power to my words, that the indendant thanked me for having so seasonably come to undeceive, and set him right. Had I not done this, he assured me the cause had been lost. As they saw the falsehood of every point, they would have condemned the plaintiff to pay the costs, if he had not been so great a prince, who lent his name to the scheme. To save the honor of the prince they ordered us to pay him fifty crowns. Hereby the two hundred thousand livres were reduced to only one hundred and fifty. My husband was exceedingly pleased at what I had done. My brother appeared as outrageous against me, as if I had caused him some great loss. Thus moderately and at once ended an affair, which had at first appeared so very weighty and alarming.

CHAPTER 21

About this time I fell into a state of total privation which lasted nearly seven years. I seemed to myself cast down like Nebuchadnezzar, to live among beasts; a deplorable state, yet of the greatest advantage to me, by the use which divine wisdom made of it. This state of emptiness, darkness, and impotency, went far beyond any trials I had ever yet met. I have since experienced, that the prayer of the heart when it appears most dry and barren, nevertheless is not ineffectual nor offered in vain. God gives what is best for us, though not what we most relish or wish for. Were people but convinced of this truth, they would be far from complaining all their lives. By causing us death He would procure us life; for all our happiness, spiritual, temporal and eternal, consists in resigning ourselves to God, leaving it to Him to do in us and with us as He pleases, and with so much the more submission; as things please us less. By this pure dependence on His Spirit, everything is given us admirably. Our very weaknesses, in His hand, prove a source of humiliation. If the soul were faithful to leave itself in the hand of God, sustaining all His operations whether gratifying or mortifying, suffering itself to be conducted, from moment to moment, by His hand, and annihilated by the strokes of His Providence, without complaining, or desiring anything but what it has; it would soon arrive at the experience of the eternal truth, though it might not at once know the ways and methods by which God conducted it there.

People want to direct God instead of resigning themselves to be directed by Him. They want to show Him a way, instead of passively following that wherein He leads them. Hence many souls, called to enjoy God Himself, and not barely His gifts, spend all their lives in running after little consolations, and feeding on them—resting there only, making all their happiness to consist therein.

If my chains and my imprisonment in any way afflict you, I pray that they may serve to engage you to seek nothing but God for Himself alone, and never to desire to possess Him but by the death of your whole selves, never to seek to be something in the ways of the Spirit, but choose to enter into the most profound nothingness.

I had an internal strife, which continually racked me—two powers which appeared equally strong seemed equally to struggle for the mastery within me. On the one hand, a desire of pleasing Thee, O my God, a fear of offending, and a continual tendency of all my powers to Thee—on the other side, the view of all my inward corruptions, the depravity of my heart, and the continual stirring and rising of self. What torrents of tears, what desolations have these cost me? "Is it possible," I cried, "that I have received so many graces and favors from God only to lose them;—that I have loved Him with so much ardor, but to be eternally deprived of Him; that His benefits have only produced ingratitude; His fidelity been repaid with infidelity; that my heart has been emptied of all creatures, and created objects, and filled with His blessed presence and love, in order now to be wholly void of divine power, and only filled with wanderings and created objects!"

I could now no longer pray as formerly. Heaven seemed shut to me, and I thought justly. I could get no consolation or make any complaint; nor had I any creature on earth to apply to. I found myself banished from all beings without finding a support of refuge in anything. I could no more practice any virtue with facility. "Alas!" said I, "is it possible that this heart, formerly all on fire, should now become like ice!" I often thought all creatures combined against me. Laden with a weight of past sins, and a multitude of new ones, I could not think God would ever pardon me, but looked on myself as a victim designed for Hell. I would have been glad to do penances, to make use of prayers, pilgrimages, and vows. But still, whatever I tried for a remedy seemed only to increase the malady. I may say that tears were my drink, and sorrow my food. I felt in myself such a pain as I never could bring any to comprehend, but such as have experienced it. I had within myself an executioner who tortured me without respite. Even when I went to church, I was not easy there. To sermons I could give no attention; they were now of no service or refreshment to me. I scarcely conceived or understood anything in them, or about them.

CHAPTER 22

As my husband drew near his end, his distempers had no intermission. No sooner was he recovered from one when he fell into another. He bore great pains with much patience offering them to God and making a good use of them. Yet his anger toward me increased, because reports and stories of me were multiplied to him, and those about him did nothing but vex him. He was the more susceptible of such impressions, as his pains gave him a stronger bent to vexation. At this time, the maid, who used to torment me sometimes took pity on me. She came to see me as soon as I was gone into my closet, and said, "Come to my master that your mother-in-law may not speak any more to him against you." I pretended to be ignorant of it all but he could not conceal his displeasure, nor even suffer me near him. My mother-in-law at the same time kept no bounds. All that came to the house were witnesses of the continual scoldings, which I was forced to bear, and which I bore with much patience, notwithstanding my being in the condition I have mentioned.

My husband having, sometime before his death,

finished the building of the chapel in the country, where we spent a part of the summer, I had the conveniency of hearing prayers every day, and of the communion. Not daring to do it openly every day, the priest privately admitted me to the communion. They solemnized the dedication of this little chapel. I felt myself all on a sudden inwardly seized, which continued more than five hours, all the time of the ceremony, when our Lord made a new consecration of me to Himself. I then seemed to myself a temple consecrated to Him, both for time and for eternity. I said within myself, (speaking both of the one and the other) "May this temple never be profaned; may the praises of God be sung therein forever!" It seemed to me at that time as if my prayer was granted. But soon all this was taken from me, and not so much as any remembrance left to console me.

When I was at this country house, which was only a little place of retreat before the chapel was built, I retired for prayer to woods and caverns. How many times, here, has God preserved me from dangerous and venomous beasts! Sometimes, unawares, I kneeled upon serpents, which were there in great plenty; they fled away without doing me any harm. Once I happened to be alone in a little wood wherein was a mad bull; but he betook himself to flight. If I could recount all the providences of God in my favor, it would appear wonderful. They were indeed so frequent and continual, that I could not but be astonished at them. God everlastingly gives to such as have nothing to repay Him. If there appears in the creature any fidelity or patience, it is He alone who gives it. If He ceases for an instant to support, if He seems to leave me to myself, I cease to be strong, and find myself weaker than any other creature. If my miseries show what I am, His favors show what He is, and the extreme necessity I am under of ever depending on Him.

After twelve years and four months of marriage, crosses as great as possible, except poverty which I never knew, though I had much desired it, God drew me out of that state to give me still stronger crosses of such a nature as I had never met with before. For if you give attention, sir, to the life which you have ordered me to write, you will remark that my crosses have been increasing till the present time, one removed to give place to another to succeed it, still heavier than the former. Amid the troubles imposed upon me, when they said, I "was in a mortal sin," I had nobody in the world to speak to. I could have wished to have had somebody for a witness of my conduct; but I had none. I had no support, no confessor, no director, no friend, no councellor. I had lost all. And after God had taken from me one after another, He withdrew also Himself. I remained without any creature; and to complete my distress, I seemed to be left without God, who alone could support me in such a deeply distressing state.

My husband's illness grew every day more obstinate. He apprehended the approach of death, and even wished for it, so oppressive was languishing life. To his other ills was great dislike to every sort of nourishment; he did not take anything necessary to sustain life. I alone had the courage to get him to take what little he did. The doctor advised him to go to the country. There for a few days at first he seemed to be better, when he was suddenly taken with a complication of diseases. His patience increased his pain. I saw plainly he could not live long. It was a great trouble to me, that my mother-in-law kept me from him as much as she could. She infused into his mind such a displeasure against me, that I was afraid lest he should die in it. I took a little interval of time when she happened not to be with him, and drawing near his bed, I kneeled down and said to him, "That if I had ever done any thing that displeased him I begged his pardon, assuring him it had not been voluntary." He appeared very much affected. As he had just come out of a sound sleep, he said to me, "It is I who beg your pardon, I did not deserve you." After that time he was not only pleased to see me, but gave me advice what I should do after his death; not to depend on the people on whom now I depended. He was for eight days very resigned and patient. I sent to Paris for the most skillful surgeon; but when he arrived my husband was dead.

No mortal could die in a more Christian disposition, or with more courage than he did, after having received the sacrament in a manner truly edifying. I was not present when he expired, for out of tenderness he made me retire. He was above twenty hours unconscious and in the agonies of his death. It was in the morning of July 21, 1676, that he died. Next day I entered into my closet, in which was the image of my divine spouse, the Lord Jesus Christ. I renewed my marriage-contract, and added thereto a vow of chastity, with a promise to make it perpetual, if M. Bertot my director, would permit me. After that I was filled with great joy, which was new to me, as for a long time past I had been plunged in the deepest bitterness

As soon as I heard that my husband had expired, "Oh, my God," I cried, "thou hast broken my bonds, and I will offer thee a sacrifice of praise." After that I remained in a deep silence, both exterior and interior, quite dry and without any support. I could neither weep nor speak. My mother-in-law said very fine things, and was very much commended for it by everyone. They were offended at my silence, which they attributed to want of resignation. A friar told me, that everyone admired the fine acts which my mother-in-law did; but as for me, they heard me say nothing; that I must sacrifice my loss to God. But I could not say one single word, let me strive as I would.

I was indeed very much exhausted. Although I was but recently delivered of my daughter, yet I attended and sat up with my husband four and twenty nights before his death. I was more than a year after in recovering from fatigue, joined to my great weakness and pain both of body and of mind. The great depression, or dryness and stupidity which I was in, was such that I could not say a word about God. It bore me down in such a manner that I could hardly speak. However, I entered for some moments into the admiration of thy goodness, O my God. I saw well that my crosses would not fail, since my mother-in-law had survived my husband. Also I was still tied, in having two children given me in so short a time before my husband's death, which evidently appeared the effect of divine wisdom; for had I only my eldest son, I would have put him in a college; and have gone myself into the convent of the Benedictines, and so frustrated all the designs of God upon me.

I was willing to show the esteem I had for my husband, in causing the most magnificent funeral to be made for him at my own expense. I paid off the legacies he had left. My mother-in-law violently opposed everything I could do for securing my own interests. I had nobody to apply to for advice or help; for my brother would not give me the least assistance. I was ignorant of business affairs; but God, independent of my natural understandings, always made me fit for everything that pleased Him, and supplied me with such a perfect intelligence that I succeeded. I omitted not the least minutia, and was surprised that in these matters I should know without ever having learned. I digested all my papers, and regulated all my affairs, without assistance from any one. My husband had abundance of writings deposited in his hands. I took an exact inventory of them, and sent them severally to their owners, which, without divine assistance, would have been very difficult for me; because, my husband having been a long time sick, everything was in the greatest confusion. This gained me the reputation of being a skillful woman.

There was one matter of great importance. A number of persons, who had been contending at law for several years, applied to my husband to settle their affairs. Though it was not properly the business of a gentleman, yet they applied to him, because he had both understanding and prudence; and as he had a love for several of them, he consented. There were twenty actions one upon another, and in all twenty-two persons concerned, who could not get any end put to their differences, by reason of new incidents continually falling out. My husband charged himself with getting lawyers to examine their papers, but died before he could make any procedure therein. After his death I sent for them to give them their papers; but they would not receive them, begging of me that I would accommodate them, and prevent their ruin. It appeared to me as ridiculous, as impossible, to undertake an affair of so great consequence, and which would require so long a discussion. Nevertheless, relying on the strength and wisdom of God, I consented. I shut myself up about thirty days for all these affairs, without ever going out, but to mass and to my meals. The arbitration being at length prepared, they all signed it without seeing it. They were all so well satisfied therewith, that they could not forbear publishing it everywhere. It was God alone who did those things; for after they were settled I knew nothing about them; and if I now hear any talk of such things, to me it sounds like Arabic.

166

CHAPTER 23

Being now a widow, my crosses, which one would have thought should have abated, only increased. That turbulent domestic I have often mentioned, instead of growing milder, now that she depended on me became more furious than ever. In our house she had amassed a good fortune, and I settled on her, besides, an annuity for the remainder of her life, for the services she had done my husband. She swelled with vanity and haughtiness. Having been used to sit up so much with an invalid, she had taken to drink wine, to keep up her spirits. This had now passed into a habit. As she grew aged and weak, a very little of it affected her. I tried to hide this fault, but it grew so that it could not be concealed. I spoke of it to her confessor, in order that he might try, softly and artfully to reclaim her from it; but instead of profiting by her director's advice, she was outrageous against me. My mother-in-law, who could hardly bear the fault of intemperance, and had often spoken to me about it, now joined in reproaching me and vindicating her. This strange creature, when any company came, would cry out with all her might, that I had dishonored her, thrown her into despair, and would be the cause of her damnation, as I was taking the ready course to my own. Yet God gave me an unbounded patience. I answered only with mildness and charity all her passionate invectives, giving her besides every possible mark of my affection. If any other maid came to wait on me, she would drive her back in a rage, crying out, that I hated her on account of the affection with which she had served my husband. When she had not a mind to come, I was obliged to serve myself; and when she did come, it was to chide me and make a noise. When I was very unwell, as was often the case, this girl would appear to be in despair. From hence I thought it was from Thee, O Lord, that all this came upon me. Without thy permission, she was scarcely capable of such unaccountable conduct. She seemed not sensible of any faults, but always to think herself in the right. All those whom Thou hast made use of to cause me to suffer, thought they were rendering service to Thee in so doing.

Before my husband's death, I went to Paris on purpose to see Monsieur Bertot, who had been of very little service to me as a director. Not knowing my state, and I being incapable of telling him of it, he grew weary of the charge. At length he gave it up, and wrote to me to take another director. I made no doubt but God had revealed to him my wicked state; and this desertion of me seemed a most certain mark of my reprobation. This was during the life of my husband. But now my renewed solicitations, and his sympathy with me on my husband's death, prevailed on him to resume my direction, which to me still proved of very little service. I went again to Paris to see him. While there, I visited him twelve or fifteen times, without being able to tell him anything of my condition. I told him, indeed, that I wanted some ecclesiastic to educate my son, to rid him of his bad habits, and of the wrong impressions he had conceived against me. He found one for me, of whom he had received very good recommendations.

I went to make a retreat with M. Bertot and Madame de C. All that time he spoke to me not a quarter of an hour at most. As he saw that I said nothing to him, for indeed I knew not what to say, as I had not spoken to him of the favors which God had conferred on me (not from a desire to conceal them, but because the Lord did not permit me to do it, as He had over me only the designs of death) he therefore spoke to such as he looked upon to be more advanced in grace. He let me alone as one for whom there was nothing to be done. So well did God hide from him the situation of my soul, in order to make me suffer, that he wanted to refer me, thinking that I had not the spirit of prayer, and that Mrs. Granger was mistaken when she told him I had. I did what I could to obey him, but it was entirely impossible. On this account I was displeased with myself, because I believed M. Bertot rather than my experience. Through this whole retreat my inclination, which I discerned only by my resistance to it, was to rest in silence and nakedness of thought. In the settling of my mind therein I feared I was disobeying the orders of my director. This made me think that I had fallen from grace. I kept myself in a state of nothingness, content with my poor low degree of prayer, without envying the higher degree of others, of which I judged myself unworthy. I would have, however, desired much to do the will of God, and to please Him, but despaired altogether of ever attaining that desirable end.

There was in the place where I lived, and had been for some years, one whose doctrine was suspected. He possessed a dignity in the church, which always obliged me to have a deference for him. As he understood how averse I was to all who were suspected of unsoundness in the faith, and knowing that I had some credit in the place, he used his utmost efforts to engage me in his sentiments. I answered him with so much clearness and energy, that he had not a word to reply. This increased his desire to win me in order to do it, to contract a friendship for me. He continued to importune me for two years and a half. As he was very polite, and of an obliging temper, and had a good share of learning, I did not mistrust him. I even conceived a hope of his conversion, in which I found myself mistaken. I then ceased going near him. He came to inquire why he could see me no more. At that time he was so agreeable to my sick husband, in his assiduities about him, that I could not avoid him though I thought the shortest and best way for me would be break off all acquaintance with him, which I did after the death of my husband. M. Bertot would not permit me to do it before. When he now saw that he could not renew it, he and his party raised up strong persecutions against me.

These gentlemen had at that time a method among them, by which they soon knew who were of their party, and who were opposite. They sent to one another circular letters, by means of which, in a very little time, they cried me down on every side, after a very strange manner. Yet this gave me little trouble. I was glad of my new liberty, intending never again to enter into an intimacy with anyone, which would give me so much difficulty to break.

This inability I was now in, of doing those exterior acts of charity I had done before, served this person with a pretext to publish that it was owing to him I had formerly done them. Willing to ascribe to himself the merit of what God alone, by His grace, had made me do, he went so far as to preach against me publicly, as one who had been a bright pattern to the town, but was now become a scandal to it. Several times he preached very offensive things. Though I was present at those sermons, and they were enough to weigh me down with confusion, for they offended all that heard them, I could not be troubled. I carried in myself my own condemnation beyond utterance. I thought I merited abundantly worse than all he could say of me, and that, if all men knew me, they would trample me under their feet. My reputation then was blasted by the industry of this ecclesiastic. He caused all such as passed for persons of piety to declare against me. I thought he and they were in the right and therefore quietly bore it all. Confused like a criminal that dares not lift up his eyes, I looked upon the virtue of others with respect. I saw no fault in others and no virtue in myself. When any happened to praise me, it was like a heavy blow struck at me, and I said in myself, "They little know my miseries, and from what state I have fallen." When any blamed me, I agreed to it, as right and just. Nature wanted sometimes to get out of such an abject condition, but could not find any way. If I tried to make an outward appearance of righteousness, by the practice of some good thing, my heart in secret rebuked me as guilty of hypocrisy, in wanting to appear what I was not; and God did not permit that to succeed. Oh, how excellent are the crosses of Providence! All other crosses are of no value.

I was often very ill and in danger of death, and knew not how to prepare myself for it. Several persons of piety, who had been acquainted with me, wrote to me about those things which the gentleman spread about me. I did not offer to justify myself, although I knew myself innocent of the things whereof they acused me. One day being in the greatest desolation and distress, I opened the New Testament on these words, "My grace is sufficient for thee, for my strength is made perfect in weakness." That for a little time gave me some relief.

CHAPTER 24

THE LORD TOOK FROM ME all the sensibility which I had for the creatures, or things created, even in an instant, as one takes off a robe. After that time I had none for any whatsoever. Though He had done me that favor, for which I can never be sufficiently grateful, I was, however, neither more contented nor less confused by it. My God seemed to be so estranged and displeased with me, that there remained nothing but the grief of having lost His blessed presence through my fault. The loss of my reputation every day increasing, became sensible to my heart, though I was not allowed to justify or bewail myself.

As I became always more impotent for every kind of exterior works, as I could not go to see the poor, nor stay at church, nor practice prayer; as I became colder toward God, in proportion as I was more sensible of my wrong steps, all this destroyed me the more both in my own eyes and in those of others. There were some very considerable gentlemen who made proposals for me, and even such persons as according to the rules of fashion ought not to think of me. They presented themselves during the very depth of my outward and inward desolation. At first it appeared to me a means of drawing me out of the distress I was in. But it seemed to me then notwithstanding my pains of body and mind, that if a king had presented himself to me, I would have refused him with pleasure, to show thee, O my God, that with all my miseries I was resolved to be thine alone.

If Thou wouldst not accept of me, I should at least have the consolation of having been faithful to Thee to the utmost of my power. For as to my inward state, I never mentioned it to anybody. I never spoke thereof, nor of the suitors, though my mother-in-law would say that if I did not marry, it was because none would have me. It was sufficient for me that Thou, O my God, knewest that I sacrificed them to Thee, (without saying a word to anybody) especially one whose high birth and amiable exterior qualities might have tempted both my vanity and inclination. Oh, could I but have hoped, to become agreeable to Thee, such a hope would have been like a change from Hell to Heaven. So far was I from presuming to hope for it, that I feared this sea of affliction might also be followed by everlasting misery, in the loss of Thee. I dared not even desire to enjoy Thee—I only desired not to offend Thee.

I was for five or six weeks at the last extremity. I could not take any nourishment. A spoonful of broth made me faint. My voice was so gone, that when they put their ears close to my mouth, they could scarcely distinguish my words. I could not see any hope of salvation, yet was not unwilling to die. I bore a strong impression that the longer I lived the more I would sin. Of the two, I thought I would rather choose Hell than sin. All the good, which God made me do, now seemed to me evil or full of faults. All my prayers, penances, alms and charities, seemed to rise up against me, and heighten my condemnation. I thought there appeared on the side of God, on my own, and from all creatures, one general condemnation, my conscience was a witness against me, which I could not appease. What may appear strange, the sins of my youth did not then give me any pain at all. They did not rise up in judgment against me, but there appeared one universal testimony against all the good I had done, and all the sentiments of evil I had entertained. If I went to confessors, I could tell them nothing of my condition. If I could have told them, they would have not understood me. They would have regarded as eminent virtues, what, O my God, thy eyes all pure and chaste rejected as infidelity. It was then that I felt the truth of what Thou hast said, that Thou judgest our righteousness. Oh, how pure art thou! Who can comprehend it? It was then that I turned my eyes on every side, to see what way succor might come to me; but my succor could come no way but from Him who made Heaven and earth. As I saw there was no safety for me, or spiritual health in myself, I entered into a secret complacency in seeing no good in myself whereon to rest, or presume for salvation. The nearer my destruction appeared, the more I found in God Himself, wherewith to augment my trust and confidence, notwithstanding

175

He seemed so justly irritated against me. It seemed to me that I had in Jesus Christ all that was wanting in myself. Oh, ye stout and righteous men! Observe as much as ye please of excellence in what ye have done to the glory of God. As for me, I only glory in my infirmities, since they have merited for me such a Saviour!

All my troubles, joined to the loss of my reputation, which yet was not so great as I apprehended, (it being only among a party) rendered me so unable to eat, that it seemed wonderful how I lived. In four days I did not eat as much as would make one very moderate repast. I was obliged to keep my bed through mere weakness, my body being no longer able to support the burden laid upon it. If I had thought, known, or heard tell, that there had ever been such a state as mine, it would have exceedingly relieved me. My very pain appeared to me to be sin. Spiritual books, when I tried to read them, all contributed only to agument it. I saw in myself none of those states which they set down. I did not so much as comprehend them. And when they treated the pains of certain states, I was very far from attributing any of them to myself. I said to myself, "These persons feel the pains of divine operations; but as to me, I sin, and feel nothing but my own wicked state." I could have wished to separate the sin from the confusion of sin, and provided I had not offended God, all would have been easy to me.

A slight sketch of my last miseries, which I am glad to let you know, because in their beginning I omitted many infidelities, having had too much of an earnest attachment, vain complaisance, unprofitable and tedious conversations, though self-love and nature made a sort of necessity for them; but toward the latter part I could not have borne a speech too human, nor the least thing of the kind.

CHAPTER 25

THE FIRST RELIGIOUS PERSON that God made use of to draw me to Himself, to whom (according to his desire) I had written from time to time, wrote to me in the depth of my distress, desiring me to write to him no more, signifying his disapprobation of what came from me, and that I displeased God greatly. A father, a Jesuit, who had esteemed me much, wrote to me in like manner. No doubt, it was by Thy permission, they thus contributed to complete my desolation. I thanked them for their charity, and commended myself to their prayers. It was then so indifferent to me to be decried of everybody, even of the greatest saints, that it added but little to my pain. The pain of displeasing God, and the strong propensity I felt in myself to all sorts of faults, caused me most lively and sensible pain.

I had been accustomed from the beginning to dryness and privation. I even preferred it to the state of abounding, because I knew that I must seek God above all. I had even at the first beginnings, an instinct of my inmost soul to pass over every manner of thing whatsoever, and to leave the gifts to run after the Giver. But at this time my spirit and senses were in such a manner struck, by Thy permission, O my Lord, who wert pleased to destroy me without mercy, that the farther I went, the more everything appeared to me a sin; even crosses appeared to me no more crosses but real faults. I thought I drew them all on myself by my imprudent words and actions. I was like those, who, looking through a colored glass, behold everything of the same color with which it is stained. Had I been able to perform any exterior acts as formerly, or penances for my evil, it would have relieved me. I was forbidden to do the latter, besides I grew so timorous, and felt in myself such a weakness, as made it appear impossible for me to do them. I looked on them with horror, I found myself now so weak and incapable of anything of the kind.

I omit many things, both of providences of the Lord in my favor, and of rugged paths through which I was obliged to pass. But as I have only one general view, I leave them in the knowledge of the Lord only. Afterward, being forsaken of my director, the coldness toward me which I remarked in the persons conducted by him, gave me no more trouble, nor indeed the estrangement of all the creatures, on account of my inward humiliation. My brother also joined with those who exclaimed against me, even though he had never seen them before. I believe it was the Lord who conducted things in this way, for my brother has worth, and undoubtedly thought he did well in acting thus.

I was obliged to go about some business to a town

where some near relations of my mother-in-law lived. How did I find things changed there! When I was there before, they entertained me in a most elegant and obliging manner, regaling me from house to house with emulation. Now they treated me with the utmost contempt, saying, they did it to revenge what I made their relation suffer. As I saw the thing went so far, and that notwithstanding all my care and endeavors to please her, I had not been able to succeed, I resolved to come to an explanation with her. I told her that there was a current report that I treated her ill, though I made it my study to give her every mark of my esteem. If the report were true, I desired her to allow me to remove from her; for that I would not choose to stay to give her pain, but only with a quite contrary view. She answered very coldly, "I might do what I would; for she had not spoken about it, but was resolved to live apart from me." This was fairly giving me my discharge, and I thought of taking my measures privately to retire. As I had not, since my widowhood, made any visits but such as were of pure necessity, or charity, there were found too many discontented spirits, who made a party with her against me. The Lord required of me an inviolable secrecy of all my pains, both exterior and interior. There is nothing which makes nature die so much, as to find neither support nor consolation. In short I saw myself obliged to go out, in the middle of winter, with my children and my daughters' nurse. At that time there was no house empty in the town, so the Benedictines offered me an apartment in theirs.

I was now in a great strait; on one side fearing lest I was shunning the cross, on the other side thinking it unreasonable to impose my stay on one to whom it was only painful. Besides what I have related of her behavior, which still continued, when I went into the country to take a little repose she complained that I left her alone. If I desired her to come thither she would not. If I said, "I dare not ask her to come, for fear of incommoding her by changing her bed," She replied, "It was only an excuse, because I would not have her go; and that I only went to be away from her." When I heard that she was displeased at my being in the country, I returned to the town. Then she could not bear to speak to me, or to see me. I accosted her without appearing to notice how she received it. Instead of making me any answer, she turned her head another way. I often sent her my coach, desiring her to come and spend a day in the country. She sent it back empty, without any answer. If I passed some days there without sending it, she complained aloud. In short, all I did to please her soured her, God so permitting it. She had in the main a good heart, but was troubled with an uneasy temper: And I do not fail to think myself under much obligation to her.

Being with her on Christmas day, I said to her with much affection: "My mother, on this day was the King of peace born, to bring it to us; I beg peace of you in His name." I think that touched her, though she would not let it appear. The ecclesiastic, whom

181

I had met with at home, far from strengthening and comforting me, did nothing but weaken and afflict me, telling me that I ought not to suffer certain things. I had not credit enough to discharge any domestic, however defective or culpable. As soon as any of them were warned to go away, she sided with them, and all her friends interferred. As I was ready to go off, one of my mother-in-law's friends, a man of worth, who had always an esteem for me, without daring to show it, having heard it, was much afraid lest I should leave the town; for the removal of my alms, he thought, would be a loss to the country. He resolved to speak to my mother-in-law in the softest manner he could for he knew her. After he had spoken to her, she said, that she would not put me away, but if I went, she would not hinder me. After this he came to see me, and desired me to go and make an excuse to her, in order to content her. I told him, I should be willing to make a hundred, although "I did not know about what; that I did it continually about everything, which made her uneasy. But that was not now the matter, for I make no complaint of her, but thought it not proper for me to continue with her, to give her pain; that it was but just that I should contribute to her ease." However, he went with me into her room. Then I told her, that I begged her pardon, if ever I had displeased her in anything, that it had never been my intention to do it; that I desired her, before this gentleman, who was her friend, to tell me wherein I had given her any offense. Here God permitted; she made a declaration of the truth in his presence. She said, "She was not a person to suffer herself to be offended; that she had no other complaint against me but that I did not love her, and that I wished her dead." I answered her that these thoughts were far from my heart, so far from it, that I should be glad, by my best care and attendance on her, to prolong her days; that my affection was real, but that she never would be persuaded to believe it, whatever testimonies I could give, so long as she hearkened to people who spoke to her against me; that she had with her a maid, who, far from showing me any respect, treated me ill, so far as to push me when she wanted to pass by. She had done it at church, making me give way to her with as much violence as contempt, several times, also, in my room grating me with her words: that I had never complained of it, because such a temper might one day give her trouble." She took the girl's part. Nevertheless we embraced and it was left so. Soon after, when I was in the country, this maid, having me no more to vent her chagrins on behaved in such a manner to my mother-in-law that she could not bear it. She immediately put her out of doors. I must say here on my mother-in-law's behalf, that she had both sense and virtue, and except certain faults, which persons who do not practice prayer are liable to, she had good qualities. Perhaps I caused crosses to her without intending it, and she to me without knowing it. I hope what I write will not be seen by any who may be offended with it, or who may not be in a condition to see these matters in God.

That gentleman who had used me so ill, for breaking off my acquaintance with him, among his penitents had one who, for affairs which befell her husband, was obliged to quit the country. He himself was accused of the same things which he had so liberally and unjustly accused me, and even things much worse, and with more noise and outcry. Though I well knew all this, God granted me the favor never to make his downfall the subject of my discourse. On the contrary, when any spoke to me of it, I pitied him, and said what I could in mitigation of his case. And God governed my heart so well, that it never offered to go into any vain joy at seeing him overtaken, and oppressed, with those kind of evils which he had been so assiduous in endeavoring to bring upon me. Though I knew that my mother-in-law was informed of it all, I never spoke to her about it, or about the sad confusions he had caused in a certain family.

CHAPTER 26

ONE DAY during my husband's life-time, laden with sorrow, not knowing what to do, I wished to speak to a person of distinction, and merit, who came often into the country. I wrote to request an opportunity with him, for that I wanted his in-struction and advice. But soon after I felt remorse for it; this voice spoke in my heart, "What,—dost thou seek for ease, and to shake off my yoke?" Here-upon I instantly sent a note again to desire him to excuse me, adding that what I had written was only from self-love, not necessity; that as he knew what it was to be faithful to God, I hoped he would not disapprove my acting with this Christian simplicity. Yet he resented it, which surprised me much, as I had conceived a high idea of his virtue. Virtues he had, but such as are full of the life and activities of nature, and unacquainted with the paths of mortifi-cation and death.

Thou, O my God, hast been my conductor even in these paths, as with admiration I have discovered since they are past. Blessed be Thy name forever. I am obliged to bear this testimony to Thy goodness.

Before I continue my narration, I must add one remark, which the Lord gave me to make upon the way by which He, in His goodness, was pleased to conduct me; which is, that this obscure path is the surest to mortify the soul, as it leaves it not any prop to lean upon for support. Though it has no application to any particular state of Jesus Christ; yet, at its coming out, it finds itself clothed with all His dispositions. The impure and selfish soul, is hereby purified, as gold in the furnace. Full of its own judgment and its own will before, but now obeys like a child and finds no other will in itself. Before, it would have contested for a trifle; now it yields at once, not with reluctance and pain by way of practicing virtue, but as it were naturally. Its own vices are vanished. This creature so vain before now loves nothing but poverty, littleness and humilation. Before, it preferred itself above everybody; now everybody above itself, having a boundless charity for its neighbor, to bear with his faults and weaknesses, in order to win him by love, which before it could not do but with very great constraint. The rage of the wolf is changed to the meekness of the lamb.

During all the time of my experiencing my miseries and my deep trials, I went after no fine sights or recreations. I wanted to see and know nothing but Jesus Christ. My closet was my only diversion. Even when the queen was near me, whom I had never seen, and whom I had desire enough to see; I had only to open my eyes, and look out to see her; yet did not do it. I had been fond of hearing others sing; yet I was once four days with one who passed for the finest voice in the world, without ever desiring her to sing; which surprised her, because she was not ignorant that, knowing her name, I must know the charming excellence of her voice. However, I committed some infidelities, in inquiring what others said of me by way of blame. I met with one who told me everything. Though I showed nothing of it, it served only to mortify me. I saw I was yet too much alive to self.

I shall never be able to express the number of my miseries. They are so vastly surmounted by the favors of God, and so swallowed up in these that I can see them no more. One of the things which gave me most pain in the seven years I have spoken of, especially the last five, was so strange a folly of my imagination that it gave me no rest. My senses bore it company. I could no more shut my eyes at church. Thus having all the gates and avenues open, I was like a vineyard exposed, because the hedges which the father of the family had planted were torn away. I saw every one that came and went, and everything that passed in the church. For the same force, which had drawn me inward to recollection, seemed to push me outward to dissipation.

Laden with miseries, weighed down with oppressions, and crushed under continual crosses, I thought of nothing but ending my days thus. There remained in me not the least hope of ever emerging. Notwithstanding, I thought I had lost grace forever, and the salvation which it merits for us, I longed at least to do what I could for God, though I feared I should never love Him. Seeing the happy state from whence

187

I had fallen, I wished in gratitude to serve Him, though I looked on myself as a victim doomed to destruction. Sometimes the view of that happy period caused secret desires to spring up in my heart, of recovering it again. I was instantly rejected and thrown back into the depth of the abyss; I judged myself to be in a state which was due to unfaithful souls. I seemed, my God, as if I was forever cast off from Thy regard, and from that of all creatures. By degrees my state ceased to be painful. I became even insensible to it, and my insensibility seemed like the final hardening of my reprobation. My coldness appeared to me a mortal coldness. It was truly so, O my God, since I thus died to self, in order to live wholly in Thee, and in thy precious love.

To resume my history, a servant of mine wanted to become a Barnabite. I wrote about it to Father de la Mothe. He answered me, that I must address Father La Combe, who was then the superior of the Barnabites of Tonon. That obliged me to write to him. I had always preserved secret respect and esteem for him, as one under grace. I was glad of this opportunity of recommending myself to his prayers. I wrote to him about my fall from the grace of God, that I had requited His favors with the blackest ingratitude; that I was miserable, and a subject worthy of compassion; and far from having advanced toward God, I was become entirely alienated from Him. He answered in such a manner, as if he had known, by a supernatural light, the frightful description I had given of myself.

In the midst of my miseries, Geneva came into my

mind, a singular manner, which caused me many fears. "What," said I, "to complete my reprobation, shall I go to such an excess of impiety, as to quit the faith through apostacy? (The inhabitants of Geneva being generally Protestant Calvinists.) Am I then about quitting that church, for which I would give a thousand lives? Or, shall I ever depart from that faith which I would even wish to seal with my blood?" I had such a distrust of myself, that I dared hope for nothing, but had a thousand reasons for fear. Nevertheless the letter which I had received from Father La Combe, in which he wrote me an account of his present disposition, somewhat similar to mine, had such an effect, as to restore peace and calmness to my mind. I felt myself inwardly united to him, as to a person of great fidelity to the grace of God. Afterward a woman appeared to me in a dream to be come down from Heaven, to tell me that God demanded me at Geneva.

About eight or ten days before Magdalene's day, 1680, it came into my mind to write to Father La Combe, and to request him, if he received my letter before that day, to pray particularly for me. It was so ordered, contrary even to my expectations, that he received my letter on St. Magdalene's eve, and when praying for me the next day, it was said to him, thrice over, with much power, "Ye shall both dwell in one and the same place." He was very much surprised, as he never had received interior words before. I believe, O my God, that that has been much more verified, both in our inward sense and experi-

189

ence, and in the same crucifying events which have befallen us, pretty much alike; and in Thyself, who art our dwelling, than in any temporal abode.

CHAPTER 27

ON THAT HAPPY MAGDALENE'S DAY my soul was perfectly delivered from all its pains. It had already begun since the receipt of the first letter from Father La Combe, to recover a new life. It was then only like that of a dead person raised, though not yet unbound from grave clothes. On this day I was, as it were, in perfect life, and set wholly at liberty. I found myself as much raised above nature, as before I had been depressed under its burden. I was inexpressibly overjoyed to find Him, whom I thought I had lost forever, returned to me again with unspeakable magnificence and purity. It was then, O God, that I found again in Thee with new advantages, in an ineffable manner, all I had been deprived of; the peace I now possessed was all holy, heavenly and inexpressible. All I had enjoyed before was only a peace, a gift of God, but now I received and possessed the God of peace. Yet the remembrance of my past miseries still brought a fear upon me, lest nature should find means to take to itself any part therein. As soon as it wanted to see or taste anything, the Spirit ever watchful crossed and repelled it. I was

191

far from elevating myself, or attributing to myself anything of this new state. My experience made me sensible of what I was.

I hoped I should enjoy this happy state for some time, but little did I think my happiness so great and immutable as it was. If one may judge of a good by the trouble which precedes it, I leave mine to be judged of by the sorrows I had undergone before my attaining it. The apostle Paul tells us, that "the sufferings of this life are not to be compared with the glory that is prepared for us." How true is that of this life! One day of this happiness was worth more than years of suffering. It was indeed, at that time well worth all I had undergone, though it was then only dawning. An alacrity for doing good was restored to me, greater than ever. It seemed to me all quite free and natural to me. At the beginning, this liberty was less extensive; but as I advanced it grew greater. I had occasion to see Mon. Bertot for a few moments, and told him, I thought my state much changed. He, seemingly attentive to something else, answered, "No." I believed him; because grace taught me to prefer the judgment of others, and rather believe them than my own opinions or experience. This did not give me any kind of trouble. Every state seemed equally indifferent if I only had the favor of God. I felt a kind of beatitude every day increasing in me. I did all sorts of good, without selfishness or premeditation. Whenever a self-reflective thought was presented to my mind, it was instantly rejected, and as it were a curtain in the soul drawn before it. My imagination was kept so fixed,

192

that I had now very little trouble on that
at the clearness of my mind and the p
whole heart.

I received a letter from Father La Combe, wherein
he wrote that God had discovered to him that he
had great designs in regard to me. "Let them be,"
then said I to myself, "either of justice or mercy, all
is equal to me." I still had Geneva deeply at heart;
but said nothing of it to anybody, waiting for God
to make known to me His all powerful will and fearing lest any stratagem of the Devil should be concealed therein, that might tend to draw me out of
my proper place, or steal me out of my condition.
The more I saw my own misery, incapacity and
nothingness, the plainer it appeared that they rendered me fitter for the designs of God, whatever
they might be. "Oh, my Lord," said I, "take the weak
and the wretched to do thy works, that Thou mayest
have all the glory and that man may attribute nothing of them to himself. If Thou shouldst take a person of eminence and great talents, one might attribute to him something; but if Thou takest me, it will
be manifest that thou alone art the Author of whatever good shall be done." I continued quiet in my
spirit, leaving the whole affair to God, being satisfied,
if He should require anything of me, that He would
furnish me with the means of performing it. I held
myself in readiness with a full resolution to execute
His orders, whenever he should make them known,
though it were to the laying down of my life. I was
released from all crosses. I resumed my care of the
sick, and dressing of wounds, and God gave me to

cure the most desperate. When surgeons could do no more, it was then that God made me cure them.

Oh, the joy that accompanied me everywhere, finding still Him who had united me to Himself, in His own immensity and boundless vastitude! Oh, how truly did I experience what He said in the Gospel, by the four evangelists, and by one of them twice over, "Whosoever will lose his life for my sake shall find it; and whosoever will save his life shall lose it."

When I had lost all created supports, and even divine ones, I then found myself happily compelled to fall into the pure divine, and to fall into it through all those very things which seemed to remove me further from it. In losing all the gifts, with all their supports, I found the Giver. In losing the sense and perception of Thee in myself—I found Thee, O my God, to lose Thee no more in Thyself, in Thy own immutability. Oh, poor creatures, who pass all your time in feeding upon the gifts of God, and think therein to be the most favored and happy. How I pity you if you stop here, short of the true rest, and cease to go forward to God Himself, through the loss of those cherished gifts which you now delight in! How many pass all their lives in this way, and think highly of themselves! There are others who, being called of God to die to themselves, yet pass all their time in a dying life, in inward agonies, without ever entering into God through death and a total loss of self, because they are always willing to retain something under plausible pretexts, and so never lose themselves to the whole extent of the designs of God.

They never enjoy God in all His fullness; which is a loss that cannot be perfectly known in this life.

Oh, my Lord, what happiness did I not largely taste in my solitude, and with my little family, where nothing interrupted my tranquillity! As I was in the country, the slender age of my children did not require my application too much, they being in good hands, I retired a great part of the day into a wood. I passed as many days of happiness as I had had months of sorrow. Thou, O my God, dealt by me as by thy servant Job, rendering me double for all thou hadst taken, and delivering me from all my crosses. Thou gavest me a marvelous facility to satisfy everyone. What was surprising now was that my mother-in-law, who had ever been complaining of me, without my doing anything more than usual to please her, declared that none could be better satisfied with me than she was. Such as before had cried me down the most, now testified their sorrow for it and became full of my praises. My reputation was established with much more advantage, in proportion as it had appeared to be lost. I remained in an entire peace, as well without as within. It seemed to me that my soul was become like New Jerusalem, spoken of in the Apocalypse, prepared as a bride for her husband and where there is no more sorrow, or sighing. I had a perfect indifference to everything that is here, a union so great with the will of God, that my own will seemed entirely lost. My soul could not incline itself on one side or the other, since another will had taken the place of its own, but only nourished itself with the daily providences of God.

It now found a will all divine, yet was so natural and easy that it found itself infinitely more free than ever it had been in its own.

These dispositions have still subsisted, and still grown stronger, and more perfect even to this hour. I could neither desire one thing nor another, but was content with whatever fell. If any in the house asked me, "Will you have this, or that?" then I was surprised to find that there was nothing left in me which could desire or choose. I was as if everything, of smaller matters, quite disappeared, a higher power having taken up and filled all their place. I even perceived no more that soul which He had formerly conducted by His crook and His staff, because now He alone appeared to me, my soul having given up its place to Him. It seemed to me, as if it was wholly and altogether passed into its God, to make but one and the same thing with Him; even as a little drop of water, cast into the sea, receives the qualities of the sea. Oh, union of unity, demanded of God by Jesus Chirst for men and merited by him! How strong is this in a soul that is become lost in its God! After the consummation of this divine unity, the soul remains hid with Christ in God. This happy loss is not like those transient ones which ecstacy operates, which are rather an absorption than union because the soul afterwards finds itself again with all its own dispositions. Here she feels that prayer fulfilled—John 17:21: "That they all may be one as thou Father art in me, and I in thee; that they also may be one in us."

CHAPTER 28

I WAS OBLIGED TO GO to Paris about some business. Having entered into a church, that was very dark, I went up to the first confessor I found, whom I did not know, nor have ever seen since. I made a simple and short confession; but to the confessor himself I said not a word. He surprised me saying, "I know not who you are whether maid, wife or widow; but I feel a strong inward motion to exhort you to do what the Lord has made known to you, that he requires of you. I have nothing else to say." I answered him, "Father, I am a widow who have little children. What else could God require of me, but to take due care of them in their education?" He replied, "I know nothing about this. You know if God manifests to you that He requires something of you; there is nothing in the world which ought to hinder you from doing His will. One may have to leave one's children to do that." This surprised me much. However, I told him nothing of what I felt about Geneva. I disposed myself submissively to quit everything, if the Lord required it of me. I did not look upon it as a good I aspired to, or a virtue

I hoped to acquire, or as anything extraordinary, or as an act that would merit some return on God's part; but only gave myself up to be led in the way of my duty, whatever it might be, feeling no distinction between my own will and the will of God in me.

In this disposition, I lived with my family in the greatest tranquillity, until one of my friends had a great desire to go on a mission to Siam. He lived twenty leagues from my house. As he was ready to make a vow to this purpose, he found himself stopped, with an impulse to come and speak to me. He came immediately, and as he had some reluctance to declare his mind to me, he went to read prayers in my chapel, hoping God would be satisfied with his making the vow. As he was performing divine service in my hearing, he was stopped again. He left the chapel to come and speak to me. He then told me his intention.

Though I had no thought of saying anything positive to him, I felt an impression in my soul to relate to him my case, and the idea I had for a long time past for Geneva. I told him a dream I had, which appeared to me supernatural. When I had done, I felt a strong impulse to say to him, "You must go to Siam; and you must also serve me in this affair. It is for that end God has sent you hither; I desire you to give me your advice." After three days, having considered the matter, and consulted the Lord in it, he told me that he believed I was to go thither; but to be the better assured of it, it would be needful to see the Bishop of Geneva. If he approved of my design, it would be a sign that it was from the

Lord; if not, I must drop it. I agreed with his sentiment. He then offered to go to Annecy, to speak to the Bishop, and to bring me a faithful account. As he was advanced in years, we were deliberating in what way he could take so long a journey, when there came two travelers, who told us the Bishop was at Paris. This I looked on as an extraordinary providence. He advised me to write to Father La Combe, and recommend the affair to his prayers, as he was in that country. He then spoke to the Bishop at Paris. I, having occasion to go thither, spoke to him also.

I told him, that "my design was to go into the country, to employ there my substance, to erect an establishment for all such as should be willing truly to serve God, and to give themselves unto him without reserve; and that many of the servants of the Lord had encouraged me thereto." The bishop approved of the design. He said, "there were New Catholics going to establish themselves at Gex, near Geneva, and that it was providential thing. I answered him, "that I had no vocation for Gex, but for Geneva." He said, "I might go from hence to that city."

I thought this was a way which divine Providence had opened, for my taking this journey with the less difficulty. As I yet knew nothing positive of what the Lord would acquire at my hand, I was not willing to oppose anything. "Who knows," said I, "but the will of the Lord is only that I should contribute to this establishment?"

I went to see the prioress of the New Catholics at Paris. She seemed much rejoiced, and assured me she would gladly join me. As she is a great servant of God, this confirmed me. When I could reflect a little, which was but seldom, I thought God would make choice of her for her virtue, and me for my worldly substance. When I inadvertantly looked at myself, I could not think God would make use of me; but when I saw the things in God, then I perceived that the more I was nothing, the fitter I was for His designs. As I saw nothing in myself extraordinary, and looked on myself as being in the lowest stage of perfection, and imagined that an extraordinary degree of inspiration was necessary for extraordinary designs, this made me hesitate, and fear deception. It was not that I was in fear of anything, as to my perfection and salvation which I had referred to God; but I was afraid of not doing His will by being too ardent and hasty in doing it. I went to consult Father Claude Martin. At that time he gave me no decisive answer, demanding time to pray about it; saying he would write to me what should appear to him to be the will of God concerning me.

I found it hard to get to speak to M. Bertot, both on account of his being difficult of access, and of my knowing how he condemned things extraordinary, or out of the common road. Being my director, I submitted, against my own views or judgment, to what he said, laying down all my own experiences when duty required me to believe and obey. I thought, however, than in an affair of this importance, I ought to address myself to him, and prefer his sense of the matter to that of every one beside. Persuaded, he would infallibly tell me the will of God. I went to him then, and he told me that my design was of God, and that he had had a sense given him of God for some time past, that he required something of me. I therefore returned home to set everything in order. I loved my childern much, having great satisfaction in being with them, but resigned all to God to follow His will.

On my return from Paris, I left myself in the hands of God, resolved not to take any step, either to make the thing succeed or to hinder it, either to advance or retard it, but singly to move as He should be pleased to direct me. I had mysterious dreams, which portended nothing but crosses, persecutions and afflictions. My heart submitted to whatever it should please God to ordain. I had one which was very significant.

Being employed in some necessary work, I saw near me a little animal which appeared to be dead. This animal I took to be the envy of some persons, which seemed to have been dead for some time. I took it up, and as I saw it strove hard to bite me, and that it magnified to the eye, I cast it away. I found thereupon that it filled my fingers with sharp-pointed prickles like needles. I came to one of my acquaintance to get him to take them out; but he pushed them deeper in, and left me so, till a charitable priest of great merit, (whose countenance is still present with me, though I have not yet seen him, but believe I shall before I die) took this animal up with a pair of pincers. As soon as he held it fast, those

201

sharp prickles fell off, of themselves. I found that I easily entered into a place, which before had seemed inaccessible. And although the mire was up to my girdle, in my way to a deserted church, I went over it without getting any dirt. It will be easy to see in the sequel what this signified.

Doubtless you will wonder that I, who makes so little account of things extraordinary, relate dreams. I do it for two reasons; first out of fidelity, having promised to omit nothing of what should come to my mind; secondly, because it is the method God makes use of to communicate Himself to faithful souls, to give them foretokens of things to come, which concern them. Thus mysterious dreams are found in many places of the holy Scriptures. They have singular properties, as—

1. To leave a certainty that they are mysterious, and will have their effect in their season.

2. To be hardly ever effaced out of the memory, though one forgets all others.

3. To redouble the certainty of their truth every time one thinks of them.

4. They generally leave a certain unction, a divine sense or savor at one's waking.

I received letters from sundry religious persons, some of whom lived far from me, and from one another, relating to my going forth in the service of God, and some of them to Geneva in particular, in such a manner as surprised me. One of them intimated that I must there bear the cross and be persecuted; and another of them that I should be eyes to the blind, feet to the lame, and arms to the maimed.

The ecclesiastic, or chaplain, of our house was much afraid lest I was under a delusion. What at that time greatly confirmed me was Father Claude Martin, whom I mentioned above, wrote to me that, after many prayers, the Lord had given him to know that He required me at Geneva, and to make a free sacrifice of everything to Him. I answered him, "that perhaps the Lord required of me nothing more than a sum of money to assist in founding an institution which was going to be established there." He replied, that the Lord had made him know that He wanted not my worldly substance but myself. At the very same time with this letter I received one from Father La Combe, who wrote to me that the Lord had given him a certainty, as he had done to several of his good and faithful servants and handmaids, that he wanted me at Geneva. The writers of these two letters lived above a hundred and fifty leagues from each other; yet both wrote the same thing. I could not but be somewhat surprised to receive at the same time two letters exactly alike, from two persons living so far distant from each other.

As soon as I became fully convinced of its being the will of the Lord, and saw nothing on earth capable of detaining me, my senses had some pain about leaving my children. And upon reflecting thereon a doubt seized my mind. O my Lord! Had I rested on myself, or on the creatures, I would have revolted; "leaned on a broken reed, which would have pierced my hand." But relying on Thee alone, what needed

I to fear? I resolved then to go, regardless of the censures of such as understand not what it is to be a servant of the Lord, and to receive and obey His orders. I firmly believed that He, by His Providence, would furnish the means necessary for the education of my children. I put everything by degrees in order, the Lord alone being my guide.

CHAPTER 29

WHILE PROVIDENCE, on the one hand, appointed my forsaking all things, it seemed on the other to make my chains the stronger, and my separation the more blameable. None could receive stronger marks of affection from one's own mother than those which I received at this time from my mother-in-law. Even the least sickness which befell me made her very uneasy. She said, "she had veneration for my virtue." I believe what contributed not a little to this change was, that she had heard that three persons had offered suit to me, and that I had refused them, although their fortune and quality were quite superior to mine. She remembered how she had upbraided me on this head, and I answered her not a word, whereby she might understand that it depended on myself to marry to advantage. She began to fear lest such rigorous treatment, as hers had been toward me, might excite me to deliver myself by such means, with honor, from her tyranny, and was sensible what damage that might be to my children. So she was now very tender to me on every occasion.

I fell extremely ill. I thought that God had accepted of my willingness to sacrifice all to him, and required that of my life. During this illness, my mother-in-law went not from my bedside; her many tears proved the sincerity of her affection. I was very much affected at it, and thought I loved her as my true mother. How, then, should I leave her now, being so far advanced in age? The maid, who till then had been my plague, took an inconceivable friendship for me. She praised me everywhere, extolling my virtue to the highest and served me with extraordinary respect. She begged pardon for all that she had made me suffer, and died of grief after my departure.

There was a priest of merit, a spiritual man, who had fallen in with temptation of taking upon him employment which I was sensible God did not call him to do. Fearing it might be a snare to him, I advised him against it. He promised me he would not do it, and yet accepted it. He then avoided me, joined in calumniating me, gradually fell away from grace, and died soon after.

There was a nun in a monastery I often went to, who was entered into a state of purification, which everyone in the house looked on as distraction. They locked her up and all who went to see her called it phrenzy or melancholy. I knew her to be devout I requested to see her. As soon as I approached, I felt an impression that she sought purity. I desired of the Superior that she should not be locked up, nor should people be admitted to see her, but that she would confide her to my care. I hoped things would change. I discovered that her greatest pain was at being counted a fool. I advised her to bear the state of foolishness, since Jesus Christ had been willing to bear it before Herod. This sacrifice gave her a calmness at once. But as God was willing to purify her soul, He separated her from all those things for which she had before the greatest attachment. At last, after she had patiently undergone her sufferings, her Superior wrote to me that "I was in the right, and that she had now come out of that state of dejection, in greater purity than ever." The Lord gave to me alone at that time to know her state. This was the commencement of the gift of discerning spirits, which I afterward received more fully.

The winter before I left home was one of the longest and hardest that had been for several years (1680). It was followed with extreme scarcity, which proved to me an occasion of exercising charity. My mother-in-law joined me heartily and appeared to me so much changed. I could not but be both surprised and overjoyed at it. We distributed at the house ninety-six dozen loaves of bread every week, but private charities to the bashful poor were much greater. I kept poor boys and girls employed. The Lord gave such blessings to my alms, that I did not find that my family lost anything by it. Before the death of my husband, my mother-in-law told him that I would ruin him with my charities, though he himself was so charitable, that in a very dear year, while he was young, he distributed a considerable sum. She repeated this to him so often, that he commanded me to set down in writing all the money I laid out, both what I gave for the expense of the house, and all that I caused to be bought, that he might better judge of what I gave to the poor. This new obligation, which I was brought under, appeared to me so much the harder, as for above eleven years we had been married I never before had this required of me. What troubled me most was the fear of having nothing to give to such as wanted. However, I submitted to it, without retrenching any part of my charities. I did not indeed set down any of my alms, and yet my account of expenses was found to answer exactly. I was much surprised and astonished, and esteemed it one of the wonders of Providence. I saw plainly it was simply given out of Thy treasury, O my Lord, that made me more liberal of what I thought was the Lord's, and not mine. Oh, if we but knew how far charity, instead of wasting or lessening the substance of the donor, blessed, increased and multiplied it profusely. How much is there in the world of useless dissipation, which, if properly applied, might amply serve for the subsistence of the poor, and would abundantly be restored, and amply rewarded to the families of those who gave it.

In the time of my greatest trials, some years after my husband's death (for they began three years before my widowhood, and lasted four years after) my footman came one day to tell me, (I was then in the country) that there was in the road a poor soldier dying. I had him brought in, and ordering a separate place to be made ready for him, I kept above a fortnight. His malady was a flux, which he had taken in the army. It was so nauseous, that though the domestics were charitably inclined, nobody could bear to come near him. I went myself to take away his vessels. But I never did anything of the kind which was so hard. I frequently made efforts for a full quarter of an hour at a time. It seemed as if my very heart was going to come up; yet I never desisted. I sometimes kept the poor people at my house to dress their putrid sores; but never met with anything so terrible as this. The poor man, after I had made him receive the sacrament, died.

What gave me now no small concern was the tenderness I had for my children, especially my younger son, whom I had strong reasons for loving. I saw him inclined to be good; everything seemed to favor the hopes I had conceived of him. I thought it running a great risk to leave him to another's education. My daughter I designed to take with me, though she was at this time ill of a very tedious fever. Providence was pleased, however, so to order it that she speedily recovered. The ties, with which the Lord held me closely united to Himself, were infinitely stronger than those of flesh and blood. The laws of my sacred marriage obliged me to give up all, to follow my spouse whithersoever it was His pleasure to call me after Him. Though I often hesitated, and doubted much before I went, I never doubted after my going of its being His will; and though men, who judge of things only according to the success they seem to have, have taken occasion from my disgraces and sufferings, to judge of my calling, and to run it down as error, illusion and imagination; it is that very persecution, and a multitude of strange crosses it has drawn upon me, (of which this imprisonment I now suffer is one,) which have confirmed me in the certainty of its truth and validity. I am more than ever convinced that the resignation which I have made of everything is in pure obedience to the divine will.

The gospel effectually in this point shows itself to be true, which has promised to those that shall leave all for the love of the Lord, "an hundred fold in this life, and persecutions also." And have not I infinitely more than an hundred fold, in so entire a possession as my Lord hast taken of me; in that unshaken firmness which is given me in my sufferings, in a perfect tranquillity in the midst of a furious tempest, which assaults me on every side; in an unspeakable joy, enlargedness and liberty which I enjoy in a most straight and rigorous captivity. I have no desire that my imprisonment should end before the right time. I love my chains. Everything is equal to me, as I have no will of my own, but purely the love and will of Him who possesses me. My senses indeed have not any relish for such things, but my heart is separated from them. My perseverance is not of myself, but of Him who is my life; so that I can say with the apostle, "It is no more I that live, but Jesus Christ that liveth in me." It is He in whom I live, move, and have my being.

To return to the subject, I say that I was not so reluctant to go with the New Catholics, as I was to engage with them, not finding a sufficient attraction, though I sought for it. I longed indeed to contribute to the conversion of wandering souls, and God made use of me to convert several families before my departure, one of which was composed of eleven or twelve persons. Besides, Father La Combe had written to me, to make use of this opportunity for setting off, but did not tell me whether I ought to engage with them or not. Thus it was the Providence of my God alone, which ordered everything, to which I was resigned without any reserve; and that hindered me from engaging with them.

One day reflecting humanly on this undertaking of mine, I found my faith staggering, weakened with a fear lest I were under a mistake, which slavish fear was increased by an ecclesiastic at our house, who told me it was a rash and ill-advised design. Being a little discouraged, I opened the Bible, and met with this passage in Isaiah, "Fear not thou worm Jacob, and ye men of Israel. I will help thee saith the Lord, and thy Redeemer, the holy one of Israel." (Chap. 61:14) and near it, "Fear not; for I have redeemed thee, I have called thee by thy name; thou art mine. When thou passest through the waters, I will be with thee."

I had a very great courage given me for going, but could not persuade myself that it would be best to settle with the New Catholics. It was, however, necessary to see Sister Garnier, their superior at Paris, in order to take our measures together. But I could not go to Paris, because that journey would have hindered me from taking another, which I had to take. She then, though much indisposed, resolved to come and see me. In what a wonderful manner, O my God, didst Thou conduct things by Thy Providence, to

211

make everything come to the point of Thy will! Every day I saw new miracles, which both amazed and still more confirmed me; for with a paternal goodness Thou tookest care of even the smallest things. As she intended setting off, she fell sick. And Thou permitted it to fall out so, to give room thereby for a person, who would have discovered everything, in the meantime to take a journey to see me. As this person had given me notice of the day she intended to set off, seeing that day was excessively hot, and so sultry that I imagined that being taken so much tender care of as she was at home, they would not suffer her to begin her journey, (which really proved to be the case, as she afterward told me,) I prayed to the Lord to be pleased to grant a wind to rise, to moderate the violent heat. Scarce had I prayed, but there arose suddenly so refreshing a wind, that I was surprised and the wind did not cease during her whole journey.

I went to meet her, and brought her to my countryhouse, in such a way that she was not seen or known of anybody. What embarrassed me a little was, that two of my domestics knew her. But as I was then endeavoring the conversion of a lady, they thought that it was on this account I had sent for her, and that it was necessary to keep it secret, that the other lady might not be discouraged from coming. Though I knew nothing of controversial points, yet God so furnished me that I did not fail to answer all her objections, and resolve all her doubts, to such a degree, that she could not but give herself up entirely to God. Though Sister Garnier had a good share of both of grace and natural understanding, yet her words had not such an effect on this soul as those with which God furnished me, as she assured me herself. She even could not forbear speaking of it. I felt a movement to beg her of God, as a testimony of His holy will concerning me. But He was pleased not to grant it then, being willing that I should go off alone without any other assurance than His divine Providence was conducting all things. Sister Garnier did not declare her thoughts to me for four days. Then she told me she would not go with me. At this I was the more surprised, as I had persuaded myself that God would grant to her virtue what He might refuse to my demerits. Besides, the reason she gave appeared to me to be merely human, and void of supernatural grace. That made me hesitate a little; then, taking new courage, through the resignation of my whole self, I said, "As I go not thither for your sake, I will not fail to go even without you." This surprised her, as she acknowledged to me; for she thought that, on her refusal, I would decline my purpose of going.

I regulated everything, wrote down the contract of association with them as I thought proper. No sooner had I done it, but I felt great perturbation and trouble of mind. I told her my pain, and that I had no doubt but the Lord demanded me at Geneva, yet did not let me see that He would have me to be of their congregation. She desired to have some time till after prayers and communion, and that then she would tell me what she thought the Lord required of me. Accordingly, He directed her contrary both to her interests and inclination. She then told me that I ought not to connect myself with her, that it was not the Lord's design; that I only ought to go with her sister's, and that when I should be there, Father La Combe, (whose letter she had seen) would signify to me the divine will. I entered at once into these sentiments, and my soul then regained the sweets of inward peace.

My first thought had been (before I heard of the New Catholics going to Gex) to go directly to Geneva. At this time there were Catholics there in service, and otherwise; to take some little room without any noise, and without declaring myself at first; and as I knew how to make up all sorts of ointments to heal wounds and especially the king's evil, of which there is abundance in that place, and for which I had a most certain cure. I hoped easily to insinuate myself by this way and with the charities which I should have done to have won over many of the people. I have no doubt but, if I had followed this impulse, things would have succeeded better. But I thought I ought to follow the sentiments of the Bishop rather than my own. What am I saying? Has not Thy eternal Word, O my Lord, had its effect and accomplishment in me? Man speaks as man; but when we behold things in the Lord, we see them in another light. Yes, my Lord, Thy design was to give Geneva not to my cares, words or works, but to my sufferings; for the more I see things appear hopeless, the more do I hope for the conversion of that city by a way known to Thee only.

Father La Combe has told me since, that he had a

strong impulse to write to me, not to engage with the New Catholics. He believed it not to be the will of the Lord concerning me; but he omitted doing it. As to my director, M. Bertot, he died four months before my departure. I had some intimations of his death, and it seemed as if he bequeathed me a portion of his spirit to help his children.

I was seized with a fear, that the check I had felt, at giving so largely in favor of the New Catholics, what I had designed for Geneva, was a stratagem of nature, which does not love to be stripped. I wrote to Sister Garnier to get a contract drawn up according to my first memorial. God permitted me to commit this fault, to make me the more sensible of His protection over me.

PART TWO

CHAPTER 1

I WENT OFF, in a strange renunciation, and in great simplicity, scarcely able to render the reason why I should in such a manner quit my family, which I most tenderly love, being without any positive assurance, yet hoping even against hope itself. I went to the New Catholics at Paris, where Providence wrought wonders to conceal me. They sent for the notary, who had drawn up the contract of engagement. When he read it to me, I felt such a repugnance to it, that I could not bear to hear it to the end, much less sign it. The notary wondered and much more so when Sister Garnier came in, and told him, that there needed no contract of engagement. I was enabled through divine assistance, to put my affairs in very good order, and to write sundry letters by the inspiration of the Spirit of God, and not by my own. This was what I had never experienced before. It was given me at that time only as a beginning, and has since been granted me much more perfectly.

I had two domestics, whom it was very difficult

for me to discharge, as I did not think to take them with me. If I had left them, they would have told of my departure; and I should have been sent after. I was when it became known. But God so ordered it that they were willing to follow me. They were of no use to me, and soon after turned into France. I took with me only my daughter, and two maids to serve us both. We set off in a boat upon the river, though I had taken places in the stage-coach, in order that, if they searched for me in the coach, they might not find me. I went to Melun to wait for it there.

It was surprising that in this boat the child could not forbear making crosses, employing a person to cut rushes for her to use for that purpose. She then put around, and all over me, above three hundred of them. I let her do it, and inwardly apprehended that it was not without its meaning. I felt an interior certainty that I was going to meet with crosses in abundance and that this child was sowing the cross for me to reap it. Sister Garnier, who saw that they could not restrain her from covering me with crosses, said to me, "What that child does appears to be significant." Turning to the little girl, she said, "Give me some crosses, too, my pretty pet." "No," she replied, "they are all for my dear mother." Soon she gave her one to stop her importunity, then continued putting more on me; after which she desired some river-flowers, which floated on the water, to be given her. Braiding a garland she put it on my head, and said to me, "After the cross you shall be crowned." I admired all this in silence, and offered myself up to the pure love of God, as a victim, free and willing to be sacrificed to Him.

Some time before my departure, a particular friend, a true servant of God, related to me a vision she had respecting me. "She saw my heart surrounded with thorns; that our Lord appeared in it well pleased; that, though the thorns seemed likely to tear it, yet, instead of doing that, they only rendered it fairer, and our Lord's approbation the stronger.

At Corbeil, (a little town on the river Seine, sixteen miles south of Paris,) I met with the priest whom God had first made use of so powerfully to draw me to His love. He approved of my design to leave all for the Lord; but he thought I should not be well suited with the New Catholics. He told me some things about them, to show that our leadings were incompatible. He cautioned me not to let them know that I walked in the inward path. If I did, I must expect nothing but persecution from them. But it is in vain to contrive to hide, when God sees it best for us to suffer, and when our wills are utterly resigned to Him, and totally passed into His.

While at Paris I gave the New Catholics all the money I had. I reserved not to myself a single penny, rejoicing to be poor after the example of Jesus Christ. I brought from home nine thousand livres. As by my donation I had reserved nothing to myself and by a contract lent them six thousand; this six thousand has returned to my children but none of it to me. That gives me no trouble; poverty, thus procured, constitutes my riches. The rest I gave entirely to the

221

sisters that were with us, as well to supply their traveling expenses, for the purchase of furniture. I did not reserve so much as my linen for my own use, putting it in the common fund. I had neither a locked coffer, nor purse. I had brought but little linen for fear of mistrust. In wanting to carry off clothes I should have been discovered. My persecutors did not fail to report that I had brought great sums from home, which I had imprudently expended, and given to the friends of Father La Combe. False as I had not a penny. On my arrival at Annecy a poor man was asking alms. I, having nothing else, gave him the buttons from my sleeves. At another time I gave a poor man a little plain ring, in the name of Jesus Christ. I had worn it as a token of marriage with Him.

We joined the flying stage at Melun where I left Sister Garnier. I went on with the other sisters with whom I had no acquaintance. The carriages were very fatiguing; I got no sleep through so long a journey. My daughter, a very tender child, only five years of age, got scarcely any. We bore great fatigue without falling sick by the way. My child had not an hour's uneasiness, although she was only three hours in bed every night. At another time half this fatigue, or even the want of rest, would have thrown me into a fit of sickness. God only knows both the sacrifices which He induced me to make, and the joy of my heart in offering up everything to Him. Had I kingdoms and empires, I think I would yield them up with still more joy, to give Him the higher marks of my love.

As soon as we arrived at the inn, I went to church and stayed there till dinner time. In the coach, my divine Lord communed with me, and in me, in a manner which the others could not comprehend, indeed not perceive. The cheerfulness I showed in the greatest dangers encouraged them. I even sang hymns of joy at finding myself disengaged from the riches, honors and entanglements of the world. God in such a manner protected us. He seemed to be to us "a pillar of fire by night, and a pillar of a cloud by day." We passed over a very dangerous spot between Lyons and Chamberry. Our carriage broke as we were coming out of it. Had it happened a little sooner, we would have perished.

We arrived at Annecy on Magdalene's eve, 1681. On Magdalene's day the Bishop of Geneva performed divine service for us, at the tomb of St. Francis de Sales. There I renewed my spiritual marriage with my Redeemer, as I did every year on this day. There also I felt a sweet remembrance of that saint, with whom our Lord gives me a singular union. I say union, for it appears to me that the soul in God is united with saints, the more so in proportion as they are conformable to Him. It is a union which it pleases God sometimes to revive after death, and awaken in the soul for His own glory. At such times departed saints are rendered more intimately present to that soul in God; and this revival is as it were an holy intercourse of friend with friend, in Him who unites them all in one immortal tie.

That day we left Annecy, and on the next went to prayers at Geneva. I had much joy at the communion. It seemed to me as if God more powerfully united me to Himself. There I prayed to Him for the conversion of that great people. That evening we arrived late at Gex, where we found only bare walls. The Bishop of Geneva had assured me that the house was furnished; undoubtedly he believed it to be. We lodged at the house of the sisters of charity, who were so kind as to give us their beds.

I was in great pain of mind for my daughter, who visibly lost weight. I had a strong desire to place her with the Ursulines at Tonon. My heart was so affected on her behalf, that I could not forbear weeping in secret for her. Next day I said, "I would take my daughter to Tonon, and leave her there, till I should see how we might be accommodated." They opposed it strongly, after a manner which seemed very hard-hearted as well as ungrateful, seeing she was a skeleton. I looked upon the child as a victim whom I had imprudently sacrificed. I wrote to Father La Combe, entreating him to come and see me, to consult together about it. I thought I could not in conscience keep her in this place any longer. Several days passed without my having any answer. In the meantime I became resigned to the will of God, whether to have succor or not.

CHAPTER 2

Our lord took pity on the lamentable condition of my daughter, and so ordered it, that the Bishop of Geneva wrote to Father La Combe, to come as speedily as possible to see us, and to console us. As soon as I saw that father, I was was surprised to feel an interior grace, which I may call communication; such as I had never had before with any person. It seemed to me that an influence of grace came from him to me, through the innermost of the soul; returned from me to him, in such a way that he felt the same effect. Like a tide of grace it caused a flux and reflux, flowing on into the divine and invisible ocean. This is a pure and holy union, which God alone operates, and which has still subsisted, and even increased. It is an union exempt from all weakness, and from all self-interest. It causes those who are blessed with it to rejoice in beholding themselves, as well as those beloved, laden with crosses and afflictions—an union which has no need of the presence of the body. At certain times absence makes not more absent, nor presence more present; a union unknown to men, but such as are come to experience it. It can never be experienced but between such souls as are united to God. As I never before felt a union of this sort with any one, it then appeared to me quite new. I had no doubt of its being from God; so far from turning the mind from Him, it tended to draw it more deeply into Him. It dissipated all my pains, and established me in the most profound peace.

God gave him at first much openness of mind toward me. He related to me the mercies God had shown him, and several extraordinary things, which gave me at first some fear. I suspected some illusion, especially in such things as flatter in regard to the future; little imagining that God would make use of me to draw him from this state and bring him into that naked faith. But the grace, which flowed from Him into my soul, recovered me from that fear. I saw that it was joined with extraordinary humility. Far from being elevated with the gifts which God had liberally conferred upon him, or with his own profound learning, no person could have a lower opinion of himself than he had. He told me as to my daughter, it would be best for me to take her to Tonon, where he thought she would be very well situated. As to myself, after I had mentioned to him my dislike to the manner of life of the New Catholics, he told me, that he did not think it would be my proper place to be long with them. It would be best for me to stay there, free from all engagements, till God, by the guidance of His Providence, should make known to me how he would dispose of me, and draw my mind to the place whither he would have me remove. I had already begun to awake regularly at midnight, in order to pray. I awoke with these words suddenly put in my mind, "It is written of me, I will do thy will, O my God." This was accompanied with the most pure, penetrating, and powerful communication of grace that I had ever experienced. Though the state of my soul was already permanent in newness of life; yet this new life was not in that immutability in which it has been since. It was a beginning life and a rising day, which goes on increasing unto the full meridan; a day never followed by night; a life which fears death no more, not even in death itself; because he who has suffered the first death, shall no more be hurt of the second. From midnight I continued on my knees till four o'clock in the morning, in prayer, in a sweet intercourse with God, and did the same also the night following.

The next day, after prayers, Father La Combe told me, that he had a very great certainty, that I was a stone which God designed for the foundation of some great building. What that building was he knew no more than I. After whatever manner then it is to be, whether His divine Majesty will make use of me in this life, for some design known to himself only, or will make me one of the stones of the new and heavenly Jerusalem, it seems to me that such stone cannot be polished, but by the strokes of the hammer. Our Lord has given to this soul of mine the qualities of the stone, firmness, resignation, insensibility, and power to endure hardness under the operations of His hand.

I carried my little daughter to the Ursulines at

Tonon. That child took a great fondness for Father La Combe, saying, "He is a good father, one from God." Here I found a hermit, whom they called Anselm. He was a person of the most extraordinary sanctity that had appeared for some time. He was from Geneva; God had miraculously drawn him from thence, at twelve years of age. He had at nineteen years of age taken the habit of hermit of St. Augustine. He and another lived alone in a little hermitage, where they saw nobody but such as came to visit their chapel. He had lived twelve years in this hut, never eating anything but pulse with salt, and sometimes oil. Three times a week he lived on bread and water. He never drank wine, and generally took but one meal in twenty-four hours. He wore for a shirt a coarse hair cloth, and lodged on the bare ground. He lived in a continual state of prayer, and in the greatest humility. God had done by him many signal miracles.

This good hermit had a great sense of the designs of God on Father La Combe and me. But God showed him at the same time that strange crosses were preparing for us both; that we were both destined for the aid of souls. I did not find, as I expected, any suitable place for my daughter at Tonon. I thought myself like Abraham, when going to sacrifice his son. Father La Combe said, "Welcome, daughter of Abraham!" I found little encouragement to leave her and could not keep her with myself, because we had no room. The little girls, whom they took to make Catholics, were all mixed and had contracted habits as were pernicious. To leave her there I thought not right. The language of the country, where scarce anyone understood French, and the food, which she could not take, being far different from ours, were great hardships. All my tenderness for her was awakened, and I looked on myself as her destroyer. I experienced what Hagar suffered when she put away her son Ishmael in the desert that she might not be forced to see him perish. I thought that even if I had ventured to expose myself, I ought at least to have spared my daughter. The loss of her education, even of her life, appeared to me inevitable. Everything looked dark in regard to her.

With her natural disposition and fine qualities, she might have attracted admiration, if educated in France, and been likely to have such offers of marriage, as she could never hope to meet with in this poor country; in which, if she should recover, she would never be likely to be fit for anything. Here she could eat nothing of what was offered her. All her subsistence was a little unpleasant and disagreeable broth, which I forced her to take against her will. I seemed like a second Abraham, holding the knife over her to destroy her. Our Lord would have me make a sacrifice to Him, without any consolation, and plunged in sorrow, night was the time in which I gave vent to it. He made me see, on one side the grief of her grandmother, if she should hear of her death, which she would impute to my taking the child away from her; the great reproach, it would be accounted among all the family. The gifts of nature she was endowed with were now like pointed darts which pierced me. I believe that God so ordered it to purify me from too human an attachment still in me. After I returned from the Ursulines at Tonon, they changed her manner of diet, and gave her what was suitable; in a short time she recovered.

CHAPTER 3

As soon as it was known in France that I was gone there was a general outcry. Father de la Mothe wrote to me, that all persons of learning and of piety united in censuring me. To alarm me still more, he informed me that my mother-in-law, with whom I had entrusted my younger son and my children's substance, was fallen into a state of childhood. This, however, was false.

I answered all these fearful letters as the Spirit dictated. My answers were thought very just, and those violent exclamations were soon changed into applauses. Father La Mothe appeared to change his censures into esteem; but it did not last. Self interest threw him back again; being disappointed in his hopes of a pension, which he expected I would have settled on him. Sister Garnier, whatever was her reason, changed and declared against me.

I both ate and slept little. The food which was given us was putrid and full of worms, by reason of the great heat of the weather, also being kept too long. What I should have formerly beheld with the greatest abhorrence, now became my only nourishment. Yet everything was rendered easy to me. In

God I found, without increase, everything which I had lost for Him. That spirit, which I once thought I had lost in a strange stupidity, was restored to me with inconceivable advantages. I was astonished at myself. I found there was nothing which I was not fit for or in which I did not succeed. Those who observed said that I had a prodigious capacity. I well knew that I had but meager capabilities, but that in God my spirit had received a quality which it had never had before. I thought I experienced something of the state which the apostles were in, after they had received the Holy Ghost. I knew, I comprehended, I understood, I was enabled to do everything necessary. I had every sort of good thing and no want of anything. When Jesus Christ, the eternal wisdom, is formed in the soul, after the death of the first Adam, it finds in Him all good things communicated to it.

Sometime after my arrival at Gex, the Bishop of Geneva came to see us. He was so clearly convinced, and so much affected, that he could not forbear expressing it. He opened his heart to me on what God had required of him. He confessed to me his own deviations and infidelities. Every time when I spoke to him he entered into what I said, and acknowledged it to be the truth. Indeed it was the Spirit of truth which inspired me to speak to him, without which I should be only a mere simpleton. Yet as soon as those persons spoke to him, who sought for preeminence, and who could not suffer any good but what came from themselves, he was so weak as to be imposed on with impressions against the truth.

This weakness has hindered him from doing all the good which otherwise he might have done.

After I had spoken to him, he said that he had it in his mind to give me Father La Combe for director; he was a man illuminated of God, who well understood the inward path, and had a singular gift of pacifying souls. Greatly was I rejoiced when the Bishop appointed him, seeing thereby his authority united with the grace which already seemed to have given him to me, by a union and effusion of supernatural life and love. The fatigues I had, and watchings with my daughter, threw me into a violent sickness attended with exquisite pain. The physicians judged me in danger, yet the sisters of the house quite neglected me; especially the stewardess. She was so penurious, that she did not give me what was necessary to sustain life. I had not a penny to help myself with, as I had reserved nothing to myself. Besides, they received all the money which was remitted to me from France, which was very considerable. I practiced poverty and was in necessity even among those to whom I had given all. They wrote to Father La Combe, desiring him to come to me, as I was so extremely ill. Hearing of my condition he was so touched with compassion as to walk on foot all night. He traveled not otherwise, endeavoring in that, as in everything else, to imitate our Lord Jesus Christ.

As soon as he entered the house my pains abated; when he had prayed and blessed me, laying his hand on my head, I was perfectly cured, to the great astonishment of my physicians; who were not willing to acknowledge the miracle.

These sisters advised me to return to my daughter. Father La Combe returned with me. A violent storm arose on the Lake, which made me very sick, and seemed likely to upset the boat. But the hand of Providence remarkably appeared in our favor; so much so, that it was taken notice of by the mariners and passengers. They looked upon Father La Combe as a saint. We arrived at Tonon, where I found myself so perfectly recovered, that, instead of making and using the remedies I had proposed, I went into a retreat, and stayed twelve days. Here I made vows of perpetual chastity, poverty and obedience, covenanting to obey whatever I should believe to be the will of God, also to obey the church, and to honor Jesus Christ in such a manner as He pleased.

At this time I found that I had the perfect chastity of love to the Lord, it being without any reserve, division, or view of interest. Perfect poverty, by the total privation of everything that was mine, both inwardly and outwardly. Perfect obedience to the will of the Lord, submission to the church, and honor to Jesus Christ in loving Himself only; the effect of which soon appeared. When by the loss of ourselves we are passed into the Lord, our will is made one and the same with that of the Lord, according to the prayer of Christ, "As thou Father art in me, and I in thee, grant that they also may be one of us." John 17:21. Oh, but it is then that the will is rendered marvelous, both because it is made the will of the Lord, which is the greatest of miracles; also because it works wonders in Him. For as it is the Lord who wills in the soul, that will has its effect. Scarcely has it willed but the thing is done.

But some may say, Why then so many oppressions endured? Why do not these souls, if they have such a power, set themselves free from them? We answer that if they had any will to do anything of that sort, against divine providence, that would be the will of flesh, or the will of man, and not the will of God, John 1:13.

I rose generally at midnight, waking at the proper time; but if I wound up my alarm-watch, then I used not to awake in time. I saw that the Lord had the care of a father and a spouse over me. When I had any indisposition, and my body wanted rest, He did not awake me; but at such times I felt even in my sleep a singular possession of Him. Some years have passed wherein I have had only a kind of half-sleep; but my soul waked the more for the Lord, as sleep seemed to steal from it every other attention. The Lord made it known also to many persons, that He designed me for a mother of great people, but a people simple and childlike. They took these intelligences in a literal sense and thought it related to some institution or congregation. But it appeared to me that the persons whom it would please the Lord that I should win over to Him, and to whom I should be as a mother, through His goodness, should have the same union of affection for me as children have for a parent, but a union much deeper and stronger; giving me all that was necessary for them, to bring them to walk in the way by which He would lead them, as I shall show.

CHAPTER 4

I WOULD WILLINGLY SUPPRESS what I am now about to write if anything of it were my own, also on account of the difficulty of expressing myself as because few souls are capable of understanding divine leadings which are so little known, and so little comprehended. I have myself never read of anything like it. I shall say something of the interior dispositions I was then in, and I shall think my time well employed, if it serves you who are willing to be of the number of my children; it serves such as are already my children, to induce them to let God glorify Himself in them after His manner, and not after their own. If there be anything which they do not comprehend, let them die to themselves. They will find it much easier to learn by experience than from anything I could say; expression never equals experience.

After I had come out of the trying condition I have spoken of I found it had purified my soul, instead of blackening it as I had feared. I possessed God after a manner so pure, and so immense, as nothing else could equal. In regard to thoughts or desires, all was so clean, so naked, so lost in the divinity, that the soul had no selfish movement, however plausible or delicate; both the powers of the mind and the very senses being wonderfully purified. Sometimes I was surprised to find that there appeared not one selfish thought. The imagination, formerly so restless, now no more troubled me. I had no more perplexity or uneasy reflections. The will, being perfectly dead to all its own appetites, was become void of every human inclination, both natural and spiritual, and only inclined to whatever God pleased, and to whatever manner He pleased. This vastness or enlargedness, which is not bounded by anything, however plain or simple it may be, increases every day. My soul in partaking of the qualities of her Spouse seems also to partake of His immensity. My prayer was in an openness and singleness inconceivable. I was, as it were, borne up on high, out of myself. I believe God was pleased to bless me with this experience. At the beginning of the new life, He made me comprehend, for the good of other souls, the simplicity and desirableness of this passage of the soul into God.

When I went to confess, I felt such an immersion of the soul into Him, that I could scarcely speak. This ascension of the spirit, wherein God draws the soul so powerfully, not into its own inmost recess, but into Himself, is not operated till after the death of self. The soul actually comes out of itself to pass into its divine object. I call it death, that is to say, a passage from one thing to another. It is truly a happy passover for the soul, and its passage into the promised land. The spirit which is created to be united to its divine Origin, has so powerful a tendency to Him, that if it were not stopped by a continual miracle, its moving quality would cause the body to be drawn after it by reason of its impetuosity and noble ascent. But God has given it a terrestrial body to serve for a counterpoise. This spirit then, created to be united to its Origin, without any medium or interstice, feeling itself drawn by its divine object, tends to it with an extreme violence; in such sort that God, suspending for sometime the power which the body has to hold back the spirit, it follows with ardency. When it is not sufficiently purified to pass into God, it gradually returns to itself; as the body resumes its own quality, it turns to the earth. The saints who have been the most perfect have advanced to that degree, as to have nothing of all this. Some have lost it toward the end of their lives, becoming single and pure as the others, because they then had in reality and permanence what they had at first only as transient fruitions, in the time of the prevalence or dominion of the body. It is certain then that the soul, by death to itself, passes into its divine Object. This is what I then experienced. I found, the farther I went, the more my spirit was lost in its Sovereign, who attracted it more and more to Himself. He was pleased at first that I should know this for the sake of others and not for myself. Indeed He drew my soul more and more into Himself, till it lost itself entirely out of sight, and could perceive itself no more. It seemed at first to pass into Him. As one sees a river pass into the ocean, lose itself in it, its water for a time distinguished from that of the sea, till it gradually becomes transformed into the same sea, and possesses all its qualities; so was my soul lost in God, who communicated to it His qualities, having drawn it out of all that it had of its own. Its life is an inconceivable innocence, not known or comprehended of those who are still shut up in themselves or only live for themselves.

The joy which such a soul possesses in its God is so great, that it experiences the truth of those words of the royal prophet, "All they who are in thee, O Lord, are like persons ravished with joy." To such a soul the words of our Lord seem to be addressed, "Your joy no man shall take from you." John 16:22. It is as it were plunged in a river of peace. Its prayer is continual. Nothing can hinder it from praying to God, or from loving Him. It amply verifies these words in the Canticles, "I sleep but my heart waketh;" for it finds that even sleep itself does not hinder it from praying. Oh, unutterable happiness! Who could ever have thought that a soul, which seemed to be in the utmost misery, should ever find a happiness equal to this? Oh, happy poverty, happy loss, happy nothingness, which gives no less than God Himself in His own immensity, no more circumscribed to the limited manner of the creature, but always drawing it out of that, to plunge it wholly into His own divine essence.

Then the soul knows that all the states of self-pleasing visions, openings, ecstasies and raptures, are rather obstacles; that they do not serve this state which is far above them; because the state which has supports, has pain to lose them; yet cannot arrive at this without such loss. In this are verified the words of an experienced saint; "When I would," says he, "possess nothing through self-love, everything was given me without going after it." Oh, happy dying of the grain of wheat, which makes it produce an hundredfold! The soul is then so passive, so equally disposed to receive from the hand of God either good or evil, as is astonishing. It receives both the one and the other without any selfish emotions, letting them flow and be lost as they come. They pass away as if they did not touch.

After I finished my retreat with the Ursulines at Tonon, I returned through Geneva and, having found no other means of conveyance, the French resident lent me a horse. As I knew not how to ride I made some difficulty of doing it; but as he assured me that it was a very quiet horse, I ventured to mount. There was a sort of a smith, who looking at me with a wild haggard look, struck the horse a blow on the back, just as I had got upon him, which made him give a leap. He threw me on the ground with such force that they thought I was killed. I fell on my temple. My cheekbone and two of my teeth were broken. I was supported by an invisible hand and in a little time I mounted as well as I could on another horse and had a man by my side to keep me up.

My relations left me in peace at Gex. They had heard at Paris of my miraculous cure; it made a great noise there. Many persons in reputation for sanctity then wrote to me. I received letters fromMadamoiselle De Lamoignon, and another young lady, who was so moved with my answer, that she sent me a hundred pistoles for our house, and let me know besides that, when we wanted money, I had only to write to her; and that she would send me all I could desire. They talked in Paris of printing an account of the sacrifice I had made, and inserting in it the miracle of my sudden recovery. I don't know what prevented it; but such is the inconstancy of the creature, that this journey, which drew upon me at that time so much applause, has served for a pretext for the strange condemnation which has since passed upon me.

CHAPTER 5

My NEAR RELATIONS did not signify any eager desire for my return. The first thing they proposed to me, a month after my arrival at Gex, was not only to give up my guardianship, but to make over all my estate to my children and to reserve an annuity to myself. This proposition, coming from people who regarded nothing but their own interest, to some might have appeared very unpleasing; but it was in no wise so to me. I had not any friend to advise with. I knew not anyone whom I could consult about the manner of executing the thing, as I was quite free and willing to do it. It appeared to me that I had now the means of accomplishing the extreme desire I had of being conformable to Jesus Christ, poor, naked, and stripped of all. They sent me an article to execute, which had been drawn under their inspection, and I innocently signed it, not perceiving some clauses which were inserted therein. It expressed that, when my children should die, I should inherit nothing of my own estate, but that it should revolve to my kindred. There were many other things, which appeared to be equally to my disadvantage. Though what I had reserved to myself was sufficient to support me in this place; yet it was scarcely enough to do so in some other places. I then gave up my estate with more joy, for being thereby conformed to Jesus Christ, than they could have who asked it from me. It is what I have never repented of, nor had any uneasiness about. What pleasure to lose all for the Lord! The love of poverty, thus contracted, is the kingdom of tranquillity.

I forgot to mention that toward the end of my miserable state of privation, when just ready to enter into newness of life, our Lord illuminated me so clearly to see that the exterior crosses came from Him, that I could not harbor any resentment against the persons who procured me them. On the contrary, I felt the tenderness of compassion for them, and had more pain for those afflictions which I innocently caused to them, than for any which they had heaped upon me. I saw that these persons feared the Lord too much to oppress me as they did, had they known it. I saw His hand in it, and I felt the pain which they suffered, through the contrariety of their humors. It is hard to conceive the tenderness which the Lord gave me for them, and the desire which I have had, with the utmost sincerity, to procure them every sort of advantage.

After the accident which befell me (fall from the horse) from which I soon wonderfully recovered, the Devil began to declare himself more openly mine enemy, to break loose and become outrageous. One night, when I least thought of it, something very monstrous and frightful presented itself. It seemed a kind face, which was seen by a glimmering blueish light. I don't know whether the flame itself composed that horrible face or appearance; for it was so mixed and passed by so rapidly, that I could not discern it. My soul rested in its calm situation and assurance, and it appeared no more after that manner. As I arose at midnight to pray, I heard frightful noises in my chamber and after I had lain down they were still worse. My bed often shook for a quarter of an hour at a time, and the sashes were all burst. Every morning while this continued, they were found shattered and torn, yet I felt no fear. I arose and lighted my waxcandle at a lamp which I kept in my room, because I had taken the office of sacristan and the care of waking the sisters at the hour they were to rise, without having once failed in it for my indispositions, ever being the first in all the observances. I made use of my little light to look all over the room and at the sashes, at the very time the noise was strongest. As he saw that I was afraid of nothing, he left off all on a sudden, and attacked me no more in person. But he stirred up men against me, and that succeeded far better with him; for he found them disposed to do what he prompted them to, zealously, inasmuch as they counted it a good thing to do me the worst of injuries.

One of the sisters whom I had brought with me, a very beautiful girl, contracted an intimacy with an ecclesiastic, who had authority in this place. At first he inspired her with an aversion for me, being well assured that if she placed confidence in me, I should advise her not to suffer his visits so frequently. She was undertaking a religious retreat. That ecclesiastic was desirous to induce her to make it, in order to gain her entire confidence, which would have served as a cloak to his frequent visits. The Bishop of Geneva had given Father La Combe for director to our house. As he was going to cause retreats to be made, I desired her to wait for him. As I had gained some share in her esteem, she submitted even against her inclination, which was to have made it under this ecclesiastic. I began to talk to her on the subject of inward prayer, and drew her into the practice of this duty. Our Lord gave such a blessing thereto, that this girl gave herself to God in right earnest, and with her whole heart and the retreat completely won her over. She then became more reserved, and on her guard, toward this ecclesiastic, which exceedingly vexed him. It enraged him both against Father La Combe and me. This proved the source of the persecutions which afterward befell me. The noise in my chamber, which may have been traced to him, ended as these commenced.

This ecclesiastic began to talk privately of me with much contempt. I knew it, but took no notice. There came a certain friar to see him, who mortally hated Father La Combe, on account of his regularity. These combined together to force me to quit the house, that they might become masters of it. All the means they could devise they used for that purpose.

My manner of life was such, that in the house I did not meddle in affairs at all, leaving the sisters to dispose of the temporalities as they pleased. Soon after my entrance into it I received eighteen hundred livres, which a lady, a friend of mine, lent me to complete our furniture, which I had repaid her at my late giving up of my estate. This sum they received, as well as what I had before given them. I sometimes spoke a little to those who retired thither to become Catholics. Our Lord favored with so much benediction what I said to them, that some, whom they knew not before what to make of, became sensible, solid women, and exemplary in piety.

I saw crosses in abundance likely to fall to my lot. At the same time these words came, "Who for the joy that was set before him endured the cross." Heb. 12:2. I prostrated myself for a long time with my face on the ground, earnestly desiring to receive all thy strokes. Oh, Thou who spared not thine own son! Thou couldst find none but Him worthy of Thee, and thou still findest in Him hearts proper for thee.

A few days after my arrival at Gex, I saw in a sacred and mysterious dream (for as such I very well distinguished it) Father La Combe fastened up to an enormous cross, stripped in like manner as they paint our Saviour. I saw around it a frightful crowd, which covered me with confusion, and threw back on me the ignominy of his punishment. He seemed to have most pain, but I more reproaches than he. I have since beheld this fully accomplished.

The ecclesiastic won over to his party one of our sisters, who was the house-steward and soon after the prioress. I was very delicate, the good inclination which I had did not give strength to my body. I had two maids to serve me; yet, as the community had need of one of them for their cook, and the other to attend the door and other occasions, I gave them up, not thinking but they would allow them to serve me sometimes. Besides this, I let them still receive all my income, they having had my first half of this year's annuity. Yet they would not permit either of my maid-servants, to do anything for me. By my office of sacristan I was obliged to sweep the church, which was large, and they would not let anyone help me. I have several times fainted over the broom and have been forced to rest in corners. This obliged me to beg them, that they would suffer it sometimes to be swept by some of the strong country girls, New Catholics, to which at last they had the charity to consent. What most embarrassed me was that I never had washed. I was now obliged to wash all the vestry linen. I took one of my maids to help me, because in attempting it I had done up the linen most awkwardly. These sisters pulled her by the arms out of my chamber, telling her she should do her own work. I let it quietly pass, without making any objection. The other good sister, the girl I just mentioned, grew more and more fervent. By the practice of prayer in her dedication of herself to the Lord she became more and more tender in her sympathy with me. It irritated this ecclesiastic. After all his impotent attempts here, he went off to Annecy, in order to sow discord, and to effect more mischief to Father La Combe.

CHAPTER 6

H<small>E</small> <small>WENT DIRECTLY</small> to the Bishop of Geneva, who till then had manifested much esteem and kindness for me. He persuaded him, that it would be proper to secure me to that house, to oblige me to give up to it the annual income I had reserved to myself; to engage me thereto, by making me prioress. He had gained such an ascendancy over the Bishop, that the people in the country called him the Little Bishop. He drew him to enter heartily and with zeal into this proposition, and to resolve to bring it about whatever it should cost.

The ecclesiastic, having so far carried his point, and being swelled with his success, no longer kept any measures in regard to me. He began with causing all the letters which I sent, and those which were directed to me, to be stopped. That was in order to have it in his power to make what impressions he pleased on the minds of others, and that I should neither be able to know it, nor to defend myself, nor to give or send to my friends any account of the manner in which I was treated. One of the maids I had brought wanted to return. She could have no rest in this place, the other that remained was infirm, too much taken up by others to help me in anything. As Father La Combe was soon to come, I thought he would soften the violent spirit of this man, and that he would give me proper advice.

In the meantime they proposed to me the engagement, and the post of prioress. I answered, that as to the engagement it was impossible for me, since my vocation was elsewhere. And I could not regularly be the prioress, till after passing through the noviticate, in which they had all served two years before their being engaged. When I should have done as much, I should see how God would inspire me. The prioress replied quite tartly, that if I would ever leave them it were best for me to do it immediately. Yet I did not offer to retire, but continued still to act as usual. I saw the sky gradually thickening and storms gathering on every side The prioress then affected a milder air. She assured me, that she had a desire, as well as I, to go to Geneva; that I should not engage, but only promise her to take her with me, if I went thither. She pretended to place a great confidence in me, and professed a high esteem for me. As I am very free, and have nothing but uprightness, I let her know that I had no attraction for the manner of life of the New Catholics, by reason of the intrigues from without. Several things did not please me, because I wanted them to be upright in everything. She signified that she did not consent to such things, but because that ecclesiastic told her they were necessary to give the house a credit in distant parts and to draw charities from Paris. I answered that if we walked uprightly God would never fail us. He would sooner do miracles for us. I remarked to her that when, instead of sincerity, they had recourse to artifice, charity grew cold, and kept herself shut up. It is God alone who inspires charity; how, then, is it to be drawn by disguises?

Soon after, Father La Combe came about the retreats. This was the third and last time that he came to Gex. The prioress, after she had been tampering a good deal with me, having written him a long letter before his coming, and received his answer, which she showed me, now went to ask him whether she would one day be united to me at Geneva. He answered with his usual uprightness, "Our Lord has made it known to me that you shall never be established at Geneva." Soon after she died. When he had uttered this declaration, she appeared enraged against both him and me. She went directly to that ecclesiastic, who was in a room with the house-steward; and they took their measures together, to oblige me either to engage or retire. They thought that I would sooner engage than retire, and they watched my letters.

With a design to lay snares for him, he requested Father La Combe to preach. He did on this text, "The King's daughter is beautiful within." That ecclesiastic, who was present with his confidant, said that it was preached against him, and was full of errors. He drew up eight propositions, and inserted in them what the other had not preached, adjusting them as maliciously as ever he could, then sent them to one of his friends in Rome, to get them examined by the

Sacred Congregation, and by the Inquisition. Though he had very illy digested them, at Rome they were pronounced good. That greatly disappointed and vexed him. After having been treated in this manner, and opprobriously reviled by him in the most offensive terms, the Father, with much mildness and humility, told him that he was going to Annecy about some affairs of the convent. If he had anything to write to the Bishop of Geneva, he would take care of his letter. He then desired him to wait awhile, as he was going to write. The good Father had the patience to wait above three hours, without hearing from him; though he had treated him exceedingly ill, so far as to snatch out of his hands a letter I had given him for that worthy hermit I have mentioned. Hearing he was not gone, but was still in the church, I went to him, and begged him to send to see if the other's packet was ready. The day was so far gone that he would be obliged to lodge by the way. When the messenger arrived, he found a servant of the ecclesiastic on horseback, ordered to go at full speed, to be at Annecy before the Father. He then returned an answer, that he had no letters to send by him. This was so contrived, that he might gain time to prepossess the Bishop for his purposes. Father La Combe then set off for Annecy, and on his arrival found the Bishop prepossessed, and in an ill humor. This was the substance of the discourse.

Bishop—You must absolutely engage this lady to give what she has to the house at Gex, and make her the prioress of it.

F. La Combe—My lord, you know what she has

told you herself of her vocation, both at Paris and in this country. I therefore do not believe that she will engage; nor is there any likelihood that, after quitting her all, in the hope of entering Geneva, she should engage elsewhere, and thereby put it out of her power to accomplish the designs of God in regard to her. She has offered to stay with those sisters as a boarder. If they are willing to keep her as such, she will remain with them; if not, she is resolved to retire into some convent, till God shall dispose of her otherwise.

BISHOP—I know all that; but I likewise know that she is so very obedient, that, if you order her, she will assuredly do it.

F. LA COMBE—It is for that reason, my lord, that one ought to be very cautious in the commands which they lay on her. Can I induce a foreign lady, who, for all her subsistence, has nothing but a small pittance she has reserved to herself, to give that up in favor of a house which is not yet established, and perhaps never will be? If the house should happen to fail, or be no longer of use, what shall that lady live on? Shall she go to the hospital? And indeed this house will not long be of any use, since there are no Protestants in any part of France near it.

BISHOP—These reasons are good for nothing. If you do not make her do what I have said, I will degrade and suspend you.

This manner of speaking somewhat surprised the Father. He well enough understands the rules of suspension, which is not executed on such things. He replied:

252

"My lord, I am ready, not only to suffer the suspension, but even death, rather than do anything against my conscience." Having said that, he retired.

He directly sent me this account by an express, to the end that I might take proper measures. I had no other course to take but to retire into a convent. I received a letter informing me that the nun to whom I had entrusted my daughter had fallen sick, and desiring me to go to her for some time. I showed this letter to the sisters of our house, telling them that I had a mind to go; but if they ceased to persecute me, and would leave Father La Combe in peace, I would return as soon as the mistress of my daughter should be recovered. Instead of this, they persecuted me more violently, wrote to Paris against me, stopped all my letters, and sent libels against me around the country.

The day after my arrival at Tonon, Father La Combe set off for the valley of Aoust, to preach there in Lent. He had come to take leave of me, and told me that he should go from thence to Rome, and perhaps not return, as his superiors might detain him there; that he was sorry to leave me in a strange country, without succor, and persecuted of everyone. I replied, "My father, that gives me no pain; I use the creatures for God, and by His order. Through His mercy, I do very well without them, when He withdraws them. I am very well contented never to see you, and to abide under persecution, if such be His will." He said he would go well satisfied to see me in such a disposition, and then departed.

As soon as I got to the Ursulines, a very aged and

pious priest, who for twenty years past had not come out of his solitude, came to find me. He told me that he had a vision relative to me; that he had seen a woman in a boat on the lake; and that the Bishop of Geneva, with some of his priests, exerted all their efforts to sink the boat she was in, and to drown her; that he continued in this vision above two hours, with pain of mind; that it seemed sometimes as if this woman were quite drowned, as for some time she quite disappeared; but afterward she appeared again, and ready to escape the danger, while the Bishop never ceased to pursue her. This woman was always equally calm; but he never saw her entirely free from him. From whence I conclude, added he, that the Bishop will persecute you without intermission.

I had an intimate friend, wife of that governor of whom I have made some mention. As she saw I had quitted everything for God, she had a warm desire to follow me. With diligence did she dispose of all her effects and settle her affairs in order to come to me; but when she heard of the persecution, she was discouraged from coming to a place, from whence she thought I should be obliged to retire. Soon after she died.

CHAPTER 7

AFTER FATHER LA COMBE WAS GONE, the persecution raised against me became more violent. But the Bishop of Geneva still showed me some civilities, as well to try whether he could prevail on me to do what he desired, as to sound out how matters passed in France, and to prejudice the minds of the people there against me, preventing me from receiving the letters sent me. The ecclesiastic and his family had twenty-two intercepted letters, opened, on their table. There was one wherein was sent me a power of attorney to sign, of immediate consequence. They were obliged to put it under another cover, and send it to me. The bishop wrote to Father La Mothe, and had no difficulty to draw him into his party. He was displeased with me on two accounts. First, that I had not settled on him a pension, as he expected, and as he told me very roughly several times. Second, I did not take his advice in everything. He at once declared against me. The bishop made him his confidant. It was he who uttered and spread abroad the news about me. They imagined, as was supposed, that I would annul the donation I had made, if I returned; that, having the support of friends in France, I would find the means of breaking it; but in that they were much mistaken. I had no thought of loving anything but the poverty of Jesus Christ. For some time yet, the Father acted with caution toward me. He wrote me some letters, which he addressed to the Bishop of Geneva, and they agreed so together, that he was the only person from whom I received any letters, to which I returned very moving answers. He, instead of being touched with them, became only more irritated against me.

The bishop continued to treat me with a show of respect; yet at the same time he wrote to many persons in Paris, as did also the sisters of the house, to all those persons of piety who had written letters to me, to bias them as much as possible against me. To avoid the blame which ought naturally to fall upon them for having so unworthily treated a person who have given up everything to devote herself to the service of that diocese. After I had done this, and was not in a condition to return to France, they treated me extremely ill in every respect. There was scarcely any kind of false or fabulous story, likely to gain any credit, which they did not invent to cry me down. Beside my having no way to make the truth known in France, our Lord inspired me with a willingness to suffer everything, without justifying myself; so that in my case nothing was heard but condemnation, without any vindication.

I was in this convent, and had seen Father La Combe no further than I have mentioned; yet they did not cease to publish, both of him and me, the most scandalous stories; as utterly false as anything could be, for he was then a hundred and fifty leagues from me.

For some time I was ignorant of this. As I knew that all my letters were kept from me, I ceased to wonder at receiving none. I lived in this house with my little daughter in a sweet repose, which was a very great favor of Providence. My daughter had forgotten her French, and among the little girls from the mountains had contracted a wild look and disagreeable manners. Her wit, sense and judgment, were indeed surprising, and her disposition exceedingly good. There were only some little fits of peevishness, which they had caused to arise in her, through certain contrarieties out of season, caresses ill applied, and for want of knowing the proper manner of education. But the Lord provided in regard to her. During this time my mind was preserved calm and resigned to God. Afterward that good sister almost continually interrupted me; I answered everything she desired of me, both out of condescension, and from a principle which I had to obey like a child.

When I was in my apartment, without any other director than our Lord by His Spirit, as soon as one of my little children came to knock at my door, he required me to admit the interruption. He showed me that it is not the actions in themselves which please Him, but the constant ready obedience to every discovery of His will, even in the minutest things, with such a suppleness, as not to stick to anything, but still to turn with Him at every call. My

257

soul was then, I thought, like a leaf, or a feather, which the wind moves what way soever it pleases and the Lord never suffers a soul so dependent upon, and dedicated to Him, to be deceived.

Most men appear to me very unjust, when they readily resign themselves to another man, and look upon that as prudence. They confide in men who are nothing, and boldly say, "Such a person cannot be deceived." But if one speaks of a soul wholly re-signed to God, which follows him faithfully, they cry aloud, "That person is deceived with his resigna-tion." Oh, divine Love! Dost thou want either strength, fidelity, love, or wisdom, to conduct those who trust in thee and who are thy dearest children? I have seen men bold enough to say, "Follow me, and you shall not be misled." How sadly are those men misled themselves by their presumption! How much sooner should I go to him who would be afraid of misleading me; who trusting neither to his learn-ing nor experience, would rely upon God only!

Our Lord showed me, in a dream, two ways by which souls steer their course, under the figure of two drops of water. The one appeared to me of an unparalleled beauty, brightness and purity; the other to have also a brightness, yet full of little streaks; both good to quench thirst; the former al-together pleasant, but the latter not so perfectly agreeable. By the former is represented the way of pure and naked faith, which pleases the Spouse much, it is so pure, so clear from all self-love. The way of emotions or gifts is not so; yet it is that in which many enlightened souls walk, and into which they had drawn Father La Combe. But God showed me, that He had given him to me, to draw him into one more pure and perfect. I spoke before the sisters, he being present, of the way of faith, how much more glorious it was to God, and advantageous for the soul, than all those gifts, emotions and assurances, which ever cause us to live to self. This discouraged them at first and him also. I saw they were pained, as they have confessed to me since. I said no more of it at that time. But, as he is a person of great humility, he bid me unfold what I had wanted to say to him. I told him a part of my dream of the two drops of water; yet, he did not then enter into what I said, the time for it being not yet come. When he came to Gex, it was to make the retreats. I told him the circumstances of a certain time past; he recollected that it was the time of so extraordinary a touch with which the Lord favored him, that he was quite overwhelmed with contrition. This gave him such an interior renovation, that, having retired to pray, in a very ardent frame of mind, he was filled with joy, and seized with a powerful emotion, which made him enter into what I had told him of the way of faith. I give these things, as they happen to come to my remembrance, without carrying them on in order.

After Easter, in 1682, the bishop came to Tonon. I had occasion to speak to him, which when I had done, our Lord so pointed my words that he appeared thoroughly convinced. But the persons who had influenced him before returned. He then pressed me very much to return to Gex and to take the place of Prioress. I gave him the reasons against it. I then appealed to him, as a bishop, desiring him to take care to regard nothing but God in what he should say to me. He was struck into a kind of confusion; and then said to me, "Since you speak to me in such a manner, I cannot advise you to it. It is not for us to go contrary to our vocations; but do good, I pray you, to this house." I promised him to do it. Having received my pension, I sent them a hundred pistoles, with a design of doing the same as long as I should be in the diocese. The bishop said to me, "I love Father La Combe. He is a true servant of God and he has told me many things to which I was forced to assent for I felt them in myself. But," added he, "when I say so, they tell me I am mistaken, and that before the end of six months he will run mad." He told me, "he approved of the nuns, which had been under the care and instruction of Father La Combe, finding them to come up fully to what he had heard of them." From thence I took occasion to tell him "that in everything he ought to refer himself to his own breast, or to the instructions there immediately received, and not to others." He agreed to what I said, and acknowledged it to be right; yet no sooner was he returned, than, so great was his weakness that he re-entered into his former dispositions. He sent the same ecclesiastic to tell me that I must engage myself at Gex; that it was his sentiment. I answered, that I was determined to follow the counsel he had given me, when he had spoken to me as from God, since now they made him speak only as man.

CHAPTER 8

My soul was in a state of entire resignation and very great content, in the midst of such violent tempests. Those persons came to tell me a hundred extravagant stories against Father La Combe. The more they said to me to his disadvantage, the more esteem I felt for him. I answered them, "Perhaps I may never see him again, but I shall ever be glad to do him justice. It is not he who hinders me from engaging at Gex. It is only because I know it to be none of my vocation." They asked me, "Who could know that better than the bishop?" They further told me, "I was under a deception, and my state was good for nothing." This gave me no uneasiness, having referred to God the care of requiring, and of exacting what He requires, and in whatever manner He demands it.

A soul in this state seeks nothing for itself, but all for God. Some may say, "What, then, does this soul?" It leaves itself to be conducted by God's providences and creatures. Outwardly, its life seems quite common; inwardly, it is wholly resigned to the divine will. The more everything appears adverse, and even desperate, the more calm it is, in spite of the annoyance and pain of the senses and of the creatures, which, for some time after the new life, raise some clouds and obstructions, as I have already signified. But when the soul is entirely passed into its original Being, all these things no more cause any separation or partition. It finds no more of that impurity which came from self-seeking, from a human manner of acting, from an unguarded word, from any warm emotion or eagerness, which caused such a mist, as it then could neither prevent nor remedy, having so often experienced its own efforts, to be useless, and even hurtful, as they did nothing else but still more and more defile it. There is in such case no other way or means of remedy, but in waiting till the Sun of Righteousness dissipate those fogs. The whole work of purification comes from God only. Afterward this conduct becomes natural; then the soul can say with the royal prophet, "Though an host should encamp against me, my heart shall not fear. Though war should rise up against me, in him will I confide." For then, though assaulted on every side, it continues fixed as a rock. Having no will but for what God sees meet to order, be it what it may, high or low, great or small, sweet or bitter, honor, wealth, life, or any other object, what can shake its peace? It is true, our nature is so crafty that it worms itself through everything; a selfish sight is like the basilisk's, it destroys.

Trials are suited to the state of the soul, whether conducted by lights, gifts, or ecstasies, or by the entire destruction of self in the way of naked faith. Both these states are found in the apostle Paul. He tells us,

"And lest I should be exalted above measure, through the abundance of revelations, there was given to me a thorn in the flesh, the messenger of Satan to buffet me." He prayed thrice, and it was said to him, "My grace is sufficient for thee; for my strength is made perfect in weakness." He proved also another state when he thus expressed himself, "Oh, wretched man that I am! who shall deliver me from the body of this death?" To which he replies, "I thank God, it is done through Jesus Christ our Lord." It is He who conquers death in us through His own life. Then there is no longer a sting in death, or thorn in the flesh, capable of paining or hurting any more.

At first indeed, and for a pretty long time after, the soul sees that nature wants to take some part with it in its trials; then its fidelity consists in withholding it, without allowing it the least indulgence, till it leaves everything to go on with God in purity as it comes from Him. Till the soul be in this state, it always sullies, by its own mixture, the operation of God; like those rivulets which contract the corruption of the places they pass through, but, flowing in a pure place, they then remain in the purity of their source. Unless God through experience, makes known His guidance to the soul, it can never comprehend it.

Oh, if souls had courage enough to resign themselves to the work of purification, without having any weak and foolish pity on themselves, what a noble, rapid and happy progress would they make! But few are willing to lose the earth. If they advance some steps, as soon as the sea is ruffled they are dejected; they cast anchor, and often desist from the prosecution of the voyage. Such disorders doth selfish interest and self-love occasion. It is of consequence not to look too much at one's own state, not to lose courage, not to afford any nourishment to self-love, which is so deep-rooted, that its empire is not easily demolished. Often the idea which a man falsely conceives of the greatness of his advancement in divine experience, makes him want to be seen and known of men, and to wish to see the very same perfection in others. He conceives too low ideas of others, and too high of his own state. Then it becomes a pain to him to converse with people too human; whereas, a soul truly mortified and resigned would rather converse with the worst, by the order of Providence, than with the best, of its own choice; wanting only to see or to speak to any as Providence directs, knowing well that all beside, far from helping, only hurt it, or at least prove very unfruitful to it.

What, then, renders this soul so perfectly content? It neither knows, nor wants to know, anything but what God calls it to. Herein it enjoys divine content, after a manner vast, immense, and independent of exterior events; more satisfied in its humiliation, and in the opposition of all creatures, by the order of Providence, than on the throne of its own choice.

It is here that the apostolic life begins. But do all reach that state? Very few, indeed, as far as I can comprehend. There is a way of lights, gifts and graces, a holy life in which the creature appears all admirable. As this life is more apparent, so it is more esteemed of such, at least, as have not the purest light. The souls which walk in the other path are often very little known, for a length of time, as it was with Jesus Christ Himself, till the last years of His life. Oh, if I could express what I conceive of this state! But I can only stammer about it.

CHAPTER 9

Being, as I have said, with the Ursulines at Tonon, after having spoken to the Bishop of Geneva, and seeing how he changed, just as others turned him, I wrote to him and to Father La Mothe; but all my efforts were useless. The more I endeavored to accommodate matters, the more the ecclesiastic tried to confound them, hence I ceased to meddle.

One day I was told that the ecclesiastic had won over the good girl whom I dearly loved· So strong a desire I had for her perfection that it had cost me much. I should not have felt the death of a child so much as her loss; at the same time I was told how to hinder it, but that human way of acting was repugnant to my inward sense; these words arose in my heart, "Except the Lord build the house."

And indeed He provided herein Himself, hindering her from yielding to this deceitful man, after a manner to be admired, and very thwarting to the designs of him and his associates. As long as I was with her she still seemed wavering and fearful; but oh, the infinite goodness of God, to preserve without our aid what without His we should inevitably lose! I was no sooner separated from her, but she became immovable.

As for me, there scarcely passed a day but they treated me with new insults; their assaults came on me at unawares. The New Catholics, by the instigation of the Bishop of Geneva, the ecclesiastic, and the sisters at Gex, stirred up all the persons of piety against me. I had but little uneasiness on my own account. If I could have had it at all, it would have been on account of Father La Combe, whom they vilely aspersed, though he was absent. They even made use of his absence, to overset all the good he had done in the country, by his missions and pious labors, which were inconceivably great. At first I was too ready to vindicate him, thinking it justice to do it. I did not do it at all for myself; and our Lord showed me that I must cease doing it for him, in order to leave him to be more thorougly annihilated; because from thence he would draw a greater glory, than ever he had done from his own reputation.

Every day then invented some new slander. No kind of stratagem, or malicious device in their power, did they omit. They came to surprise and ensnare me in my words; but God guarded me so well, that therein they only discovered their own malevolence. I had no consolation from the creatures. She who had the care of my daughter behaved roughly to me. Such are the persons who regulate themselves only by their gifts and emotions. When they do not see things succeed, and as they regard them only by their success, and are not willing to have the affront of their pretensions being though uncertain, and liable to mistake, they seek without for supports. As for me who pretended to nothing, I thought all succeeded well, inasmuch as all tended to self-annihilation. On another side, the maid I had brought, and who stayed with me, grew tired out. Wanting to go back again, she stunned me with her complaints, thwarting and chiding me from morning till night, upbraiding me with what I had left, and coming to a place where I was good for nothing. I was obliged to bear all her ill-humor and the clamor of her tongue.

My own brother, Father La Mothe, wrote to me that I was rebel to my bishop, staying in his diocese only to give him pain. Indeed, I saw there was nothing for me to do here, so long as the bishop should be against me. I did what I could to gain his goodwill, but this was impossible on any other terms than the engagement he demanded, and that I knew to be my duty not to do. This, joined to the poor education of my daughter, affected my heart. When any glimmering of hope appeared, it soon vanished; and I gained strength from a sort of despair.

During this time Father La Combe was at Rome, where he was received with so much honor, and his doctrine was so highly esteemed, that the Sacred Congregation was pleased to take his sentiments on some points of doctrine, which were found to be so just, and so clear, that it followed them. Meanwhile the sister would take no care of my daughter; when I took care of her she was displeased. I was not able, by any means, to prevail on her to promise me that she would try to prevent her contracting bad habits.

However, I hoped that Father La Combe, at his return, would bring everything into order, and renew my consolation. Yet I left it all to God.

About July, 1682, my sister, who was an Ursuline, got permission to come. She brought a maid with her, which was very seasonable. My sister assisted in the education of my daugther, but she had frequent jarring with her tutoress—I labored but in vain for peace. By some instances which I met with in this place, I saw clearly that it is not great gifts which sanctify, unless they be accompanied with a profound humility; that death to everything is infinitely more beneficial; for there was one who thought herself at the summit of perfection, but has discovered since, by the trials which have befallen her, that she was yet very far from it. O, my God, how true it is that we may have of Thy gifts, and yet be very imperfect, and full of ourselves!

How very straight is the gate which leads to a life in God! How little one must be to pass through it, it being nothing else but death to self! But when we have passed through it, what enlargement do we find! David said, (Psalm 18:19) "He brought me forth into a large place." And it was through humiliation and abasement that he was brought thither.

Father La Combe, on his arrival, came to see me. The first thing he said was about his own weakness, and that I must return. He added, "that all seemed dark, and there was no likelihood that God would make use of me in this country." The Bishop of Geneva wrote to Father La Mothe to get me to return; he wrote to me accordingly to do it. The first Lent which I passed with the Ursulines, I had a very great pain in my eyes; for that same imposthume which I formerly had between the eye and the nose, returned upon me three times. The bad air, and the noisome room which I was in, contributed hereto. My head was frightfully swelled, but great was my inward joy. It was strange to see so many good creatures, who did not know me, love and pity me; all the rest enraged against me, and most of them on reports entirely false, neither knowing me, nor why they so hated me. To swell the stream of affliction yet more, my daughter fell sick and was likely to die; there was but little hope of her recovery, when her mistress also fell ill. My soul, leaving all to God, continued to rest in a quiet and peaceable habitation. Oh, Principal and sole object of my love! Were there never any other reward of what little services we do, or of the marks of homage we render Thee, than this fixed state above the vicissitudes in the world, is it not enough? The senses indeed are sometimes ready to start aside, and to run off like truants; but every trouble flies before the soul which is entirely subjected to God. By speaking of a fixed state, I do not mean one which can never decline or fall, that being only in Heaven. I call it fixed and permanent, compared with the states which have preceded it, which were full of vicissitudes and variations. I do not exclude a state of suffering in the senses, or arising from superficial impurity, which remains to be done away, and which one may compare to refined but tarnished gold. It has no more need to be purified in the fire, having undergone that operation; but needs only to be burnished. So it seemed to be with me at that time.

CHAPTER 10

My DAUGHTER HAD THE SMALLPOX. They sent for a physician from Geneva, who gave her over. Father La Combe then came in to visit, and pray with her. He gave her his blessing; soon after she wonderfully recovered. The persecution of the New Catholics against me continued and increased; yet, for all that, I did not fail to do them all the good in my power. My daughter's mistress came often to converse with me, but much imperfection appeared in her discourses, though they were on religious subjects. Father La Combe regulated many things in regard to my daughter, which vexed her mistress so much, that her former friendship was turned into coldness. She had grace, but suffered nature too frequently to prevail. I told her my thought on her faults, as I was inwardly directed to do; but though, at that time, God enlightened her to see the truth of what I said, and she has been more enlightened since, yet the return of her coldness toward me ensued upon it. The debates between her and my sister grew more tart and violent. My daughter, who was only six years and a half old, by her little dexterities found a way to please them both, choosing to do her exercises twice over, first with the one, then with the other, which continued not long; for as her mistress generally neglected her, doing things at one time, and leaving them at another, she was reduced to learn only what my sister and I taught her. Indeed the changeableness of my sister was so excessive, that, without great grace, it was hard to suit one's self to it; yet she appeared to me to surmount herself in many things. Formerly, I could scarce bear her manners; but I have since loved everything in God, who has given me a very great facility to bear the faults of my neighbor, with a readiness to please and oblige everyone and such a compassion for their calamities or distresses as I never had before.

I have no difficulty to use condescension with imperfect persons; I should be secretly smitten if I failed therein; but with souls of grace I cannot bear this human manner of acting, nor suffer long and frequent conversations. It is a thing of which few are capable. Some religious persons say that these conversations are of great service. I believe it may be true for some, but not for all; for there is a period wherein it hurts, especially when it is of our own choice; the human inclination corrupting everything. The same things which would be profitable, when God, by His Spirit, draws to them, become quite otherwise, when we of ourselves enter into them. This appears to me so clear, that I prefer being a whole day with the worst of persons, in obedience to God, before being one hour with the best, only from my own choice and inclination.

The order of divine providence makes the whole rule and conduct of a soul entirely devoted to God. While it faithfully gives itself up thereto, it will do all things right and well, and will have everything it wants, without its own care; because God in whom it confides, makes it every moment do what He requires, and furnishes the occasions proper for it. God loves what is of His own order, and of His own will, not according to the idea of the merely rational or even enlightened man; for He hides these persons from the eyes of others, in order to preserve them in that hidden purity for Himself.

But how comes it that such souls commit any faults; because they are not faithful, in giving themselves up to the present moment. Often too eagerly bent on something, or wanting to be over-faithful, they slide into many faults, which they can neither foresee nor avoid. Does God then leave souls which confide in Him? Surely not. Sooner would He work a miracle to hinder them from falling, if they were resigned enough to Him. They may be resigned as to the general will, and yet fail as to the present moment. Being out of the order of God, they fall. They renew such falls as long as they continue out of that divine order. When they return into it, all goes right and well.

Most assuredly if such souls were faithful enough, not to let any of the moments of the order of God slip over, they would not thus fall. This appears to n.e as clear as the day. As a dislocated bone out of the place in which the economy of divine wisdom

274

had fixed it, gives continual pain till restored to its proper order, so the many troubles in life come from the soul not abiding in its place, and not being content with the order of God, and what is afforded therein from moment to moment. If men rightly knew this secret, they would all be fully content and satisfied. But alas! instead of being content with what they have, they are ever wishing for what they have not; while the soul, which enters into divine light begins to be in paradise. What is it that makes paradise? It is the order of God, which renders all the saints infinitely content, though very unequal in glory! From whence comes it that so many poor indigent persons are so contented, and that princes and potentates, who abound to profusion, are so wretched and unhappy? It is because the man who is not content with what he has, will never be without craving desires; and he who is the prey of an unsatisfied desire, can never be content.

All souls have more or less of strong and ardent desires, except those whose will is lost in the will of God. Some have good desires, so as to suffer martyrdom for God; others thirst for the salvation of their neighbor, and some pant to see God in glory. All this is excellent. But he who rests in the divine will, although he may be exempt from all these desires, is infinitely more content, and glorifies God more. It is written concerning Jesus Christ, when he drove out of the temple those who profaned it. "The zeal of thine house hath eaten me up." John 2:17. It was in that moment of the order of God, that these words had their effect. How many times had Jesus Christ been in the temple without such a conduct? Does not He occasionally say of Himself, that His hour was not yet come?

CHAPTER 11

AFTER FATHER LA COMBE returned from Rome, well approved, and furnished with testimonials of life ad doctrine, he performed his functions of preaching and confessing as usual. I gave him an account of what I had done and suffered in his absence, and what care God had taken of all my concerns. I saw his providence incessantly extended to the very smallest things. After having been several months without any news of my papers, when some pressed me to write, and blamed my neglect, an invisible hand held me back; my peace and confidence were great. I received a letter from the ecclesiastic at home, which informed me that he had orders to come and see me, and bring my papers. I had sent to Paris for a pretty considerable bundle of things for my daughter. I heard they were lost on the lake, and could learn no further tidings about them.

I gave myself no trouble; I always thought they would be found. The man who had taken charge of them made a search after them a whole month, in all the environs, without hearing any news. At the end of three months they were brought to me, having been found in the house of a poor man, who had not opened them, nor knew who brought them there. Once I had sent for all the money which was to serve me a whole year; the person who had been to receive cash for the bill of exchange, having put that money in two bags on horseback, forgot that it was there, and gave the horse to a little boy to lead. The money fell from the horse in the middle of the market at Geneva. That instant I arrived, coming on the other side, and having alighted from my litter, the first thing I found was my money. What was surprising, a great throng was in this place and not one had perceived it. Many such things have attended me. These accounts may suffice to show the continual protection of God

The Bishop of Geneva continued to persecute me. When he wrote, it was with politeness and thanks for my charities at Gex; while at the same time he said to others that I "gave nothing to that house." He wrote against me to the Ursulines with whom I lived, charging them to hinder me from having any conferences with Father La Combe. The superior of the house, a man of merit, and the prioress, as well as the community, were so irritated at this, that they could not forbear testifying it to him. He then excused himself with a pretended respect, saying, he did not mean it that way. They wrote to him that "I did not see the Father but at the confessional, and not in conference; that they were so much edified by me, as to think themselves happy in having me, and to esteem it a greater favor from God." What

278

they said out of pure charity was not pleasing to the Bishop, who, seeing they loved me in this house, said, that I won over everybody to myself and that he wished I were out of the diocese. Though I knew all this, and these good sisters were troubled at it, I could have no trouble by reason of the calm establishment which I was in. The will of God rendering everything equal to me. The creatures, however unreasonable or passionate they appear, not being regarded in themselves but in God; an habitual faith causes everything to be seen in God without distinction. Thus, when I see poor souls so ruffled for discourses in the air, so uneasy for explanations, I pity them. They have reasons, I know, which self-love causes to appear very just.

To relieve myself a little from the fatigue of continual conversation, I desired Father La Combe to allow me a retreat. It was then that I let myself be consumed by love all the day long. Also I perceived the quality of a spiritual mother; for the Lord gave me what I cannot express for the perfection of souls. This I could not hide from Father La Combe. It seemed to me as if I entered into the inmost recesses of his heart. Our Lord showed me he was His servant, chosen among a thousand, singularly to honor Him; but that He would lead him through total death, and the entire destruction of the old man. He would have me contribute thereto and be instrumental to cause him to walk in the way in which He had led me first; in order that I might be in a condition to direct others, to tell them the way through which I have passed. The Lord would have us to be conformed, and to become both one in Him; though my soul was more advanced now, yet he should one day pass beyond it, with a bold and rapid flight. God knows with what joy I would see my spiritual children surpass their mother.

In this retreat I felt a strong propensity to write, but resisted it till I fell sick. I had nothing to write about, not one idea to begin with. It was a divine impulse, with such a fulness of grace as was hard to contain. I opened this disposition of mine to Father La Combe. He answered that he had a strong impulse to command me to write, but had not dared to do it yet, on account of my weakness. I told him, that "weakness was the effect of my resistance," and I believed it would, through my writing, go off again. He asked, "But what is it you will write?"

I replied, "I know nothing of it, nor desire to know, leaving it entirely to God to direct me."

He ordered me to do so. At my taking the pen I knew not the first word I should write; when I began, suitable matter flowed copiously, nay, impetuously. As I was writing I was relieved and grew better. I wrote an entire treatise on the interior path of faith, under the comparison of torrents, or of streams and rivers.

As the way, wherein God now conducted Father La Combe, was very different from that in which he had formerly walked (all light, knowledge, ardor, assurance, sentiment) now the poor, low, despised path of faith, and of nakedness; he found it very hard to submit thereto. Who could express what it has cost my heart before he was formed according to the will of God?

Meanwhile, the possession which the Lord had of my soul became every day stronger, insomuch that I passed whole days without being able to pronounce one word. The Lord was pleased to make me pass wholly into Him by an entire internal transformation. He became more and more the absolute master of my heart, to such a degree as not to leave me a movement of my own. This state did not hinder me from condescending to my sister, and the others in the house. Nevertheless, the useless things with which they were taken up could not interest me. That was what induced me to ask leave to make a retreat, to let myself be possessed of Him who holds me so closely to Himself after an ineffable manner.

CHAPTER 12

I HAD AT THAT TIME so ardent a desire for the perfection of Father La Combe, and to see him thoroughly die to himself, that I could have wished him all the crosses and afflictions imaginable, that might conduce to this great and blessed end. Whenever he was unfaithful, or looked at things in any other light than the true one—to tend to this death of self—I felt myself on the rack, which, as I had till then been so indifferent, very much surprised me. To the Lord I made my complaint; He graciously encouraged me, both on this subject and on that entire dependence on Himself which He gave me, which was such that I was like a new born infant.

My sister had brought me a maid, whom God was willing to give me to fashion according to His will, not without some crucifixion to myself. I believe it never is to fall out, that our Lord will give me any persons without giving them wherewith to make me suffer, whether it be for the purpose of drawing them into a spiritual life, or never to leave me without the cross. She was one on whom the Lord had conferred very singular graces. She was in high reputation in the country, where she passed for a saint. Our Lord brought her to me, to let her see the difference between the sanctity conceived and comprised in those gifts, with which she was endowed, and that which is obtained by our entire destruction, even by the loss of those very gifts, and of all that raised us in the esteem of men. Our Lord had given her the same dependence on me, as I had in regard to Father La Combe.

This girl fell grievously sick. I was willing to give her all the assistance in my power, but I found I had nothing to do but to command her bodily sickness, or the disposition of her mind; all that I said was done. It was then that I learned what it was to command by the Word, and to obey by the Word. It was Jesus Christ in me equally commanding and obeying.

She, however, continued sick for sometime. One day, after dinner, I was moved to say to her, "Rise and be no longer sick." She arose and was cured. The nuns were very much astonished. They knew nothing of what had passed, but saw her walking, who in the morning had appeared to be in the last extremity. They attributed her disorder to a vivid imagination.

I have at sundry times experienced, and felt in myself, how much God respects the freedom of man, even demands his free concurrence; for when I said, "Be healed," or, "Be free from your troubles," if such persons acquiesced, the Word was efficacious, and they were healed. If they doubted, or resisted, though under fair pretexts, saying, "I shall be healed when it pleases God, I will not be healed till He wills it;"

or, in the way of despair, "I cannot be healed; I will not quit my condition," then the Word had no effect. I felt in myself that the divine virtue retired in me. I experienced what our Lord said, when the woman afflicted with the issue of blood touched him. He instantly asked, "Who touched me?" The apostles said, "Master, the multitude throng thee, and press thee; and sayest thou, Who touched me?" He replied, "It is because virtue hath gone out of me" (Luke 8:45,46). Jesus Christ had caused that healing virtue to flow, through me, by means of His Word. When that virtue met not with a correspondence in the subject, I felt it suspended in its source. That gave me some pain. I should be, as it were, displeased with those persons; but when there was no resistance, but a full acquiescence, this divine virtue had its full effect. Healing virtue has so much power over things inanimate, yet the least thing in man either restrains it, or stops it entirely.

There was a good nun much afflicted and under a violent temptation. She went to declare her case to a sister whom she thought very spiritual, and in a condition capable of assisting her. But far from finding succor, she was very much discouraged and cast down. The other despised and repulsed her, and treating her with contempt and rigor, she said, "Don't come near me, since you are that way." This poor girl, in a frightful distress, came to me thinking herself undone on account of what the sister had said to her. I consoled her and our Lord relieved her immediately. But I could not forbear telling her that assuredly the other would be punished, and would

284

fall into a state worse than hers. The sister who had used her in such a manner came also to me, highly pleased with herself in what she had done, saying, she abhorred such tempted creatures. As for herself, she was proof against such sorts of temptations, and that she never had a bad thought." I said to her, "My sister, from the friendship I have for you I wish you the pain of her who spoke to you, and even one still more violent."

She answered haughtily, "If you were to ask it from God for me, and I ask of Him the contrary, I believe I shall be heard at least as soon as you."

I answered with great firmness, "If it be only my own interests which I ask, I shall not be heard; but if it be those of God only, and yours too, I shall be heard sooner than you are aware." That very night she fell into so violent a temptation that one equal to it has seldom been known. It was then she had ample occasion to acknowledge her own weakness, and what she would be without grace. She conceived at first a violent hatred for me, saying that I was the cause of her pain. But it served her, as the clay did to enlighten him who had been born blind. She soon saw very well what had brought on her so terrible a state.

I fell sick even to extremity. This sickness proved a means to cover the great mysteries which it pleased God to operate in me. Scarce ever was a disorder more extraordinary, or of longer continuance in its excess. Several times I saw in dreams Father La Mothe raising persecutions against me. Our Lord let me know that this would be and that Father La

Combe would forsake me in the time of persecution. I wrote to him, and it disquieted him greatly. He thought his heart was united to the will of God and too desirous of serving me, to admit such desertion; yet it has since been found quite true. He was now to preach during Lent, and was so much followed, that people came five leagues, to pass several days for the benefit of his ministry. I heard he was so sick that he was thought to die. I prayed to the Lord to restore his health, and enable him to preach to the people, who were longing to hear him. My prayer was heard, and he soon recovered, and resumed his pious labors.

During this extraordinary sickness, which continued more than six months, the Lord gradually taught me that there was another manner of conversing among souls wholly His, than by speech. Thou madest me conceive, O divine Word, that as Thou art ever speaking and operating in a soul, though therein thou appearest in profound silence; so there was also a way of communication in thy creatures, in an ineffable silence. I heard then a language which before had been unknown to me. I gradually perceived, when Father La Combe entered, that I could speak no more. There was formed in my soul the same kind of silence toward him, as was formed in it in regard to God. I comprehended that God was willing to show me that men might in this life learn the language of angels. I was gradually reduced to speak to him only in silence. It was then that we understood each other in God, after a manner unutterable and divine. Our hearts spoke to each other, communicating a grace which no words can express. It was like a new country, both for him and for me; but so divine, that I cannot describe it. At first this was done in a manner so perceptible, that is to say, God penetrated us with Himself in a manner so pure and so sweet, that we passed hours in this profound silence, always communicative, without being able to utter one word. It was in this that we learned, by our own experience, the operations of the heavenly Word to reduce souls into unity with itself, and what purity one may arrive at in this life. It was given me to communicate this way to other good souls, but with this difference: I did nothing but communicate to them the grace with which they were filled, while near me, in this sacred silence, which infused into them an extraordinary strength and grace; but I received nothing from them; whereas with Father La Combe there was a flow and return of communication of grace, which he received from me, and I from him, in the greatest purity.

In this long malady the love of God, and of Him alone, made up my whole occupation, I seemed so entirely lost to Him, as to have no sight of myself at all. It seemed as if my heart never came out of that divine ocean, having been drawn into it through deep humiliations. Oh, happy loss, which is the consummation of bliss, though operated through crosses and through deaths!

Jesus was then living in me and I lived no more. These words were imprinted in me, as a real state into which I must enter, (Matt. 8:20) "The foxes have holes, and the birds of the air have nests, but the Son of man hath not where to lay his head." This I have since experienced in all its extent, having no sure abode, no refuge among friends, who were ashamed of me, and openly renounced me, when universally decried; nor among my relations, most of whom declared themselves my adversaries, and were my greatest persecutors; while others looked on me with contempt and indignation. I might as David say, "For thy sake I have borne reproach; shame hath covered my face; I am become a stranger to my brethren, and an alien unto my mother's children; a reproach to men, and despised of the people."

He showed me all the world in a rage against me, without anyone daring to appear for me and assured me in the ineffable silence of His eternal Word, that He would give me vast numbers of children, which I should bring forth by the cross. I left it to Him to do with me whatever He pleased, esteeming my whole and sole interest to be placed entirely in His divine will. He gave me to see how the Devil was going to stir up an outrageous persecution against prayer, yet it should prove the source of the same prayer, or rather the means which God would make use of to establish it. He gave me to see farther how He would guide me into the wilderness, where He would cause me to be nourished for a time. The wings, which were to bear me thither, were the resignation of my whole self to His holy will. I think I am at present in that wilderness, separated from the whole world in my imprisonment. I see already accomplished in part what was then shown me. Can I ever express the mercies which my God has bestowed on me? No; they must ever remain in Himself, being of a nature not to be described, by reason of their purity and immensity.

I was often to all apearance at the point of death. I fell into convulsions from violent pains which lasted a long time with violence. Father La Combe administered the sacrament to me, the Prioress of the Ursulines having desired him to do it. I was well satisfied to die, as was he also in the expectation of my departure. For, being united in God after a manner so pure, and so spiritual, death could not separate us. On the contrary it would have more closely united us. Father La Combe, who was on his knees at my bedside, remarking the change of my countenance, and how my eyes faded, seemed ready to give me up, when God inspired him to lift up his hands, and with a strong voice, which was heard by all who were in my room, at that time almost full, to command death to relinquish its hold. Instantly it seemed to be stopped. Thus God was pleased wonderfully to raise me up again; yet for a long time I continued extremely weak, during all of which our Lord gave me new testimonies of His love. How many times was He pleased to make use of His servant to restore me to life, when I was almost on the very point of expiring! As they saw that my sickness and pain did not entirely end, they judged that the air of the lake on which the convent was situated, was very prejudicial to my constitution. They concluded that it would be necessary for me to remove.

During my indisposition, our Lord put it into the heart of Father La Combe to establish a hospital in this place for the poor people seized with maladies, to institute also a committee or congregation of ladies to furnish such as could not leave their families to go to the hospital with the means of subsistence during their illness, after the manner of France, there having been yet no institution of this kind in that country. Willingly did I enter into it; and without any other fund than Providence and some useless rooms which a gentleman of the town gave us, we began it. We dedicated it to the holy Child Jesus, and He was pleased to give the first beds to it from my pension. He gave such a blessing that several other persons joined us in this charity. In a short time there were nearly twelve beds in it and three persons of great piety gave themselves to this hospital to serve it, who, without any salary, consecrated themselves to the service of the poor patients. I supplied them with ointments and medicines, which were freely given to such of the poor people of the town as had need of them. These good ladies were so hearty in the cause, that, through their charity, and the care of the young women, this hospital was very well maintained and served. These ladies joined together also in providing for the sick who could not go to the hospital. I gave them some little regulations such as I had observed when in France, which they continued to keep up with tenderness and love.

All these little things, which cost but little, and which owed all their success to the blessing which God gave them, drew upon us new persecutions. The Bishop of Geneva was offended with me more than ever, especially in seeing that these small matters rendered me beloved. He said that I won over everybody. He openly declared, "he could not bear me in his diocese," though I had done nothing but good, or rather God by me. He extended the persecution to those good religious women who had been my assistants. The prioress in particular had her own share to bear, though it did not last long. As I was obliged, on account of the air, to remove, after having been there about two years and a half, they were then more in peace and quietness. On another side, my sister was very weary of this house; and as the season for the waters approached, they took occasion from thence to send her away with the maid which I brought with me, who had molested me exceedingly in my late illness. I only kept her whom Providence had sent me by means of my sister. I have ever thought that God had ordered my sister's journey only to bring her to me, as one chosen of Him and proper for the state which it was His pleasure to cause me to bear.

While I was yet indisposed, the Ursulines, with the Bishop of Verceil, earnestly requested the Father-general of the Barnabites, to seek among the religious, a man of merit, piety and learning, in whom he might place confidence, and who might serve him for a prebend and a counselor. At first he cast his eyes on Father La Combe; yet before he absolutely engaged him with the said bishop, he wrote to him, to know whether he had any objection thereto. Father La Combe replied that he had no other will but that of obeying him, and that he might command him herein as he should think best in the case. He gave me an account of this, and that we were going to be entirely separated. I was glad to find that our Lord would employ him, under a bishop who knew him, and would be likely to do him justice. Yet it was some time before he went, matters not being all arranged.

CHAPTER 13

I THEN WENT OFF from the Ursulines and they sought for a house for me at a distance from the lake. There was but one to be found empty which had the look of the greatest poverty. It had no chimney but in the kitchen, through which one was obliged to pass. I took my daughter with me and gave up the largest room for her and the maid who was to take care of her. I was lodged in a little hole on straw, to which I went up by ladder. As we had no other furniture but our beds, quite plain and homely, I brought some straw chairs and some Dutch earthen and wooden ware. Never did I enjoy a greater content than in this little hole, which appeared so very conformable to the state of Jesus Christ. I fancied everything better on wood than on plate. I laid in all my provisions, hoping to stay there a long time; but the Devil did not leave me long in such sweet peace. It would be difficult for me to tell the persecutions which were stirred up against me. They threw stones in at my windows which fell at my feet. I had put my little garden in order. They came in the night, tore it all up, broke down the arbor, and overturned everything in it, as if it had been ravaged by soldiers. They came to abuse me at the door all night long, making such a racket as if they were going to break it open. These persons have since told who the person was that put them on such work.

Though from time to time I continued my charities at Gex, I was not the less persecuted for it. They offered one person a warrant to compel Father La Combe to stay at Tonon, thinking he would otherwise be a support to me in the persecution, but we prevented it. I knew not then the designs of God, and that He would soon draw me from that poor solitary place, in which I enjoyed a sweet and solid satisfaction, notwithstanding the abuse. I thought myself happier here than any sovereign on earth. It was for me like a nest and a place of repose and Christ was willing that I should be like Him. The Devil, as I have said, irritated my persecutors. They sent to desire me to go out of the diocese. All the good which the Lord had caused me to do in it was condemned, more than the greatest crimes. Crimes they tolerated, but me they could not endure. All this while I never had any uneasiness or repentance for my having left all; not that I was assured of having done the will of God therein. Such an assurance would have been too much for me. But I could neither see nor regard anything, receiving everything alike from the hand of God, who directed and disposed of these crosses for me either in justice or in mercy.

The Marchioness of Prunai, sister of the chief Secretary of State to his Royal Highness (the Duke of

Savoy) and his prime minister, had sent an express from Turin, in the time of my illness, to invite me to come to reside with her; and to let me know that, "being so persecuted as I was in this diocese, I should find an asylum with her; that during that time things might grow better; that when they should be well disposed she would return with me and join me with a friend of mine from Paris, who was willing also to come to labor there, according to the will of God," I was not at that time in a condition to execute what she desired and expected to continue with the Ursulines till things should change. She then wrote to me about it no more. This lady is one of extraordinary piety, who had quitted the splendor and noise of the Court, for the more silent satisfaction of a retired life, and to give herself up to God. With an eminent share of natural advantages, she has continued a widow twenty-two years; has refused every offer of marriage to consecrate herself to our Lord entirely and without any reserve. When she knew that I had been obliged to leave the Ursulines, yet without knowing anything of the manner in which I had been treated, she procured a letter to oblige Father La Combe to go to pass some weeks at Turin, for her own benefit, and to bring me with him thither, where I should find a refuge. All this she did unknown to us. As she has told us since, a superior force moved her to do it, without knowing the cause. If she had deliberately reflected on it, being such a prudent lady, she probably would not have done it; because the persecutions, which the Bishop of Geneva procured us in that place, cost her more than a little of humiliations. Our Lord permitted him to pursue me, after a surprising manner, into all the places I have been in, without giving me any relaxation. I never did him any harm, but on the contrary, would have laid down my life for the good of his diocese.

As this fell out without any design on our part, we, without hesitation, believed it was the will of God; and thought it might be the means of His appointment to draw us out of the reproach and persecution we labored under, seeing myself chased on the one side, desired on the other. It was concluded that Father La Combe should conduct me to Turin, and that he should go from thence to Verceil.

Beside him, I took with me a religious man of merit, who had taught theology for fourteen years past, to take away from our enemies all cause for slander. I also took with me a boy whom I had brought out of France. They took horses, and I hired a carriage for my daughter, my chambermaid and myself. But all precautions are useless, when it pleases God to permit them to be frustrated. Our adversaries immediately wrote to Paris. A hundred ridiculous stories were circulated about this journey; comedies were acted on it, things invented at pleasure, and as false as anything in the world could be. It was my brother, Father de la Mothe, who was so active in uttering all this stuff. Had he believed it to be true, he ought out of charity to have concealed it; much more, being so very false. They said that I was gone all alone with Father La Combe, strolling about the country, from province to province, with many such fables, as weak and wicked as they were incoherent and badly put together. We suffered all with patience, without vindicating ourselves, or making any complaint.

Scarcely were we arrived at Turin, but the Bishop of Geneva wrote against us. As he could pursue us no other way, he did it by letters. Father La Combe repaired to Verceil, and I staid at Turin, with the Marchioness of Prunai. But what crosses was I assaulted with in my own family, from the Bishop of Geneva, from the Barnabites, and from a vast number of persons besides! My eldest son came to find me on the death of my mother-in-law, which was an augmentation of my troubles. After we had heard all his accounts of things and how they had made sales of all the moveables, chosen guardians, and settled every article, without consulting me. I seemed to be there entirely useless. It was judged not proper for me to return, considering the rigor of the season.

The Marchioness of Prunai, who had been so warmly desirous of my company, seeing my great crosses and reproaches, looked coldly upon me. My childlike simplicity, which was the state wherein God at that time kept me, passed with her for stupidity. For when the question was to help anyone, or about anything which God required of me, He gave me, with the weakness of a child, the evident tokens of divine strength. Her heart was quite shut up to me all the time I was there. Our Lord, however, made me foretell events which should happen, which since that time have actually been fulfilled, as well to herself as to her daughter, and to the virtuous ecclesiastic who lived at her house. She did not fail, at last, to conceive more friendship for me, seeing then that Christ was in me. It was the force of self-love, and fear of reproach, which had closed up her heart. Moreover, she thought her state more advanced than in reality it was, by reason of her being without tests; but she soon saw by experience that I had told her the truth. She was obliged for family reasons to leave Turin, and go to live on her own estate. She solicited me to go with her; but the education of my daughter did not permit. To stay at Turin without her seemed improper, because, having lived very retired in this place, I made no acquaintance in it. I knew not which way to turn. The Bishop of Verceil, where Father La Combe was, most obligingly wrote to me, earnestly entreating me to come, promising me his protection, and assuring me of his esteem, adding, "that he should look upon me as his own sister; that he wished extremely to have me there." It was his own sister, one of my particular friends, who had written to him about me, as had also a French gentleman, an acquaintance of his. But a point of honor kept me from it. I would not have it said that I had gone after Father La Combe, and that I had come to Turin only for the purpose of going to Verceil. He had also his reputation to preserve, which was the cause that he could not agree to my going thither, however importunate the Bishop was for it. Had we believed it to be the will of God, we would both of us have passed over these considerations. God kept us both in so great a dependence on His orders, that He did not let us foreknow them;

but the divine moment of His providence determined everything. This proved of very great service to Father La Combe, who had long walked in assurances, to die to them and to Himself. God by an effect of His goodness, that he might thus die without any reserve, took them all from him.

During the whole time of my residence at Turin, our Lord conferred on me very great favors. I found myself every day more transformed into Him, and had continually more knowledge of the state of souls, without ever being mistaken or deceived therein, though some were willing to persuade me to think the contrary. I had used my utmost endeavors to give myself other thoughts, which has caused me not a little pain. When I told, or wrote to Father La Combe about the state of some souls, which appeared to him more perfect and advanced than the knowledge given to me of them, he attributed it to pride. He was angry with me, and prejudiced against my state. I had no uneasiness on account of his esteeming me the less, for I was not in a condition to reflect whether he esteemed me or not. He could not reconcile my willing obedience in most things, with so extraordinary a firmness, which in certain cases he looked upon as criminal. He admitted a distrust of my grace; he was not yet sufficiently confirmed in his way, nor did he duly comprehend, that it did not in any wise depend on me to be one way or another. If I had any such power I should have suited myself to what he said, to spare myself the crosses which my firmness caused me. Or, at least, I would have artfully dissembled my real sentiments. I could do neither.

Were all to perish by it, I was in such a manner constrained, that I could not forbear telling him the things, just as our Lord directed me to tell them to him. In this he had given me an inviolable fidelity to the very last. No crosses or pains have ever made me fail a moment therein. These things then, which appeared to him to be the strong prejudice of a conceited opinion, set him at variance against me. Though he did not openly show it, on the contrary tried to conceal it from me; yet how far distant soever he were from me, I could not be ignorant of it. My spirit felt it, and that more or less, as the opposition was stronger or weaker; as soon as it abated or ended, my pain, occasioned thereby, ceased. He also, on his side, experienced the same. He has told me and written to me many times over, "When I stand well with God, I find I am well with you. When I am otherwise with Him, I then find myself to be so with you also." Thus he saw clearly that when God received him, it was always in uniting him to me, as if He would accept of nothing from him but in this union.

While he was at Turin, a widow who was a good servant of God, all in the brightness of sensibility, came to him to confess. She uttered wonderful things of her state. I was then at the other side of the confessional. He told me, "He had met with a soul given up to God; that it was she who was present; that he was very much edified by her; that he was far from finding the like in me; that I operated nothing but death upon his soul." At first I rejoiced at his having met with such a holy soul. It ever gives me the highest joy to see my God glorified. As I was returning, the Lord showed me clearly the state of that soul, as only a beginning of devotion mixed with affection and a little silence, filled with a new sensation. This and more, as it was set before me, I was obliged to write to him. On his first reading of my letter he discovered the stamp of truth in it; but soon after, letting in again his old reflections, he viewed all I wrote in the light of pride. He still had in his mind the ordinary rules of humility conceived and comprised after our manner. As to me, I let myself be led as a child, who says and does, without distinction, whatever it is made to say and do. I left myself to be led wheresoever my heavenly Father pleased, high or low; all was alike good to me.

He wrote to me, that, at his first reading of my letter there appeared in it something of truth; but that on reading it over again, he found it to be full of pride, and of preference of my own discernments to that of others. Some time after he was more enlightened in regard to the state I was in. He then said, "continue to believe as you have done; I encourage and exhort you to do it." Some time after he sufficiently discovered, by that person's manner of acting, that she was very far from what he had thought. I give this as only one instance. I might give many others, but this may suffice.

CHAPTER 14

ONE NIGHT IN A DREAM our Lord showed me, that He would also purify the maid whom He had given me, make her truly enter into death to herself. I freely resolved to suffer for her, as I did for Father La Combe. As she resisted God much more than he, and was much more under the power of self-love, she had more to be purified from. What I could not tolerate in her was her regard for herself. I saw clearly that the devil cannot hurt us only so far as we retain some fondness for this corrupt self. This sight was from God. He gave me the discerning of spirits, which would ever accept what was from Him, or reject what was not; that not from any common methods of judging, not from any outward information, but by an inward principle which is His gift alone.

It is needful to mention here that souls which are yet in themselves, whatever degree of light and ardor they have attained, are unqualified for it. They often think they have this discernment, when it is nothing else but sympathy or antipathy of nature. Our Lord destroyed in me every sort of natural antipathy. The soul must be very pure, and depending on God alone, that all these things may be experienced in Him. In proportion as this maid became inwardly purified, my pain abated, till the Lord let me know her state was going to be changed, which soon happily ensued. In comparison of inward pain for souls, outward persecutions, though ever so violent, scarce gave me any.

The Bishop of Geneva wrote to different persons. He wrote in my favor to such as he thought would show me his letters, and quite the contrary in the letters which he thought I would never see. It was so ordered that these persons, having showed each other their letters received from him, were struck with indignation to see in him so shameful a duplicity. They sent me those letters that I might take proper precautions. I kept them two years, and then burned them, not to hurt the prelate. The strongest battery he raised against me was what he did with the Secretary of State, who held that post in conjunction with the Marchioness of Prunai's brother. He used all imaginable endeavors to render me odious. He employed certain abbots for that purpose, insomuch that, though I appeared very little abroad, I was well known by the description this bishop had given of me. This did not make so much impression as it would have done, if he had appeared in a better light at Court. Some letters of his, which her royal highness found after the prince's death, written to him against her, had effect on the princess, that, instead of taking any notice of what he now wrote against me, she showed me great respect. She sent her request to me to come to see her. Accordingly I waited on her. She assured me of her protection, and that she was glad of my being in her dominions.

It pleased God here to make use of me to the conversion of two or three ecclesiastics. But I had much to suffer from their repugnances and many infidelities —one of whom had villified me greatly—and even after his conversion turned aside into his old ways. God at length graciously restored him.

As I was undetermined whether I should place my daughter at the Visitation of Turin, or take some other course; I was exceedingly surprised, at a time I least expected it, to see Father La Combe arrive from Verceil. He told me that I must return to Paris without any delay. It was in the evening, and he said, "set off the next morning." I confess this sudden news startled me. It was for me a double sacrifice to return to a place where they had cried me down so much; also toward a family which held me in contempt, and who had represented my journey, caused by pure necessity, as a voluntary course, pursued through human attachments. Behold me then disposed to go off, without offering a single word in reply, with my daughter and my maid, without anybody to guide and attend us. Father La Combe was resolved not to accompany me, not so much as passing the mountains. The Bishop of Geneva had written on all sides that I was gone to Turin to run after him. But the Father Provincial, who was a man of quality, and well acquainted with the virtue of Father La Combe, told him, that it was improper and unsafe to venture on these mountains, without some person of acquaintance; the more as I had my little daughter with me. He therefore ordered him to accompany me. Father La Combe confessed to me that he had some reluctance to do it, and only obedience, and the danger to which I should have been exposed, made him surmount it. He was only to accompany me to Grenoble, and from thence to return to Turin. I went off then, designing for Paris, there to suffer whatever crosses and trials it should please God to inflict.

What made me go by Grenoble was the desire I had to spend two or three days with a lady, an eminent servant of God, and one of my friends. When I was there Father La Combe and that lady spoke to me not to go any farther. God would glorify Himself in me and by me in that place. He returned to Verceil, and I left myself to be conducted as a child by Providence. This lady took me to the house of a good widow, there not being accommodations at the inn. As I was ordered to stop at Grenoble, at her house I resided. I placed my daughter in a convent, and resolved to employ all this time in resigning myself to be possessed in solitude by Him who is the absolute Sovereign of my soul. I made not any visit in this place; no more had I in any of the others where I had sojourned. I was greatly surprised when, a few days after my arrival, there came to see me several persons who made profession of a singular devotion to God. I perceived immediately a gift which He had given me, of administering to each that which suited their states. I felt myself invested, all of a sudden, with the apostolic state. I discerned the conditions of the souls of such persons as spoke to me, and that with so much facility, that they were surprised at it, and said one to another, that I gave every one of them "the very thing they had stood in need of." It was thou, O my God, who didst all these things; some of them sent others to me. It came to such excess, that, generally from six in the morning till eight in the evening, I was taken up in speaking of the Lord. People flocked on all sides, far and near, friars, priests, men of the world, maids, wives, widows, all came one after another. The Lord supplied me with what was pertinent and satisfactory to them all, after a wonderful manner, without any share of my study or meditation therein. Nothing was hid from me of their interior state, and of what passed within them. Here, O my God, Thou madest an infinite number of conquests known to Thyself only. They were instantly furnished with a wonderful facility of prayer. God conferred on them His grace plentifully, and wrought marvelous changes in them. The most advanced of these souls found, when with me, in silence, a grace communicated to them which they could neither comprehend, nor cease to admire. The others found an unction in my words, and that they operated in them what I said. Friars of different orders, and priests of merit, came to see me, to whom our Lord granted very great favors, as indeed He did to all, without exception, who came in sincerity.

One thing was surprising; I had not a syllable to say to such as came only to watch my words, and to criticize them. Even when I thought to try to speak to them, I felt that I could not, and that God would not have me do it. Some of them in return said, "The people are fools to go to see that lady. She cannot speak." Others of them treated me as if I were only a stupid simpleton. After they left me there came one and said, "I could not get hither soon enough to apprize you not to speak to those persons; they come from such and such, to try what they can catch from you to your disadvantage." I answered them, "Our Lord has prevented your charity; for I was not able to say one word to them."

I felt that what I spoke flowed from the fountain, and that I was only the instrument of Him who made me speak. Amid this general applause, our Lord made me comprehend what the apostolic state was, with which He had honored me; that to give one's self up to the help of souls, in the purity of His Spirit, was to expose one's self to the most cruel persecutions. These very words were imprinted on my heart: "To resign ourselves to serve our neighbor is to sacrifice ourselves to a gibbet. Such as now proclaim, 'Blessed is he who cometh in the name of the Lord,' will soon cry out, 'Away with him, crucify him.'" When one of my friends speaking of the general esteem the people had for me, I said to her, "Observe what I now tell you, that you will hear curses out of the same mouths which at present pronounce blessings." Our Lord made me comprehend that I must be conformable to Him in all His states; and that, if He had continued in a private life with His parents, He never had been crucified; that, when He would resign any of His servants to crucifixion, He

307

employed such in the ministry and service of their neighbors. It is certain that all the souls employed herein by apostolic destination from God, and who are truly in the apostolic state, are to suffer extremely. I speak not of those who put themselves into it, who, not being called of God in a singular manner, and having nothing of the grace of the apostleship, have none of its crosses; but of those only who surrender themselves to God without any reserve, and who are willing with their whole hearts to be exposed, for His sake, to sufferings without any mitigation.

CHAPTER 15

AMONG SO GREAT A NUMBER of good souls, on whom our Lord wrought much by me, some were given me only as plants to cultivate. I knew their state, but had not that near connection with, or authority over them, which I had over others. It was then that I comprehended the true maternity beyond what I had done before; for those of the latter kind were given me as children, of whom some were faithful. I knew they would be so; they were closely united to me in pure charity. Others were unfaithful; I knew that of these some would never return from their infidelity, and they were taken from me. Some, after slipping aside, were recovered. Both of them cost me much distress and inward pain, when, for want of courage to die to themselves, they gave up the point; and revolted from the good beginning they had been favored with.

Our Lord, among such multitudes as followed Him on earth, had few true children. Wherefore He said to His Father, "Those that thou gavest me I have kept, and none of them is lost but the son of perdition," showing that He lost not any beside of His apostles, or disciples, though they sometimes made false steps.

Among the friars who came to see me, there was one order which discovered the good effects of grace more than any other. Some of that very order had before this, in a little town where Father La Combe was in the exercise of his mission, been actuated with a false zeal, and violent in persecuting all the good souls which had sincerely dedicated themselves to God, plaguing them after such a manner as can scarce be conceived. They burned all their books which treated of silence and inward prayer, refusing absolution to such as were in the practice of it, driving into consternation, and almost into despair, such as had formerly led wicked lives, but were now reformed, and preserved in grace by means of prayer, becoming spotless and blameless in their conduct. These friars had proceeded to such an excess of wild zeal as to raise a sedition in that town, in which a father of the oratory, a person of distinction and merit, received strokes with a stick in the open street, because he prayed extempore in the evenings, and on Sundays made a short fervent prayer, which insensibly habituated these good souls to the use and practice of the like.

I never had so much consolation as to see in this little town so many pious souls who with a heavenly emulation gave up their whole hearts to God. There were girls of twelve or thirteen years of age, who industriously followed their work almost all the day long, in silence, and in their employments enjoyed a communion with God, having acquired a fixed habit.

310

As these girls were poor, they placed themselves two and two together, and such as could do it read to the others who could not. One saw there the innocence of the primitive Christians revived. There was in that town a poor laundress who had five children, and a husband paralytic, lame in the right arm, and yet worse distempered in mind than in body. He had little strength left for anything else than to beat her. This poor woman bore it with all the meekness and patience of an angel, while she by her labor supported him and his five children. She had a wonderful gift of prayer, and amid her great suffering and extreme poverty, preserved the presence of God, and tranquility of mind. There was also a shopkeeper, and one who made locks, very much affected with God. These were close friends. Sometimes the one and sometimes the other read to this laundress; and they were surprised to find that she was instructed by the Lord Himself in all they read to her, and spoke divinely of it.

Those friars sent for this woman, and threatened her much if she did not leave off prayer, telling her it was only for churchmen to pray, and that she was very bold to practice it. She replied, that "Christ had commanded all to pray," that He had said, "What I say unto you I say unto all" (Mark 13:33, 37), without specifying either priests or friars; that without prayer she could not support her crosses and poverty; that formerly she had lived without it, and then was very wicked; that since she had been in the exercise of it, she had loved God with all her soul; so that to leave off prayer was to renounce her salvation,

311

which she could not do. She added that they might take twenty persons who had never practiced prayer, and twenty of those who were in the practice of it. Then, said she, "Inform yourselves of the lives of both sorts, and ye will see if ye have any reason to cry out against prayer." Such words as these, from such a woman, one would think might have fully convinced them; but instead of that, it only irritated them the more. They assured her that she should have no absolution till she promised them to desist from prayer. She said that depended not on her, and that Christ is master of what He communicates to His creatures, and of doing with it what He pleases. They refused her absolution; and after railing at a good tailor, who served God with his whole heart, they ordered all the books without exception, which treated on prayer to be brought to them. They burned them with their own hands in the public square. They were very much elated with their performance; but all the town presently arose in an uproar. The principal men went to the Bishop of Geneva, and complained to him of the scandals of these new missionaries, so different from the others. Speaking of Father La Combe, who had been there before them on his mission, they said that these seemed as if they were sent to destroy all the good he had done. The bishop was forced to come himself to that town, and there to mount the pulpit, protesting that he had no share in it, and that these fathers had pushed their zeal too far. The friars, on the other side declared, they had done all they did, pursuant to the orders given them.

There were also at Tonon young women who had retired together, being poor villagers, the better to earn their livelihood and to serve God. One of them read from time to time, while the others were at work, and not one went out without asking leave of the eldest. They wove ribbands, or spun, the strong supporting the weak. They separated these poor girls, and others beside them, in several villages, and drove them out of the church.

It was the friars of the very order whom our Lord made use of to establish prayer in (I know not how) many places. Into the places where they went, they carried a hundred times more books of prayer than those which their brethren had burned. The hand of God appeared to me wonderfully in these things.

One day when I was sick, a brother who had skill in curing diseases, came for a charitable collection, but hearing I was ill, came in to see me, and gave me medicines proper for my disorder. We entered into a conversation which revived in him the love he had for God, which he acknowledged had been too much stifled by his occupations. I made him comprehend that there was no employment which should hinder him from loving God, and from being occupied within himself. He readily believed me, as he already had a good share of piety, and of an interior disposition. Our Lord conferred on him many favors, and gave him to be one of my true children.

I saw at this time, or rather experienced the ground on which God rejects sinners from His bosom. All the cause of God's rejection is in the will of the sinner. If that will submits, how horrible soever he be, God purifies him in his love, and receives him into his grace; but while that will rebels, the rejection continues. For want of ability seconding his inclination, he should not commit the sin he is inclined to, yet he never can be admitted into grace till the cause ceases, which is this wrong will, rebellious to the divine law. If that once submits, God then totally removes the effects of sin, which stain the soul, by washing away the defilements which he has contracted. If that sinner dies in the time that his will is rebellious and turned toward sin, as death fixes forever the disposition of the soul, and the cause of its impurity is ever subsisting, such soul can never be received into God. Its rejection must be eternal, as there is such an absolute opposition between essential purity and essential impurity. And as this soul, from its own nature necessarily tends to its own center, it is continually rejected of the Lord, by reason of its impurity, subsisting not only in the effects, but in their cause. It is the same way in this life. This cause, so long as it subsists, absolutely hinders the grace of God from operating in the soul. But if the sinner comes to die truly penitent, then the cause, which is the wrong will, being taken away, there remains only the effect or impurity caused by it. He is then in a condition to be purified. God of his infinite mercy has provided a laver of love and of justice, a painful laver indeed, to purify this soul. And as the defilement is greater or less, so is the pain; but when the cause is utterly taken away, the pain entirely ceases. Souls, are received into grace, as soon as the cause of sin ceases; but they do not pass into the Lord Himself, till all its effects are washed away. If they have not courage to let Him, in His own way and will, thoroughly cleanse and purify them, they never enter into the pure divinity in this life.

The Lord incessantly solicits this will to cease to be rebellious, and spares nothing on His side for this good end. The will is free, yet grace follows it still. As soon as the will ceases to rebel, it finds grace at the door, ready to introduce its unspeakable benefits. O, the goodness of the Lord and baseness of the sinner, each of them amazing when clearly seen!

Before I arrived at Grenoble, the lady, my friend, saw in a dream that our Lord gave me an infinite number of children all uniformly clad, bearing on their habits the marks of candor and innocence. She thought I was coming to take care of the children of the hospital. But as soon as she told me, I discerned that it was not that which the dream meant; but that our Lord would give me, by a spiritaul fruitfulness, a great number of children; that they would not be my true children, but in simplicity, candor and innocence. So great an aversion I have to artifice and disguise.

CHAPTER 16

THE PHYSICIAN of whom I have spoken, was disposed to lay open his heart to me. Our Lord gave him through me all that was necessary for him; for though disposed to the spiritual life, yet for want of courage and fidelity he had not duly advanced in it.

He had occasion to bring to me some of his companions who were friars; and the Lord took hold of them all. It was at the very same time, that the others of the same order were making all the ravages I have mentioned, and opposing with all their might the Holy Spirit of the Lord. I could not but admire to see how the Lord was pleased to make amends for former damages, pouring out His Spirit in abundance on these men, while the others were laboring vehemently against it, doing all they could to destroy its dominion and efficacy in their fellow-mortals. But those good souls instead of being staggered by persecutions, grew the stronger by it. The Superior, and the master of the novices of the house in which this doctor was declared against me, without knowing me. They were grievously chagrined that a woman, as they said, should be so much flocked to, and so much sought after. Looking at things as they were in themselves, and not as they were in the Lord, who does whatever pleases Him, they had contempt for the gift which was lodged in so mean an instrument, instead of esteeming the Lord and His grace. Yet this good brother at length got the superior to come to see me, and thank me for the good which he said I had done. Our Lord so ordered, that he found something in my conversation which reached and took hold of him. At length he was completely brought over. He it was, who some time after, being visitor, dispersed such a number of those books, bought at their own charge, which the others had tried utterly to destroy. Oh, how wonderful art Thou, my God! In all Thy ways how wise, in all Thy conduct how full of love! How well Thou canst frustrate all the false wisdom of men, and triumph over their vain pretentions!

There were in this noviciate many novices. The eldest of them grew so very uneasy under his vocation, that he knew not what to do. So great was his trouble that he could neither read, study, pray, nor do scarcely any of his duties. His companion brought him to me. We spoke awhile together, and the Lord discovered to me both the cause of his disorder and its remedy. I told it to him; and he began to practice prayer, even that of the heart. He was on a sudden wonderfully changed, and the Lord highly favored him. As I spoke to him grace wrought in his heart, and his soul drank it in, as the parched ground does the gentle rain. He felt himself relieved of his pain

317

before he left the room. He then readily, joyfully, and perfectly performed all his exercises, which before were done with reluctance and disgust. He now both studied and prayed easily, and discharged all his duties, in such a manner, that he was scarce known to himself or to others. What astonished him most was a remarkable gift of prayer. He saw that there was readily given him what he could never have before, whatever pains he took for it. This enlivening gift was the principle which made him act, gave him grace for his employments, and an inward fruition of the grace of God, which brought all good with it. He gradually brought me all the novices, all of whom partook of the effects of grace, though differently, according to their different temperaments. Never was there a more flourishing noviciate.

The master and superior could not forbear admiring so great a change in their novices, though they did not know the cause of it. One day, as they were speaking of it to the collector, for they esteemed him highly on account of his virtue, he said, "My fathers, if you will permit me, I will tell you the reason of it. It is the lady against whom you have exclaimed so much without knowing her, whom God has made use of for all of this." They were very surprised; and both the master, though advanced in age, and his superior then submitted humbly to practice prayer, after the manner taught by a little book, which the Lord inspired me to write, and of which I shall say more hereafter. They reaped such benefit from it, that the superior said to me, "I am become quite a new man. I could not practice prayer before, because my reasoning faculty was grown dull and exhausted; but now I do it as often as I will, with ease, with much fruit, and a quite different sensation of the presence of God." And the master said, "I have been a friar these forty years, and can truly say that I never knew how to pray; nor have I ever known or tasted of God, as I have done since I read that little book."

Many others were gained to God, whom I looked on to be my children. He gave me three famous friars, of an order by which I have been, and still am, very much persecuted. He made me also of service to a great number of nuns, of virtuous young women, and even men of the world; among the rest a young man of quality, who had quitted the order of the knights of Malta, to take that of the priesthood. He was the relation of a bishop near him, who had other designs of preferment for him. He has been much favored of the Lord, and is constant in prayer. I could not describe the great number of souls which were then given me, as well maids, as wives, priests and friars. But there were three curates, one canon, and one grand-vicar, who were more particularly given me. There was one priest for whom I suffered much, through his not being willing to die to himself, and loving himself too much. With a sad regret I saw him decaying, falling away. As for the others there are some of them who have continued stedfast and immovable, and some whom the tempest has shaken a little, but not torn away. Though these start aside, yet they still return. But those who are snatched quite away return no more.

319

There was one true daughter given me, whom our Lord made use of to gain many others to Him. She was in a strange state of death when I first saw her, and by me He gave her life and peace. She afterward, fell extremely ill. The doctors said she would die; but I had an assurance of the contrary, and that God would make use of her to gain souls, as he has done. There was in a monastery a young woman confined in a state of distraction. I saw her, knew her case, and that it was not what they thought it was. As soon as I had spoken to her she recovered. But the prioress did not like that I should tell her my thoughts of it, because the person who had brought her thither was her friend. They plagued her more than before, and threw her back again into her distraction.

A sister of another monastery had been for eight years in a deep melancholy, unrelieved by anyone. Her director increased it, by practicing remedies contrary to her disorder. I had never been in that monastery; for I did not go into such places, unless I was sent for, as I did not think it right to intrude, but left myself to be conducted of Providence. I was very much surprised that at eight o'clock at night one came for me from the prioress. It was in the long days of summer, and being near, I went. I met with a sister who told me her case. She had gone to such excess, that seeing no remedy for it, she had taken a knife to kill herself. The knife fell out of her hand and a person coming to see her had advised her to speak to me. Our Lord made me know at first what the matter was; and that He required her to resign herself to Him, instead of resisting Him as they had made her do for eight years. I was instrumental to draw her into such a resignation, that she entered at once into a peace of paradise; all her pains and troubles were instantly banished; and never returned again. She has the greatest capacity of any in the house. She was presently so changed as to be the admiration of the whole community. Our Lord gave her a very great gift of prayer and His continual presence, with a faculty and readiness for everything. A domestic also, who had troubled her for twenty-two years past, was delivered from her troubles. That produced a close tie of friendship between the prioress and me, as the wonderful change and the peace of this sister surprised her, she having so often seen her in her terrible sorrow. I also contracted other such ties in this monastery, where there are souls under the Lord's special regard, whom He drew to Himself by the means He had been pleased to make choice.

I was specially moved to read the Holy Scriptures. When I began I was impelled to write the passage, and instantly its explication was given me, which I also wrote, going on with inconceivable expedition, light being poured in upon me in such a manner, that I found I had in myself latent treasures of wisdom and knowledge which I had not yet known of. Before I wrote I knew not what I was going to write. And after I had written, I remembered nothing of what I had penned; nor could I make use of any part of it for the help of souls. The Lord gave me, at the time I spoke to them (without any study or reflection of mine) all that was necessary for them. Thus the Lord made me go on with an explanation of the holy internal sense of the Scriptures. I had no other book but the Bible, nor ever made use of any but that, and without even seeking for any. When, in writing on the Old Testament, I made use of passages of the New, to support what I had said, it was without seeking them, they were given me along with the explication; and in writing on the New Testament, therein making use of passages of the Old, they were given me in like manner without my seeking anything. I had scarce any time for writing but in the night, allowing only one or two hours to sleep. The Lord made me write with so much purity, that I was obliged to leave off or begin again, as He was pleased to order. When I wrote by day, often suddenly interrupted, I left the word unfinished, and He afterward gave me what He pleased. If I gave way to reflection I was punished for it, and could not proceed. Yet sometimes I was not duly attentive to the divine Spirit, thinking I did well to continue when I had time, even without feeling His immediate impulse or enlightning influence, from whence it is easy to see some places clear and consistent, and others which have neither taste nor unction; such is the difference of the Spirit of God from the human and natural spirit. Although they are left just as I wrote them, yet I am ready, if ordered, to adjust them according to my present light.

Didst thou not, O my God, turn me a hundred ways, to prove whether I was without any reserve, through every kind of trial, or whether I had not yet some little interest for myself? My soul became hereby readily too pliable to every discovery of the divine will, and whatever kind of humiliations attended me to counterbalance my Lord's favors, till everything, high or low, was rendered alike to me.

Methinks the Lord acts with His dearest friends as the sea with its waves. Sometimes it pushes them against the rocks where they break in pieces, sometimes it rolls them on the sand, or dashes them on the mire, then instantly it retakes them into the depths of its own bosom, where they are absorbed with the same rapidity that they were first ejected. Even among the good the far greater part are souls only of mercy; surely that is well; but to appertain to divine justice, oh, how rare and yet how great! Mercy is all distributive in favor of the creature, but justice destroys everything of the creature, without sparing anything.

The lady, who was my particular friend, began to conceive some jealousy on the applause given me, God so permitting if for the farther purification of her soul, through this weakness, and the pain it caused her. Also some confessors began to be uneasy, saying that it was none of my business to invade their province, and to meddle in the helps of souls; that there were some of the penitents which had a great affection for me." It was easy for me to observe the difference between those confessors who, in their conducting of souls, seek nothing but God, and those who seek themselves therein. The first came to see me, and rejoiced greatly at the grace of God bestowed on their penitents, without fixing their attention on the instrument. The others, on the contrary, tried underhand to stir up the town against me. I saw that they would be in the right to oppose me, if I had intruded of myself; but I could do nothing but what the Lord made me do. At times there came some to dispute and oppose me. Two friars came, one of them a man of profound learning and a great preacher. They came separately, after having studied a number of difficult things to propose to me. Though they were matters far out of my reach, the Lord made me answer as justly as if I had studied them all my life; after which I spoke to them as He inspired me. They went away not only convinced and satisfied, but affected with the love of God.

I still continued writing with a prodigious swiftness; for the hand could scarcely follow fast enough the Spirit which dictated. Through the whole progress of so long a work I never altered my manner nor made use of any other book than the Bible itself. The transcriber, whatever diligence he used, could not copy in five days what I wrote in one night. Whatever is good in it comes from God only. Whatever is otherwise from myself; I mean from the mixture which I have made, without duly attending to it, of my own impurity with his pure and chaste doctrine. In the day I had scarcely time to eat, by reason of the vast numbers of people which came thronging to me. I wrote the canticles in a day and a half, and received several visits besides.

Here I may add to what I have said about my writings, that a considerable part of the book of

Judges happened by some means to be lost. Being desired to render that book complete, I wrote again the places lost. Afterward when the people were about leaving the house, they were found. My former and latter explications, on comparison, were found to be perfectly conformable to each other, which greatly surprised persons of knowledge and merit, who attested the truth of it.

There came to see me a counselor of the parliament, a servant of God, who finding on my table a tract on prayer, which I had written long before, desired me to lend it. Having read it and liked it much, he lent it to some friends, to whom he thought it might be of service. Everyone wanted copies of it. He resolved therefore to have it printed. The impression was begun, and proper approbations given to it. They requested me to write a preface, which I did, and thus was that little book printed. This counselor was one of my intimate friends, and a pattern of piety. The book has already passed through five or six editions; and our Lord has given a very great benediction to it. Those good friars took fifteen hundred of them. The devil became so enraged against me on account of the conquest which God made by me, that I was assured he was going to stir up against me a violent persecution. All that gave me no trouble. Let him stir up against me ever so strange persecutions. I know they will all serve to the glory of my God.

CHAPTER 17

A POOR GIRL of very great simplicity, who earned her livelihood by her labor, and was inwardly favored of the Lord, came all sorrowful to me, and said, "Oh my mother, what strange things have I seen!" I asked what they were, "Alas" said she, "I have seen you like a lamb in the midst of a vast troop of furious wolves. I have seen a frightful multitude of people of all ranks and robes, of all ages, sexes and conditions, priests, friars, married men, maids and wives, with pikes, halberts and drawn swords, all eager for your instant destruction. You let them alone without stirring, or being surprised and without offering any way to defend yourself. I looked on all sides to see whether anyone would come to assist and defend you; but I saw not one."

Some days after, those, who through envy were raising private batteries against me, broke forth. Libels began to spread. Envious people wrote against me, without knowing me. They said that I was a sorceress, that it was by a magic power I attracted souls, that everything in me was diabolical; that if

I did charities, it was because I coined, and put off false money, with many other gross accusations, equally false, groundless and absurd.

As the tempest increased every day, some of my friends advised me to withdraw, but before I mention my leaving Grenoble, I must say something farther of my state while here.

It seemed to me that all our Lord made me do for souls, would be in union with Jesus Christ. In this divine union my words, had wonderful effect, even the formation of Jesus Christ in the souls of others. I was in no wise able of myself to say the things I said. He who conducted me made me say what He pleased, and as long as He pleased. To some I was not permitted to speak a word; and to others there flowed forth as it were a deluge of grace, and yet this pure love admitted not of any superfluity, or a means of empty amusement. When questions were asked, to which an answer were useless, it was not given me. It was the same in regard to such as our Lord was pleased to conduct through death to themselves, and who came to seek for human consolation. I had nothing for them but what was purely necessary, and could proceed no farther. I could at least only speak of indifferent things, in such liberty as God allows, in order to suit everyone, and not to be unsociable or disagreeable to any; but for His own word, He Himself is the dispenser of it. Oh, if preachers were duly careful to speak only in that spirit what fruits would they bring forth in the lives of the hearers! With my true children I could communicate best in silence, in the spiritual language of the divine Word. I had the consolation some time before to hear one read in St. Augustine a conversation he had with his mother. He complains of the necessity of returning from that heavenly language to words. I sometimes said, "Oh, my Love, give me hearts large enough to receive and contain the fulness bestowed on me."

After this manner, when the Holy Virgin approached Elizabeth, a wonderful commerce was maintained between Jesus Christ and St. John the Baptist, who after this manifested no eagerness to come to see Christ, but was drawn to retire into the desert, to receive the like communications with the greatest plenitude. When he came forth to preach repentance, he said, not that he was the Word, but only a Voice which was sent to make way, or open a passage into the hearts of the people for Christ the Word. He baptized only with water, for that was his function; for, as the water in running off leaves nothing, so does the Voice when it is past. But the Word baptized with the Holy Ghost, because He imprinted Himself on souls, and communicated with them by that Holy Spirit. It is not observed that Jesus Christ said anything during the whole obscure part of His life, though it is true that not any of His words shall be lost. Oh Love, if all thou hast said and operated in silence were to be written, I think the whole world could not contain the books that should be written. John 21:25.

All that I experienced was shown me in the Holy Scripture. I saw with admiration that there passed nothing within my soul which was not in Jesus

Christ and in the Holy Scriptures. I must pass over very many things in silence, because they cannot be expressed. If they were expressed they could not be understood or comprehended.

I often felt much for Father La Combe, who was not yet fixed in his state of interior death, but often rose and fell into alternatives. I was made sensible that Father La Combe was a vessel of election, whom God had chosen to carry His name among the Gentiles, and that He would show him how much he must suffer for that name. A carnal world judges carnally of them, and imputes to human attachment what is from the purest grace. If this union by any deviation be broken, the more pure and perfect it is, the more painfully will it be felt; the separation of the soul from God by sin being worse than that from the body of death. For myself I may say I had a continual dependence on God, in every state; my soul was ever willing to obey every motion of His Spirit. I thought there could not be anything in the world which He could require from me, to which I would not give myself up readily and with pleasure. I had no interest at all for myself. When God requires anything from this wretched nothing, I find no resistance left in me to do His will, how rigorous soever it may appear. If there is a heart in the world of which Thou art the sole and absolute master, mine seems to be one of that sort. Thy will, however rigorous, is its life and its pleasure.

To resume the thread of my story, the Bishop of Grenoble's Almoner persuaded me to go for some time to Marseilles, to let the storm pass over. He told me that I would be well received there, it being his native soil, and that many people of merit were there. I wrote to Father La Combe for his consent. He readily gave it. I might have gone to Verceil; for the Bishop of Verceil had written me very obliging letters, earnestly pressing me to come. But a human respect, and fear of affording a handle to my enemies, gave me an extreme aversion thereto.

Beside the above, the Marchioness of Prunai, who, since my departure from her, had been more enlightened by her own experience, having met with a part of the things which I thought would befall her, had conceived for me a very strong friendship and intimate union of spirit, in such a manner that no two sisters could be more united than we. She was extremely desirous that I would return to her, as I had formerly promised her. But I could not resolve upon this, lest it should be thought that I was gone after Father La Combe. There had been no room given to anybody to accuse me of any indirect attachment to him; for when it depended on myself not to continue with him, I did not do it. The Bishop of Geneva had not failed to write against me to Grenoble, as he had done to other places. His nephew had gone from house to house to cry me down. All this was indifferent to me; and I did not cease to do to his diocese all the good in my power. I even wrote to him in a respectful manner; but his heart was too much closed to yield to anything.

Before I left Grenoble, that good girl I have spoken of came to me weeping, and told me that I was going, and that I hid it from her, because I would have nobody know it; but that the Devil would be before me in all the places I should go to; that I was going to a town, where I would scarce be arrived, before he would stir up the whole town against me, and would do me all the harm he possibly could. What had obliged me to conceal my departure, was my fear of being loaded with visits, and testimonies of friendship from a number of good persons, who had a very great affection for me.

I embarked then upon the Rhone, with my maid and a young woman of Grenoble, whom the Lord has highly favored through my means. The Bishop of Grenoble's Almoner also accompanied me, with another very worthy ecclesiastic. We met with many alarming accidents and wonderful preservations; but those instant dangers, which affrighted others, far from alarming me, augmented my peace. The Bishop of Grenoble's Almoner was much astonished. He was in a desperate fright, when the boat struck against a rock, and opened at the stroke. In his emotion looking attentively at me, he observed that I did not change my countenance, or move my eyebrows, retaining all my tranquillity. I did not so much as feel the first emotions of surprise, which are natural to everybody on those occasions, as they depend not on ourselves. What caused my peace in such dangers as terrify others, was my resignation to God, and because death is much more agreeable to me than life, if such were His will, to which I desire to be ever patiently submissive.

A man of quality, a servant of God, and one of my intimate friends had given me a letter for a knight of Malta, who was very devout, and whom I have esteemed since I have known him, as a man whom our Lord designed to serve the order of Malta greatly, and to be its ornament and support by his holy life. I had told him that I thought he should go thither, and that God would assuredly make use of him to diffuse a spirit of piety into many of the knights. He has actually gone to Malta, where the first places were soon given him. This man of quality sent him my little book of prayer and printed at Grenoble. He had a chaplain very averse to the spiritual path. He took this book, and condemning it at once, went to stir up a part of the town, and among the rest a set of men who called themselves the seventy-two disciples of St. Cyran. I arrived at Marseilles at ten o'clock in the morning, and that very afternoon all was in a noise against me. Some went to speak to the bishop, telling him that, on account of that book, it was necessary to banish me from the city. They gave him the book which he examined with one of his prebends. He liked it well. He sent for Monsieur Malaval and a father Recollect, who he knew had come to see me a little after my arrival, to inquire of them from whence that great tumult had its rise, which indeed had no other effect on me than to make me smile, seeing so soon accomplished what that young woman had foretold me. Monsieur Malaval and that good father told the bishop what they thought of me; after which he testified much uneasiness at the insult given me. I was obliged to go to see him. He received me with extraordinary respect, and begged my excuse for what had happened; desired me to stay at Marseilles, and assured me that he would protect me. He even asked where I lodged, that he might come to see me.

Next day the Bishop of Grenoble's Almoner went to see him, with that other priest who had come with us. The Bishop of Marseilles again testified to them his sorrow for the insults given me without any cause; and told them, that it was usual with those persons to insult all such as were not of their cabal, that they had even insulted himself. They were not content with that. They wrote to me the most offensive letters possible, though at the same time they did not know me. I apprehended that our Lord was beginning in earnest to take from me every place of abode; and those words were renewed in my mind, "The foxes have holes, and the birds of the air have nests, but the Son of man hath not where to lay his head."

In the short time of my stay at Marseilles, I was instrumental in supporting some good souls, and among others an ecclesiastic, who till then was unacquainted with me. After having finished his thanksgiving in the church, seeing me go out, he followed me into the house in which I lodged. Then he told me that the Lord had inspired him to address me, and to open his inward state to me. He did it with as much simplicity as humility, and the Lord gave him through me all that was necessary for him, from whence he was filled with joy, and thankful acknowledgments to God. Although there were many spiritual persons there, and even of his intimate friends, he never had been moved to open his mind to any of them. He was a servant of God, and favored by Him with a singular gift of prayer. During the eight days I was at Marseilles, I saw many good souls there. Through all my persecutions, our Lord always struck some good stroke of His own right hand, and that good ecclesiastic was delivered from an anxiety of mind, which had much afflicted him for some years.

After I had left Grenoble, those who hated me, without knowing me, spread libels against me. A woman for whom I had great love, and whom I had even extricated from an engagement which she had continued in for several years, and contributed to her discarding the person to whom she had been attached, suffered her mind to resume its fondness for that pernicious engagement. She became violently enraged against me for having broken it off. Although I had freely been at some expense to procure her freedom, still she went to the Bishop of Grenoble, to tell him that I had counseled her to do an act of injustice. She then went from confessor to confessor, repeating the same story, to animate them against me. As they were too susceptible of the prejudices infused, the fire was soon kindled in all quarters. There were none but those who knew me, and who loved God, that took my part. They became more closely united to me in sympathy through my persecution. It would have been very easy for me to destroy the calumny, as well with the Bishop of Grenoble. I needed only to tell who the person was, and show the fruits of her disorder. I could not declare the guilty person, without making known at the same time the other who had been her accomplice, who now, being touched of God, was very penitent, I thought it best for me to suffer and be silent. There was a very pious man who knew all her history, from the beginning to the end of it, who wrote to her, that if she did not retract her lies, he would publish the account of her wicked life, to make known both her gross iniquity and my innocence. She continued some time in her malice, writing that I was a sorceress, with many other falsehoods. Some time after she had such a cruel remorse of conscience on this account, that she wrote both to the bishop and others to retract what she had said. She induced one to write to me, to inform me that she was in despair for what she had done; that God had punished her. After these recantations the outcry abated, the bishop disabused, and since that time he has testified a great regard for me. This creature had, among other things, said that I caused myself to be worshiped; also other unparalleled follies.

From Marseilles I knew not how or whither I should turn next. I saw no likelihood either of staying or of returning to Grenoble, where I had left my daughter in a convent. Father La Combe had written to me that he did not think I ought to go to Paris. I even felt a strong repugnance to the idea of going, which made me think it was not yet the time for it. One morning I felt myself inwardly pressed to go somewhere. I took a conveyance to go to see the Marchioness of Prunai, which was, I thought, the most honorable refuge for me in my present condi-

tion. I thought I might pass through Nice on my way
to her habitation, as some had assured me I might.
But when I arrived at Nice, I was greatly surprised
to learn that the conveyance could not pass the moun-
tain. I knew not what to do, nor which way to turn,
alone, forsaken of everybody, and not knowing what
God required of me. My confusion and crosses seemed
to increase. I saw myself, without refuge or retreat,
wandering as a vagabond. All the tradesmen, whom
I saw in their shops, appeared to me happy, in having a dwelling of their own in which to retire. Nothing in the world seemed harder than this wandering
life to me, who naturally loved propriety and deco-
rum. As I was in this uncertainty, not knowing what
course to take, one came to tell me that next day a
sloop would set off, which used to go in one day to
Genoa; and that if I chose it, they would land me
at Savona, from whence I might get myself carried
to the Marchioness of Prunai's house. To that I consented, as I could not be supplied with any other
way.

I had some joy at embarking on the sea. I said in
myself, "If I am the dregs of the earth, the scorn
and offscouring of nature, I am now going to embark
on the element which above all others is the most
treacherous; if it be the Lord's pleasure to plunge
me in the waves, it shall be mine to perish in them."
There came a tempest in a place dangerous for a
small boat; and the mariners were some of the wick-
edest. The irritation of the waves gave a satisfaction
to my mind. I pleased myself in thinking that those
mutinous billows might probably supply me with a

grave. Perhaps I carried the point too far in the pleasure I took, at seeing myself beaten and bandied by the waters. Those who were with me, took notice of my intrepidity, but knew not the cause of it. I asked some little hole of a rock to be placed in, there to live separate from all creatures. I figured to myself, that some uninhabited island would have terminated all my disgraces, and put me in a condition of infallibly doing Thy will. Thou designedst me a prison far different from that of the rock, and quite another banishment than that of the uninhabited island. Thou reservest me to be battered by billows, more irritated than those of the sea. Calumnies proved to be the unrelenting waves, to which I was to be exposed, in order to be lashed and tossed by them without mercy. By the tempest we were kept back, and instead of a short day's passage to Genoa, we were eleven days making it. How peaceable was my heart in so violent an agitation! We could not land at Savona. We were obliged to go on to Genoa. We arrived there in the beginning of the week before Easter.

While I was there I was obliged to bear the insults of the inhabitants, caused by the resentment they had against the French because of the havoc of a late bombardment. The Doge was newly gone out of the city, and had carried off with him all the coaches. I could not get one, and was obliged to stay several days at excessive expenses. The people there demanded of us exorbitant sums, and as much for every single person as they would have asked for a company at the best eating place in Paris. I had

337

little money left, but my store in Providence could not be exhausted. I begged with the greatest earnestness for a carriage at any price, to pass the feast of Easter at the Marchioness of Prunai's house. It was then within three days of Easter. I could scarce any way get myself to be understood. By the force of entreaty, they brought me at length a sorry coach with lame mules, and told me that they would take me readily to Verceil, which was only two days journey, but demanded an enormous sum. They would not engage to take me to the Marchioness of Prunai's house, as they knew not where her estate lay. This was to me a strong mortification; for I was very willing to go to Verceil; nevertheless the proximity of Easter; and want of money, in a country where they used every kind of extortion and tyranny, left me no choice. I was under an absolute necessity of submitting to be thus conveyed to Verceil.

Thus Providence led me whither I would not. Our muleteer was one of the most brutal men; and for an increase of my affliction, I had sent away to Verceil the ecclesiastic who accompanied us, to prevent their surprise at seeing me there, after I had protested against going. That ecclesiastic was very coarsely treated on the road, through the hatred they bore to the French. They made him go part of the way on foot, so that, though he set off the day before me, he arrived there only a few hours sooner than I did. As for the fellow who conducted us, seeing he had only women under his care, he treated us in the most insolent and boorish manner.

We passed through a wood infested with robbers.

The muleteer was afraid, and told us, that, if we met any of them on the road, we should be murdered. They spared nobody. Scarcely had he uttered these words, when there appeared four men well armed. They immediately stopped us! The man was exceedingly frightened. I made a light bow of my head, with a smile, for I had no fear, and was so entirely resigned to Providence, that it was all one to die this way or any other; in the sea, or by the hands of robbers. When the dangers were most manifest, then was my faith the strongest, as well as my intrepidity, being unable to wish for anything else than what should fall out, whether to be dashed against the rocks, drowned, or killed in any other way; everything in the will of God being equal to me. The people who used to convey or attend me said that they had never seen a courage like mine; for the most alarming dangers, and the time when death appeared the most certain, were those which seemed to please me the most. Was it not thy pleasure, O my God, which guarded me in every imminent danger, and held me back from rolling down the precipice, on the instant of sliding over its dizzy brow? The more easy I was about life, which I bore only because Thou wast pleased to bear it, the more care Thou tookest to preserve it. There seemed a mutual emulation between us, on my part to resign it, and on thine to maintain it. The robbers then advanced to the coach; but I had no sooner saluted them, than God made them change their design. Having pushed off one another, as it were, to hinder each of them from doing any harm; they respectfully saluted me, and, with an air of compassion, unusual to such sorts of persons, retired. I was immediately struck to the heart with a full and clear conviction that it was a stroke of Thy right hand, who had other designs over me than to suffer me to die by the hand of robbers. It is Thy sovereign power which takes away their all from Thy devoted lovers; and destroys their lives with all that is of self without pity or sparing anything.

The muleteer, seeing me attended only with two young women, thought he might treat me as he would, perhaps expecting to draw money from me. Instead of taking me to the inn, he brought me to a mill, in which there was a woman. There was but one single room with several beds in it, in which the millers and muleteers lay together. In that chamber they forced me to stay. I told the muleteer I was not a person to lie in such a place and wanted to oblige him to take me to the inn. Nothing of it would he do. I was constrained to go out on foot, at ten o'clock at night, carrying a part of my clothes, and to go a good way more than a quarter of a league in the dark, in a strange place, not knowing the way, crossing one end of the wood infested with robbers, to endeavor to get to the inn. That fellow, seeing us go off from the place, where he had wanted to make me lodge, hooted after us in a very abusive manner. I bore my humiliation cheerfully, but not without feeling it. But the will of God and my resignation to it rendered everything easy to me. We were well received at the inn; and the good people there did the best in their power for our recovery from the fatigue we had undergone. They assured us the place we had left was very dangerous. Next morning we were obliged to return on foot to the carriage for that man would not bring it to us. On the contrary, he gave us a shower of fresh insults. To consummate his base behavior, he sold me to the post, whereby I was forced to go the rest of the way in a post-chaise instead of a carriage.

In this equipage I arrived at Alexandria, a frontier town, subject to Spain, on the side of the Milanese. Our driver took us, according to their custom, to the posthouse. I was exceedingly astonished when I saw the landlady coming out not to receive him, but to oppose his entrance. She had heard there were women in the chaise, and taking us for a different sort of women from what we were, she protested against our coming in. On the other hand, the driver was determined to force his entrance in spite of her. Their dispute rose to such a height, that a great number of the officers of the garrison, with a mob, gathered at the noise, who were surprised at the odd humor of the woman in refusing to lodge us. With earnestness I entreated the post to take us to some other house, but he would not; so obstinately was he bent on carrying his point. He assured the landlady we were persons of honor and piety too; the marks whereof he had seen. At last, by force of pressing entreaties, he obliged her to come to see us. As soon as she had looked at us, she acted as the robbers had done; she relented at once and admitted us.

No sooner had I alighted from the chaise, than she said, "Go shut yourselves up in that chamber hard by, and do not stir, that my son may not know you are here; as soon as he knows it he will kill you." She said it with so much force, as did also the servant maid, that, if death had not so many charms for me, I should have been ready to die with fear. The two poor girls with me were under frightful apprehensions. When any stirred, or came to open the door, they thought they were coming to kill them. In short they continued in a dreadful suspense, between life and death, till next day, when we learned that the young man had sworn to kill any woman who lodged at the house. A few days before, an event had fallen out, which had like to have ruined him; a woman of a bad life having there privately murdered a man in some esteem, that had cost the house a heavy fine; and he was afraid of any more such persons coming, not without reason.

CHAPTER 18

AFTER THESE ADVENTURES, and others which it would be tedious to recite, I arrived at Verceil. I went to the inn, where I was badly received. I sent for Father La Combe, who I thought had been already apprised of my coming, by the ecclesiastic whom I had sent before, and who would be of so much service to me. This ecclesiastic was only a little while arrived. How much better on the road should I have fared, if I had him with me! For in that country they look upon ladies, accompanied with ecclesiastics, with veneration, as persons of honor and piety. Father La Combe came in a strange fret at my arrival, God so permitting it. He said that every one would think I was come after him, and that would injure his reputation, which in that country was very high. I had no less pain to go. It was necessity only which had obliged me to submit to such a disagreeable task. The father received me with coolness, and in such a manner as let me sufficiently see his sentiments, and indeed redoubled my pain. I asked him if he required me to return, adding, if he did, "I would go off that moment however oppressed and spent, both with fatigues and fastings." He said that he did not know how the Bishop of Verceil would take my arrival, after he had given over all his expectations of it, and after I had so long, and so obstinately, refused the obliging offers he had made me; since which he no longer expressed any desire to see me.

It seemed to me then as if I were rejected from the face of the earth, without being able to find any refuge, and as if all creatures were combined to crush me. I passed that night without sleep, not knowing what course I should be obliged to take, being persecuted by my enemies, and a subject of disgrace to my friends.

When it was known at the inn, that I was one of Father La Combe's acquaintance, they treated me with greatest respect and kindness. They esteemed him as a saint. The father knew not how to tell the bishop of my arrival, and I felt his pain more than my own. As soon as that Prelate knew that I was arrived, he sent his niece, who took me in her coach, and carried me to her house. These things were only done out of ceremony; and the bishop, not having seen me yet, knew not what to think of a journey so very unexpected, after I had thrice refused, though he sent expresses on purpose to bring me to him. He was out of humor with me. Nevertheless, as he was informed that my design was not to stay at Verceil, but to go to the Marchioness of Prunai's house, he gave orders for me to be well treated. He could not see me till Easter Sunday was over. He officiated all the eve and all that day. After it was over, he came in a chaise to his niece's house to see me. Though he understood French hardly any better than I did Italian, he was very well satisfied with the conversation he had with me. He appeared to have as much favor for me as he had of indifference before.

He conceived as strong a friendship for me as if I had been his sister; and his only pleasure, amid his continual occupations, was to come and pass half an hour with me in speaking of God. He wrote to the Bishop of Marseilles to thank him for having protected me in the persecutions there. He wrote to the Bishop of Grenoble; and he omitted nothing to manifest his regard for me. He now seemed to think alone of finding out means to detain me in his diocese. He would not hear of my going to see the Marchioness of Prunai. On the contrary, he wrote to her to come and settle with me in his diocese. He sent Father La Combe to her, on purpose to exhort her to come; assuring her that he would unite us all to make a congregation. The Marchioness entered into it readily, and so did her daughter. They would have come with Father La Combe, but the Marchioness was sick. The bishop was active and earnest in collecting and establishing a society of us, and found several pious persons and some very devout young ladies, who were all ready to come to join us. But it was not the will of God to fix me thus, but to crucify me yet more.

The fatigue of traveling made me sick. The girl also whom I brought from Grenoble fell sick. Her relations, who were covetous took it in their heads that, if she should die in my service, I would get her to make a will in my favor. They were much mistaken. Far from desiring the property of others, I had given up my own. Her brother, full of this apprehension, came with all speed; the first thing he spoke to her about, although he found her recovered, was to make a will. That made a great noise in Verceil. He wanted her to return with him, but she refused. I advised her to do what her brother desired. He contracted a friendship with some of the officers of the garrison, to whom he told ridiculous stories, as that I wanted to use his sister badly. He pretended she was a person of quality. They gave out what I was still afraid of,—that I was come after Father La Combe. They even persecuted him on my account. The bishop was much troubled, but could not remedy it. The friendship he had for me increased every day; because, as he loved God, so he did all those whom he thought desired to love God. As he saw me so much indisposed, he came to see me with assiduity and charity, when at leisure from his occupations. He made me little presents of fruits and other things. His relations were jealous. They said that I was come to ruin him, and to carry off his money into France, which was farthest from my thoughts. The bishop patiently bore these affronts, hoping still to keep me in his diocese, when I should be recovered.

Father La Combe was the bishop's prebend and his confessor. He esteemed him highly. God made use of him to convert several of the officers and soldiers, who, from being men of scandalous lives, became patterns of piety. In that place everything was mixed with crosses, but souls were gained to God. There were some of his friars, who, after his example, were advancing toward perfection. Though I neither understood their language nor they mine, the Lord made us understand each other in what concerned His service. The Rector of the Jesuits took his time, when Father La Combe was gone out of town, to prove me, as he said. He had studied theological matters, which I did not understand. He propounded several questions. The Lord inspired me to answer him in such a manner, that he went away both surprised and satisfied. He could not forbear speaking of it.

The Barnabites of Paris, or rather Father de la Mothe took it in head to try to draw Father La Combe to go and preach at Paris. He wrote to the Father-general about it, because they had no one at Paris to support their house, that their church was deserted; that it was a pity to leave such a man as Father La Combe in a place where he only corrupted his language. It was necessary to make his fine talents appear at Paris, where he himself could not bear the burden of the house, if they did not give him an assistant of such qualifications and experience. Who would not have thought all this to be sincere? The Bishop of Verceil, who was very much a friend of Father-general, having advice thereof, opposed it, and answered that it would be doing him the greatest injury to take from him a man who was so exceedingly useful to him, and at a time when he had the greatest need of him.

The Father-general of the Barnabites would not

agree to the request of Father de la Mothe, for fear of offending the Bishop of Verceil. As to me, my indisposition increased. The air, which is there extremely bad, caused me a continual cough, with frequent returns of fever. I grew so much worse that it was thought I could not get over it. The Bishop was afflicted to see it, but, having consulted the physicians, they assured him that the air of the place was mortal to me, whereupon he said to me, "I had rather have you live, though distant from me, than see you die here." He gave up his design of establishing his congregation, for my friend would not settle there without me. The Genoese lady could not easily leave her own city, where she was respected. The Genoese besought her to set up there what the Bishop of Verceil had wanted her to set up. It was a congregation almost like that of Madame de Miramion. When the Bishop had first proposed this, however agreeable it appeared, I had a presentiment that it would not succeed, and that it was not what our Lord required of me, though I submissively yielded to the good proposal, were it only to acknowledge the many special favors of this prelate. I was assured that the Lord would know well how to prevent what He should now require of me. As this good prelate saw he must resign himself to let me go, he said to me, "You were willing to be in the diocese of Geneva, and there they persecuted and rejected you; I, who would gladly have you, cannot keep you." He wrote to Father La Mothe that I should go in the spring, as soon as the weather would permit. He was sorry to be obliged to let me go. Yet he still hoped to have kept Father La Combe, which probably might have been, had not the death of the Father-general given it another turn.

Here it was that I wrote upon the Apocalypse, and that there was given me a greater certainty of all the persecutions of the most faithful servants of Cod. Here also I was strongly moved to write to Madame De Ch———. I did it with great simplicity; and what I wrote was like the first foundation of what the Lord required of her, having been pleased to make use of me to help to bring her into His ways, being one to whom I am much united, and by her to others.

The Bishop of Verceil's friend, the Father-general of the Barnabites, departed this life. As soon as he was dead, Father La Mothe wrote to the Vicar-general who now held his place till another should be elected renewing his request to have Father La Combe as an assistant. The father, hearing that I was obliged on account of my indisposition to return into France, sent an order to Father La Combe to return to Paris, and to accompany me in my journey, as his doing that would exempt their house at Paris, already poor, from the expenses of so long a journey. Father La Combe, who did not penetrate the poison under this fair outside, consented thereto; knowing it was my custom to have some ecclesiastic with me in traveling. Father La Combe went off twelve days before me, in order to transact some business, and to wait for me at the passage over the mountains, as the place where I had most need of an escort. I set off in Lent, the weather then being fine. It was a sorrowful parting to the Bishop. I pitied him; he was so much affected at losing both Father La Combe and me. He caused me to be attended, at his own expense, as far as Turin, giving me a gentleman and one of his ecclesiastics to accompany me.

As soon as the resolution was taken that Father La Combe should accompany me, Father La Mothe reported everywhere "that he had been obliged to do it, to make him return into France." He expatiated on the attachment I had for Father La Combe, pretending to pity me. Upon this everyone said that I ought to put myself under the direction of Father La Mothe. In the meantime he deceitfully palliated the malignity of his heart, writing letters full of esteem to Father La Combe, and some to me of tenderness, "desiring him to bring his dear sister, and to serve her in her infirmities, and in the hardships of so long a journey; that he should be sensibly obliged to him for his care;" with many other things of the like nature.

I could not resolve to depart without going to see my good friend, the Marchioness of Prunai, notwithstanding the difficulty of the roads. I caused myself to be carried, it being scarcely possible to go otherwise on account of the mountains. She was extremely joyful at seeing me arrive. Nothing could be more cordial than what passed between us. It was then that she acknowledged that all I had told her had come to pass. A good ecclesiastic, who lives with her, told me the same. We made ointments and plasters together, and I gave her the secret of my remedies, I encouraged her, and so did Father La

Combe, to establish an hospital in that place; which was done while we were there. I contributed my mite to it which has ever been blest to all the hospitals, which have ever been established in reliance on Providence.

I believe I had forgotten to tell, that the Lord had made use of me to establish one near Grenoble, which subsists without any other fund than the supplies of Providence. My enemies made use of that afterward to slander me, saying that I had wasted my children's substance in establishing hospitals, though, far from spending any of their substance, I had even given them my own. All those hospitals have been established only on the fund of divine Providence, which is inexhaustible. But so it has been ordered for my good, that all our Lord has made me to do His glory has ever been turned into crosses for me.

As soon as it was determined that I should come into France, the Lord made known to me, that it was to have greater crosses than I ever had. Father La Combe had the like sense. He encouraged me to resign myself to the divine will, and to become a victim offered freely to new sacrifices. He also wrote to me, "Will it not be a thing very glorious to God, if He should make us serve in that great city, for a spectacle to angels and to men?" I set off then with a spirit of sacrifice, to offer myself up to new kinds of punishments, if pleasing to my dear Lord. All along the road something within me repeated the very words of St. Paul, "I go bound in the Spirit unto Jerusalem, not knowing the things should befall me

351

there, save that the Holy Ghost witnesseth, saying, that bonds and afflictions abide me. But none of these things move me; neither count I my life dear unto myself, so that I might finish my course with joy." (Acts 20:22,23,24.) I could not forbear to testify it to my most intimate friends, who tried hard to prevail on me to stop, and not to proceed. They were all willing to contribute a share of what they had, for my settlement there, and to prevent my coming to Paris. But I found it my duty to hold on my way, and to sacrifice myself for Him who first sacrificed Himself for me.

At Chamberry we saw Father La Mothe, who was going to the election of a Father-general. Though he affected an appearance of friendship, it was not difficult to discover that his thoughts were different from his words, and that he had conceived dark designs against us. I speak not of his intentions, but to obey the command given me to omit nothing. I shall necessarily be obliged often to speak of him. I could wish with all my heart it were in my power to suppress what I have to say of him. If what he has done respected only myself, I would willingly bury all; but I think I owe it to truth, and to the innocence of Father La Combe, so cruelly oppressed, and grievously crushed so long, by wicked calumnies, by an imprisonment of several years, which in all probability will last as long as life. Though Father La Mothe may appear heavily charged in what I say of him, I protest solemnly, and in the presence of God, that I pass over in silence many of his bad actions.

CHAPTER 19

Scarcely had I arrived at Paris,
when I readily discovered the black designs entertained against both Father La Combe and me. Father
La Mothe who conducted the whole tragedy, artfully
dissembled, according to his custom; flattering me to
my face, while he was aiming the keenest wounds
behind my back. He and his confederates wanted,
for their own interest, to persuade me to go to
Montargis (my native place), hoping, thereby, to
get the guardianship of my children, and to dispose
of both my person and effects. All the persecutions
from Father La Mothe and my family have been attended on their part with views of interest; those
against Father La Combe have sprung from rage
and revenge, because he, as my director, did not
oblige me to do what they wanted; as well as out of
jealousy. I might enter into a long detail on this,
sufficient to convince all the world; but I suppress, to
avoid prolixity. I shall only say, that they threatened
to deprive me of what little I had reserved to myself. To this I only replied that I would not go to
law, that if they were resolved to take from me little

I had left (little indeed in comparison of what I had given up) I would surrender it entirely to them; being quite free and willing not only to be poor, but to be even in the very extremity of want in imitation of our Lord Jesus Christ.

I arrived at Paris on Magdalene's eve, 1686, exactly five years after my departure from that city. After Father La Combe arrived, he was soon followed and much applauded. I perceived some jealously in Father La Mothe hereupon, but did not think that matters would be carried so far as they have been. The greater part of the Barnabites of Paris, and its neighborhood, joined against Father La Combe, induced from several causes that particularly related to their order. But all their calumnies and evil attempts were overthrown by the unaffected piety he manifested, and the good which multitudes reaped from his labors.

I had deposited a little sum of money in his hands (with the consent of his superior) to serve for the entrance of a nun. I thought myself obliged in conscience to do it. She had, through my means, quitted the New Catholics. It was that young woman whom I mentioned before, whom the priest of Gex wanted to win over. As she is beautiful, though very prudent, there always continues a cause for fear, when such an one is exposed in the world. La Mothe wanted to have that money, and signified to La Combe that, if he did not make me give it to him for a wall, which he had to rebuild in his convent, he would make him suffer for it. But the latter, who is always upright, answered that he could not in conscience advise me to do anything else, but what I had already resolved, in favor of that young woman. Hence he and the provincial ardently longed to satisfy their desire of revenge. They employed all their thoughts on the means of effecting it.

A very wicked man who was employed for that purpose, wrote defamatory libels, declaring that the propositions of Molinos, which had been current for two year past in France, were the sentiments of Father La Combe. These libels were spread about in the community. Father La Mothe and the provincial, acting as persons well affected to the church, carried them to the official, or judge of the ecclesiastical court, who joined in the dark design. They showed them to the Archbishop, saying, "It was out of their zeal, and that they were exceedingly sorry that one of their fraternity was an heretic, and as such execrable. They also brought me in, but more moderately, saying Father La Combe was almost always at my house, which was false. I could scarcely see him at all except at the confessional, and then for a very short time. Several other things equally false they liberally gave out concerning both of us.

They bethought themselves of one thing further likely to favor their scheme. They knew I had been at Marseilles, and thought they had a good foundation for a fresh calumny. They counterfeited a letter from a person at Marseilles (I heard it was from the Bishop) addressed to the Archbishop of Paris, or to his official, in which they wrote the most abominable scandal. Father La Mothe came to try to draw me into his snare, and to make me say, in the presence of the people whom he had brought, that I had been at Marseilles with Father La Combe. "There are," said he, "shocking accounts against you, sent by the Bishop of Marseilles. You have there fallen into great scandal with Father La Combe. There are good witnesses of it." I replied with a smile, "The calumny is well devised; but it would have been proper to know first whether Father La Combe had been at Marseilles, for I do not believe he was ever there in his life. While I was there, Father La Combe was laboring at Verceil." He was confounded and went off, saying, "There are witnesses of its being true." He went immediately to ask Father La Combe if he had not been at Marseilles. He assured him he never had been there. They were struck with disappointment. They then gave out that it was not Marseilles but Seisel. Now this Seisel is a place I have never been at, and there is no bishop there.

Every imaginable device was used to terrify me by threats, forged letters, and by memorials drawn up against me, accusing me of teaching erroneous doctrines, and of living a bad life and urging me to flee the country to escape the consequences of exposure. Failing in all these, at length La Mothe took off the mask, and said to me in the church, before La Combe, "It is now, my sister, that you must think of fleeing, you are charged with crimes of a deep dye." I was not moved in the least, but replied with my usual tranquillity, "If I am guilty of such crimes I cannot be too severely punished; wherefore I will not flee or go out of the way. I have made an open profession of dedicating myself to God entirely. If I have done things offensive to Him, whom I would wish both to love, and to cause to be loved by the whole world, even at the expense of my life, I ought by my punishment to be made an example to the world; but if I am innocent, for me to flee is not the way for my innocence to be believed."

Similar attempts were made to ruin Father La Combe. He was grossly misrepresented to the king, and an order procured for his arrest and imprisonment in the Bastile.

Although on his trial he appeared quite innocent, and they could not find anything whereupon to ground a condemnation, yet they made the king believe he was a dangerous man in the article of religion. He was then shut up in a certain fortress of the Bastile for life; but as his enemies heard that the captain in that fortress esteemed him, and treated him kindly, they had him removed into a much worse place. God, who beholds everything, will reward every man according to his works. I know by an interior communication that he is very well content, and fully resigned to God.

La Mothe now endeavored more than ever to induce me to flee, assuring me that, if I went to Montargis, I should be out of all trouble; but that if I did not, I should pay for it. He insisted on my taking himself for my director, to which I could not agree. He decried me wherever he went, and wrote to his brethren to do the same. They sent me very abusive letters, assuring me that, if I did not put myself under his direction, I was undone. I have the letters by me still. One father desired me in this case to make a virtue of necessity. Nay, some advised me to pretend to put myself under his direction, and to deceive him. I abhorred the thought of deceit. I bore everything with the greatest tranquillity, without taking any care to justify or defend myself, leaving it entirely to God to order as he should please about me. Herein he was graciously pleased to increase the peace of my soul, while every one seemed to cry against me, and to look on me as an infamous creature, except those few who knew me well by a near union of spirit. At church I heard people behind me exclaim against me, and even some priests say it was necessary to cast me out of the church. I left myself to God without reserve, being quite ready to endure the most rigorous pains and tortures, if such were His will.

I never made any solicitation either for Father La Combe or myself, though charged with that among other things. Willing to owe everything to God, I have no dependence on any creature. I would not have it said that any but God had made Abraham rich. Gen. 14:23. To lose all for Him is my best gain; and to gain all without Him would be my worst loss. Although at this time so general an outcry was raised against me, God did not fail to make use of me to gain many souls to Himself. The more persecution raged against me the more children were given me, on whom the Lord conferred great favors through His handmaid.

One must not judge of the servants of God by what their enemies say of them, nor by their being oppressed under calumnies without any resource.

Jesus Christ expired under pangs. God uses the like conduct toward His dearest servants, to render them conformable to His Son, in whom He is always well pleased. But few place that conformity where it ought to be. It is not in voluntary pains or austerities, but in those which are suffered in a submission ever equal to the will of God, in a renunciation of our whole selves, to the end that God may be our all in all, conducting us according to His views, and not our own, which are generally opposite to His. All perfection consists in this entire conformity with Jesus Christ, not in shining things which men esteem. It will only be seen in eternity who are the true friends of God. Nothing pleases Him but Jesus Christ, and that which bears His mark or character.

They were continually pressing me to flee, though the Archbishop had spoken to myself, and bidden me not to leave Paris. But they wanted to give the appearance of criminality both to me and to Father La Combe by my flight. They knew not how to make me fall into the hands of the official. If they accused me of crimes, it must be before other judges. Any other judge would have seen my innocence; the false witnesses would have run the risk of suffering for it. They continually spread stories of horrible crimes; but the official assured me that he had heard no mention of any. He was afraid lest I should retire out of his jurisdiction. They then made the king believe that I was an heretic, that I carried on a literary correspondence with Molinos (I, who never knew there was a Molinos in the world, till the Gazette had told me of it) that I had written a dangerous book;

and that on those accounts it would be necessary to issue an order to put me in a convent, that they might examine me. I was a dangerous person, it would be proper for me to be locked up, to be allowed no commerce with any one; since I continually held assemblies," which was very false. To support this calumny my handwriting was counterfeited, and a letter was forged as from me, importing, that I had "great designs, but feared that they would prove abortive, through the imprisonment of Father La Combe, for which reason I had left off holding assemblies at my house, being too closely watched; but that I would hold them at the houses of other persons. This forged letter they showed the king, and upon it an order was given for my imprisonment.

This order would have been put in execution two months sooner than it was, had I not fallen very sick. I had inconceivable pains and a fever. Some thought that I had a gathering in my head. The pain I suffered for five weeks made me delirious. I had also a pain in my breast and a violent cough. Twice I received the holy sacrament, as I was thought to be expiring. One of my friends had acquainted Father La Mothe, (not knowing him to have had any hand in F. La Combe's imprisonment) that she had sent me a certificate from the inquisition in Father La Combe's favor, having heard that his own was lost. This answered a very good purpose; for they had made the king believe that he had run away from the inquisition; but this showed the contrary.

Father La Mothe then came to me, when I was in excessive pain, counterfeiting all the affection and tenderness in his power, and telling me "that the affair of Father La Combe was going on very well, that he was just ready to come out of prison with honor, that he was very glad of it. If he had only this certificate, he would soon be delivered. Give me it then," said he, "and he will be immediately released." At first I made a difficulty of doing it. "What! said he, will you be the cause of ruining poor Father La Combe, having it in your power to save him, and cause us that affliction, for want of what you have in your hands." I yielded, ordering it to be brought and given him. But he suppressed it, and gave out that it was lost. It never could be got from him again. The Ambassador from the Court of Turin sent a messenger to me for this certificate, designing the proper use of it to serve Father La Combe. I referred him to Father La Mothe. The messenger went to him and asked him for it. He denied I had given it to him, saying, "Her brain is disordered which makes her imagine it." The man came back to me and told me his answer. The persons in my chamber bore witness that I had given it to him. Yet all signified nothing; it could not be got out of his hands; but on the contrary, he insulted me, and caused others also to do it, though I was so weak that I seemed to be at the very gates of death.

They told me they only waited for my recovery to cast me into prison. He made his brethren believe that I had treated him ill. They wrote to me that it was for my crimes that I suffered; and that I should put myself under the control of Father La Mothe, otherwise I should repent it; that I was mad and ought to be bound; and was a monster of pride, since I would not suffer myself to be conducted by Father La Mothe. Such was my daily feast in the extremity of my pain; deserted of my friends, and oppressed by my enemies; the former being ashamed of me, through the calumnies which were forged and industriously spread; the latter let loose to persecute me; under all which I kept silence, leaving myself to the Lord.

There was not any kind of infamy, error, sorcery, or sacrilege, of which they did not accuse me. As soon as I was able to be carried to the church in a chair, I was told I must speak to the prebend. (It was a snare concerted between Father La Mothe and the Canon at whose house I lodged). I spoke to him with much simplicity, and he approved of what I said. Yet, two days after they gave out that I had uttered many things, and accused many persons; and from hence they procured the banishment of sundry persons with whom they were displeased, persons whom I had never seen or of whom I never heard. They were men of honor. One of them was banished, because he said my little book is a good one. It is remarkable that they say nothing to those who prefixed their approbations, and that, far from condemning the book, it has been reprinted since I have been in prison, and advertisements of it have been posted up at the Archbishop's palace, and all over Paris. In regard to others, when they find faults in their books, they condemn the books and leave the person at liberty; but as for me, my book is approved, sold and spread, while I am kept a prisoner for it.

The same day that those gentlemen were banished, I received a lettre de cachet, or sealed order to repair to the Convent of the Visitation of St. Mary's, in a suburb of St. Antoine. I received it with a tranquillity which surprised the bearer exceedingly. He could not forbear expressing it, having seen the extreme sorrow of those who were only banished. He was so touched with it as to shed tears. And although his order was to carry me off directly, he was not afraid to trust me, but left me all the day, desiring me to repair to St. Mary's in the evening. On that day many of my friends came to see me, and found me very cheerful, which surprised such of them as knew my case. I could not stand, I was so weak, having the fever every night, it being only a fortnight since I was thought to be expiring. I imagined they would leave me my daughter and maid to serve me.

CHAPTER 20

On JANUARY 29, 1688, I went to St. Mary's. There they let me know I must neither have my daughter nor a maid to serve me, but must be locked up alone in a chamber. Indeed it touched me to my heart when my daughter was taken from me. They would neither allow her to be in that house, nor anybody to bring me any news of her. I was then obliged to sacrifice my daughter, as if she were mine no longer. The people of the house were prepossessed with so frightful an account of me, that they looked at me with horror. For my jailer they singled out a nun, who, they thought, would treat me with the greatest rigor, and they were not mistaken therein.

They asked me who was now my confessor. I named him; but he was seized with such a fright that he denied it; though I could have produced many persons who had seen me at his confessional. So then they said they had caught me in a lie; I was not to be trusted. My acquaintance then said they knew me not, and others were at liberty to invent stories, and say all manner of evil of me. The woman, appointed for my keeper, was gained over by my enemies, to torment me as an heretic, an enthusiast, one crackbrained and an hypocrite. God alone knows what she made me suffer. As she sought to surprise me in my words, I watched them, to be more exact in them; but I fared the worse for it. I made more slips and gave her more advantages over me thereby, beside the trouble in my own mind for it. I then left myself as I was, and resolved, though this woman would bring me to the scaffold, by the false reports she was continually carrying to the prioress, that I would simply resign myself to my lot; so I re-entered into my former condition.

Monsieur Charon the Official, and a Doctor of Sorbonne, came four times to examine me. Our Lord did me the favor which He promised to His apostles, to make me answer much better than if I had studied. Luke 21:14,15. They said to me, if I had explained myself, as I now did, in the book entitled, Short and Easy Method of Prayer, I would not now have been here. My last examination was about a counterfeit letter, which they read and let me see. I told them the hand was no way like mine. They said it was only a copy; they had the original at home. I desired a sight of it, but could not obtain it. I told them I never wrote it, nor did I know the person to whom it was addressed; but they took scarcely any notice of what I said.

After this letter was read, the official turned to me and said, "You see, madam, that after such a letter there was foundation enough for imprisoning you." "Yes, sir," said I, "if I had written it." I showed them its falsehoods and inconsistencies, but all in vain. I was left two months, and treated worse and worse, before either of them came again to see me. Till then I had always some hope that, seeing my innocence, they would do me justice; but now I saw that they did not want to find me innocent, but to make me appear guilty.

The official alone came the next time, and told me, "I must speak no more of the false letter; that it was nothing." "How nothing," said I, "to counterfeit a person's writing, and to make one appear an enemy to the State!" He replied, "We will seek out the author of it." "The author," said I, "is no other than the Scrivener Gautier." He then demanded where the papers were which I wrote on the Scriptures. I told him, "I would give them up when I should be out of prison; but was not willing to tell with whom I had lodged them."

About three or four days before Easter he came again, with the doctor, and a verbal process was drawn up against me for rebelling, in not giving up papers. Copies of my writings were then put into their hands; for I had not the originals. I know not where those who got them from me have put them; but I am firm in the faith that they will all be preserved, in spite of the storm. The prioress asked the official how my affair went. He said, very well, and that I should soon be discharged; this became the common talk; but I had a presentiment of the contrary.

I had an inexpressible satisfaction and joy in suffering, and being a prisoner. The confinement of my body made me better relish the freedom of my mind.

St. Joseph's day was to me a memorable day; for then my state had more of Heaven than of earth beyond what any expression can reach. This was followed, as it were, with a suspension of every favor then enjoyed, a dispensation of new sufferings. I was obliged to sacrifice myself anew, and to drink the very dregs of the bitter draught.

I never had any resentment against my persecutors, though I well knew them, their spirit and their actions. Jesus Christ and the saints saw their persecutors, and at the same time saw that they could have no power except it were given them from above. John 19:11.

Loving the strokes which God gives, one cannot hate the hand which He makes use of to strike with.

A few days after, the official came, and told me he gave me the liberty of the cloister, that is, to go and come in the house. They were now very industrious in urging my daugther to consent to a marriage, which had it taken place, would have been her ruin. To succeed herein, they had placed her with a relation of the gentleman whom they wanted her to marry. All my confidence was in God, that He would not permit it to be accomplished, as the man had no tincture of Christianity, being abandoned both in his principles and morals.

To induce me to give up my daughter they promised me an immediate release from prison and from every charge under which I labored. But if I refused, they threatened me with imprisonment for life and with death on the scaffold. In spite of all their promises and threatenings, I persistently refused.

367

Soon after, the official and doctor came to tell the prioress I must be closely locked up. She represented to them that the chamber I was in, was small, having an opening to the light or air, only on one side, through which the sun shone all the day long, and being the month of July, it must soon cause my death. They paid no regard. She asked why I must be thus closely locked up. They said I had committed horrible things in her house, even within the last month, and had scandalized the nuns. She protested the contrary, and assured them the whole community had received great edification from me, and could not but admire my patience and moderation. But it was all in vain. The poor woman could not refrain from tears, at a statement so remote from the truth.

They then sent for me, and told me I had done base things in the last month. I asked what things? They would not tell me. I said then that I would suffer as long and as much as it should please God; that this affair was begun on forgeries against me, and so continued. That God was witness of everything. The doctor told me, that to take God for a witness in such a thing was a crime. I replied nothing in the world could hinder me from having recourse to God. I was then shut up more closely than at first, until I was absolutely at the point of death, being thrown into a violent fever, and almost stifled with the closeness of the place, and not permitted to have any assistance.

In the time of the ancient law, there were several of the Lord's martyrs who suffered for asserting and trusting in the one true God. In the primitive church of Christ the martyrs shed their blood, for maintaining the truth of Jesus Christ crucified. Now there are martyrs of the Holy Ghost, who suffer for their dependence on Him, for maintaining His reign in souls, and for being victims of the Divine will.

It is this Spirit which is to be poured out on all flesh, as saith the prophet Joel. The martyrs of Jesus Christ have been glorious martyrs, He having drunk up the confusion of that martyrdom; but the martyrs of the Holy Spirit are martyrs of reproach and ignominy. The Devil no more exercises his power against their faith or belief, but directly attacks the dominion of the Holy Spirit, opposing His celestial motion in souls, and discharging his hatred on the bodies of those whose minds he cannot hurt. Oh, Holy Spirit, a Spirit of love, let me ever be subjected to Thy will, and, as a leaf is moved before the wind, so let me be moved by Thy Divine breath. As the impetuous wind breaks all that resists it, so break thou all that opposes Thy empire.

Although I have been obliged to describe the procedure of those who persecute me, I have not done it out of resentment, since I love them at my heart, and pray for them, leaving to God the care of defending me, and delivering me out of their hands, without making any movement of my own for it. I have apprehended and believed that God would have me write everything sincerely, that His name may be glorified; that the things done in secret against His servants should one day be published on the housetops; for the more they strive to conceal them from the eyes of men, the more will God in His own time make them all manifest.

August 22, 1688, it was thought I was about coming out of prison, and everything seemed to tend toward it. But the Lord gave me a sense that, far from being willing to deliver me they were only laying new snares to ruin me more effectually, and to make Father La Mothe known to the king, and esteemed by him. On the day mentioned, which was my birthday, being forty years of age, I awaked under an impression of Jesus Christ in an agony, seeing the counsel of the Jews against Him. I knew that none but God could deliver me out of prison, and I was satisfied that He would do it one day by His own right hand, though ignorant of the manner, and leaving it wholly to Himself.

In the order of Divine Providence my case was laid before Madame de Maintenon, who became deeply interested in the account given her of my sufferings, and at length procured my release. A few days afterward I had my first interview with the Abbe Fenelon.

Coming out of St. Mary's I retired into the community of Mad. Miramion, where I kept my bed of a fever three months, and had an imposthume in my eye. Yet at this time I was accused of going continually out, holding suspected assemblies, together with other groundless falsehoods. In this house my daughter was married to Mons. L. Nicholas Fouquet, Count de Vaux. I removed to my daughter's house, and on account of her extreme youth, lived with her two years and an half. Even there my enemies were ever forging one thing after another against me. I then wanted to retire quite secretly, to the house of the Benedictines at Montargis, (my native place) but it was discovered, and both friends and enemies jointly prevented it.

The family in which my daughter was married being of the number of Abbe Fenelon's friends, I had the opportunity of often seeing him at our house. We had some conversations on the subject of a spiritual life, in which he made several objections to my experiences therein. I answered them with my usual simplicity, which, as I found, gained upon him. As the affair of Molinos at that time made a great noise, the plainest things were distrusted, and the terms used by mystic writers exploded. But I so clearly expounded everything to him, and so fully solved all his objections, that no one more fully inbibed my sentiments than he; which has since laid the foundation of that persecution he has suffered. His answers to the Bishop of Meaux evidently show this to all who have read them.

I now took a little private house, to follow the inclination I had for retirement; where I sometimes had the pleasure of seeing my family and a few particular friends. Certain young ladies of St. Cyr. having informed Mad. Maintenon, that they found in my conversation something which attracted them to God, she encouraged me to continue my instructions to them. By the fine change in some of them with whom before she had not been well pleased, she found she had no reason to repent of it. She then treated me with much respect; and for three years after, while this lasted, I received from her every mark of esteem and confidence. But that very thing afterward drew on me the most severe persecution. The free entrance I had into the house, and the confidence which some young ladies of the Court, distinguished for their rank and piety, placed in me, gave no small uneasines to the people who had persecuted me. The directors took umbrage at it, and under pretext of the troubles I had some years before, they engaged the Bishop of Chartres, Superior of St. Cyr, to present to Mad. Maintenon that, by my particular conduct, I troubled the order of the house; that the young women in it were so attached to me, and to what I said to them, that they no longer hearkened to their superiors. I then went no more to St. Cyr. I answered the young ladies who wrote to me, only by letters unsealed, which passed through the hands of Mad. Maintenon.

Soon after I fell sick. The physicians, after trying in vain the usual method of cure, ordered me to repair to the waters of Bourbon. My servant had been induced to give me some poison. After taking it, I suffered such exquisite pains that, without speedy succor, I should have died in a few hours. The man immediately ran away, and I have never seen him since. When I was at Bourbon, the waters which I threw up burned like spirits of wine. I had no thought of being poisoned, till the physicians of Bourbon assured me of it. The waters had but little effect. I suffered from it for above seven years.

God kept me in such a disposition of sacrifice, that I was quite resigned to suffer everything, and to receive from His hand all that might befall me, since for me to offer in any way to vindicate myself, would be only beating the air. When the Lord is willing to make any one suffer, He permits even the most virtuous people to be readily blinded toward them; and I may confess that the persecution of the wicked is but little, when compared with that of the servants of the church, deceived and animated with a zeal which they think right. Many of these were now, by the artifices made use of, greatly imposed on in regard to me. I was represented to them in an odious light, as a strange creature. Since, therefore, I must, O my Lord, be conformable to Thee, to please Thee; I set more value on my humiliation, and on seeing myself condemned of everybody, than if I saw myself on the summit of honor in the world. How often have I said, even in the bitterness of my heart, that I should be more afraid of one reproach of my conscience, than of the outcry and condemnation of all men!

CHAPTER 21

AT THIS TIME I had my first acquaintance with the Bishop of Meaux. I was introduced by an intimate friend, the Duke of Chevreuse. I gave him the foregoing history of my life, and he confessed, that he had found therein such an unction as he had rarely done in other books, and that he had spent three days in reading it, with an impression of the presence of God on his mind all that time.

I proposed to the bishop to examine all my writings, which he took four or five months to do, and then advanced all his objections; to which I gave answers. From his unacquaintance with the interior paths, I could not clear up all the difficulties which he found in them.

He admitted that looking into the ecclesiastical histories for ages past, we may see that God has sometimes made use of laymen, and of women to instruct, edify, and help souls in their progress to perfection. I think one of the reasons of God's acting thus, is that glory may not be ascribed to any, but to Himself alone. For this purpose, He has chosen the weak things of this world, to confound such as are mighty. 1 Cor. 1:27.

Jealous of the attributes which men pay to other men, which are due only to Himself, He has made a paradox of such persons, that He alone may have the glory of His own works. I pray God, with my whole heart, sooner to crush me utterly, with the most dreadful destruction, than to suffer me to take the least honor to myself, of anything which He has been pleased to do by me for the good of others. I am only a poor nothing. God is all-powerful. He delights to operate, and exercise His power by mere nothings.

The first time that I wrote a history of myself, it was very short. In it I had particularized my faults and sins, and said little of the favors of God. I was ordered to burn it, to write another, and in it to omit nothing anyway remarkable that had befallen me. I did it. It is a crime to publish secrets of the King; but it is a good thing to declare the favors of the Lord our God, and to magnify His mercies.

As the outcry against me became more violent, and Madame Maintenon was moved to declare against me, I sent to her through the Duke of Beauvilliers, requesting the appointment of proper persons to examine my life and doctrines, offering to retire into any prison until fully exculpated. My proposal was rejected. In the meantime, one of my most intimate friends and supporters, Mons. Fouquet, was called away by death. I felt his loss very deeply, but rejoiced in his felicity. He was a true servant of God.

Determined to retire out of the way of giving offense to any, I wrote to some of my friends, and bade them a last farewell; not knowing whether I were to be carried off by the indisposition which I then had, which had been a constant fever for forty days past, or to recover from it.

Referring to the Countess of G. and the Duchess of M., I wrote, "When these ladies and others were in the vanities of the world, when they patched and painted, and some of them were in the way to ruin their families by gaming and profusion of expense in dress, nobody arose to say anything against it; they were quietly suffered to do it. But when they have broken off from all this, then they cry out against me, as if I had ruined them. Had I drawn them from piety into luxury, they would not make such an outcry. The Duchess of M. at her giving herself up to God, thought herself obliged to quit the court, which was to her like a dangerous rock, in order to bestow her time on the education of her children and the care of her family, which, till then, she had neglected. I beseech you, therefore, to gather all the memorials you can against me; if I am found guilty of the things they accuse me of, I ought to be punished more than any other, since God has brought me to know Him and love Him, and I am well asured that there is no communion between Christ and Belial."

I sent them my two little printed books, with my commentaries on the Holy Scriptures. I also, by their order, wrote a work to facilitate their examination, and to spare them as much time and trouble as I could, which was to collect a great number of passages out of approved writers, which showed the conformity of my writings with those used by the holy penmen. I caused them to be transcribed by the quire, as I had written them, in order to send them to the three commissioners. I also, as occasion presented, cleared up the dubious and obscure places. I had written them at a time when the affairs of Molinos had not broken out, I used the less precaution in expressing my thoughts, not imagining that they would ever be turned into an evil sense. This work was entitled, 'THE JUSTIFICATIONS.' It was composed in fifty days, and appeared to be very sufficient to clear up the matter. But the Bishop of Meaux would never suffer it to be read.

After all the examinations, and making nothing out against me, who would not have thought but they would have left me to rest in peace? Quite otherwise, the more my innocence appeared, the more did they, who had undertaken to render me criminal, put every spring in motion to effect it. I offered the Bishop of Meaux to go to spend some time in any community within his diocese, that he might be better acquainted with me. He proposed to me that of St. Mary de Meaux, which I accepted; but in going in the depth of winter I had like to have perished in the snow, being stopped four hours, the coach having entered into it, and being almost buried in it, in a deep hollow. I was taken out at the door with one maid. We sat upon the snow, resigned to the mercy of God, and expected nothing but death. I never had more tranquillity of mind, though chilled and soaked with the snow, which melted on us. Occasions like these are such as show whether we are perfectly resigned to God or not.

This poor girl and I were easy in our minds, in a state of entire resignation, though sure of dying if we passed the night there, and seeing no likelihood of anyone coming to our succor. At length some waggoners came up, who with difficulty drew us through the snow.

The bishop, when he heard of it, was astonished, and had no little self-complacency to think that I had thus risked my life to obey him so punctually. Yet afterward he denounced it as artifice and hypocrisy.

There were times indeed when I found nature overcharged; but the love of God and His grace rendered sweet to me the very worst of bitters. His invisible hand supported me; else I had sunk under so many probations. Sometimes I said to myself, "All thy waves and thy billows are gone over me," (Psa. 42:7). "Thou hast bent thy bow and set me as a mark for the arrow; thou has caused all the arrows of thy quiver to enter into my reins" (Lam. 3:12,13). It seemed to me as if everyone thought he was in the right to treat me ill, and rendered service to God in doing it. I then comprehended that it was the very manner in which Jesus Christ suffered. He was numbered with the transgressors, (Mark 15:28). He was condemned by the sovereign pontiff, chief priests, doctors of the law, and judges deputed by the Romans, who valued themselves on doing justice. Happy they who by suffering for the will of God under all the like circumstances, have so near a relation to the sufferings of Jesus Christ!

For six weeks after my arrival at Meaux, I was in

a continual fever, nor had I recovered from my indisposition, when I was waited on by the bishop, who would fain have compelled me to give it under my hand, that I did not believe the Word incarnate, (or Christ manifest in the flesh). I answered him, that "through the grace of God, I know how to suffer, even to death, but not how to sign such a falsehood." Several of the nuns who overheard this conversation, and perceiving the sentiments of the bishop, they joined with the Prioress, in giving a testimonial, not only of my good conduct, but of their belief in the soundness of my faith.

The bishop some days after, brought me a confession of faith, and a request to submit my books to the church, that I may sign it, promising to give me a certificate, which he had prepared. On my delivering my submission signed, he, notwithstanding his promise, refused to give the certificate. Some time after, he endeavored to make me sign his pastoral letter, and acknowledge that I had fallen into those errors, which he there lays to my charge, and made many demands of me of the like absurd and unreasonable nature, threatening me with those persecutions I afterward endured, in case of non-compliance. However, I continued resolute in refusing to put my name to falsehoods. At length, after I had remained about six months at Meaux, he gave me the certificate. Finding Mad. Maintenon disapproved of the certificate he had granted, he wanted to give me another in place of it. My refusal to deliver up the first certificate enraged him, and as I understood they intended to push matters with the utmost violence, "I thought that although I were resigned to whatever might fall out, yet I ought to take prudent measures to avoid the threatening storm." Many places of retreat were offered me; but I was not free in my mind to accept of any, nor to embarrass anybody, nor involve in trouble my friends and my family, to whom they might attribute my escape. I took the resolution of continuing in Paris, of living there in some private place with my maids, who were trusty and sure, and to hide myself from the view of the world. I continued thus for five or six months. I passed the day alone in reading, in praying to God, and in working. But the December 27, 1695, I was arrested, though exceedingly indisposed at that time, and conducted to Vincennes. I was three days in the custody of Mons. des Grez, who had arrested me; because the king would not consent to my being put into prison; saying several times over, that a convent was sufficient. They deceived him by still stronger calumnies. They painted me in his eyes, in colors so black, that they made him scruple his goodness and equity. He then consented to my being taken to Vincennes.

I shall not speak of that long persecution, which has made so much noise, for a series of ten years imprisonments, in all sorts of prisons, and of a banishment almost as long, and not yet ended, through crosses, calumnies, and all imaginable sorts of sufferings. There are facts too odious on the part of divers persons, which charity induces me to cover.

I have borne long and sore languishings, and oppressive and painful maladies without relief. I have been also inwardly under great desolations for several months, in such sort that I could only say these words, "My God, my God, why hast thou forsaken me!" All creatures seemed to be against me. I then put myself on the side of God, against myself.

Perhaps some will be surprised at my refusing to give the details of the greatest and strongest crosses of my life, after I have related those which were less. I thought it proper to tell something of the crosses of my youth, to show the crucifying conduct which God held over me. I thought myself obliged to relate certain facts, to manifest their falsehood, the conduct of those by whom they had passed, and the authors of those persecutions of which I have been only the accidental object, as I was only persecuted, in order to involve therein persons of great merit; whom, being out of their reach by themselves, they, therefore, could not personally attack, but by confounding their affairs with mine. I thought I owed this to religion, piety, my friends, my famliy, and myself.

While I was prisoner at Vincennes, and Monsieur De La Reine examined me, I passed my time in great peace, content to pass the rest of my life there, if such were the will of God. I sang songs of joy, which the maid who served me learned by heart, as fast as I made them. We together sang thy praises, O, my God! The stones of my prison looked in my eyes like rubies; I esteemed them more than all the gaudy brilliancies of a vain world. My heart was full of that joy which Thou givest to them who love Thee, in the midst of their greatest crosses.

When things were carried to the greatest extremities, being then in the Bastile, I said, "O, my God, if thou art pleased to render me a new spectacle to men and angels, Thy holy will be done!

DECEMBER, 1709.

Here she left off her narrative, though she lived a retired life above seven years after this date. What she had written being only done in obedience to the commands of her director. She died June 9, 1717, at Blois, in her seventieth year.

Moody Press, a ministry of the Moody Bible Institute, is designed for education, evangelization and edification. If we may assist you in knowing more about Christ and the Christian life, please write us without obligation to: Moody Press, c/o MLM, Chicago, Illinois 60610.